*Disjunctive Poetics* examines some of the most interesting and experimental contemporary writers whose work forms a counterpoint to the mainstream writing of our time. Peter Quartermain suggests that the explosion of noncanonical modern writing is linked to the severe political, social, and economic dislocation of non-English-speaking immigrants who, bringing alternative culture with them as they passed through Ellis Island in their hundreds of thousands at the turn of the century, found themselves uprooted from their traditions and dissociated from their cultures. The line of American poetry that runs from Gertrude Stein through Louis Zukofsky and the Objectivists to the Language Writers, Quartermain contends, is not the constructive but the deconstructive aspect, which emphasizes the materiality and ambiguity of the linguistic medium and the arbitrariness and openness of the creative process. Providing close reading of Gertrude Stein, Louis Zukofsky, Robert Creeley, Basil Bunting, Guy Davenport, Robert Duncan, and Susan Howe, the book explains how these writers describe the modern experience in a multicultural world by displacing commonly accepted cultural icons and by loading their language with multiple potential meanings.

CAMBRIDGE STUDIES IN AMERICAN LITERATURE AND CULTURE

# Disjunctive Poetics: From Gertrude Stein and Louis Zukofsky to Susan Howe

CAMBRIDGE STUDIES IN AMERICAN LITERATURE AND CULTURE



*Selected books in the series*

58 Paul Giles, *Roman Catholicism in American Literature: Ideology and Aesthetics*
57 Ann-Janine Morey, *Religion and Sexuality in American Fiction*
56 Philip Weinstein, *A Cosmos No One Owns: Gender, Race, and Culture in the Faulknerian Canon*
55 Stephen Fender, *Sea Changes: British Emigration and American Literature*
54 Peter Stoneley, *Mark Twain and the Feminine Aesthetic*
53 Joel Porte, *In Respect to Egotism: Studies in American Romantic Writing*
52 Charles Swann, *Nathaniel Hawthorne: Tradition and Revolution*
51 Ronald Bush (ed.), *T. S. Eliot: The Modernist in History*
50 Russell B. Goodman, *American Philosophy and the Romantic Tradition*
49 Eric J. Sundquist (ed.), *Frederick Douglass: New Literary and Historical Essays*
48 Susan Stanford Friedman, *Penelope's Web: Gender, Modernity, H. D.'s Fiction*
47 Timothy Redman, *Ezra Pound and Italian Fascism*
46 Ezra Greenspan, *Walt Whitman and the American Reader*
45 Michael Oriard, *Sporting with the Gods: The Rhetoric of Play and Game in American Culture*

*Continued on pages following the Index*

# Disjunctive Poetics:

## From Gertrude Stein and Louis Zukofsky to Susan Howe

PETER QUARTERMAIN

Published by the Press Syndicate of the University of Cambridge
The Pitt Building, Trumpington Street, Cambridge CB2 1RP
40 West 20th Street, New York, NY 10011-4211, USA
10 Stamford Road, Oakleigh, Victoria 3166, Australia



First published 1992

Printed in the United States of America

*Library of Congress Cataloging-in-Publication Data*

Quartermain, Peter.

Disjunctive poetics : from Gertrude Stein and Louis Zukofsky to Susan Howe / Peter Quartermain.

p. cm. – (Cambridge studies in American literature and culture)

Includes index.

ISBN 0-521-41268-4

1. American poetry – 20th century – History and criticism.
2. Experimental poetry, American – History and criticism.
3. Poetics. I. Title. II. Series.

PS323.5.Q37 1992
811'.509–dc20 91–33743
CIP

A catalog record for this book is available from the British Library.

ISBN 0-521-41268-4 hardback

*This book is for*
*MEREDITH*

Democratic nations naturally stand more in need of forms than other nations, and they naturally respect them less.

*Alexis de Tocqueville*

# Contents

# *Preface*

*Language is much more like a sort of being than a means.*
Maurice Merleau-Ponty[1]

Close readings. Somewhat belatedly discovering the poetry of William Carlos Williams and Louis Zukofsky in the middle 1960s and thus beginning to read poetry at all seriously, I had the great good fortune through the kindness of Ellen Tallman and Warren Tallman to meet Robert Duncan on one of his many visits to Vancouver. The sheer excitement and revelation of that encounter drilled home to me as could perhaps nothing else the very real news that reading poetry is not a matter of qualifying for membership in a literary or intellectual elite, and that the great pleasures poetry affords are intensely personal as well as oppositional in radical and far-reaching ways. The great undoing this discovery of the poem as a series of possibilities in meaning afforded was reinforced in 1970 by the sheer serendipity of renewing acquaintance with Robert Creeley (who had just come to teach in Vancouver when I arrived there in 1962) at precisely the time of Basil Bunting's sojourn in Vancouver in 1970. Bunting's insistence on the primacy of sound, coinciding as it did with the ear-opening discovery of Creeley's preciseness of line, was the final stage of an education that led to the writing of this book. My indebtedness to those named, and especially to the close friendship of the Tallmans and Bunting, is beyond words.

Including Bunting in a book of essays about American writers of this century has its ironies, for he is emphatically an English poet. His very Northumbrianness, however, served to separate him from the English koiné and from the English modernist tradition; his reinvention (with Hugh MacDiarmid and David Jones) of an older and regional poetic strain has much in common with Gertrude Stein, William Carlos Williams, Louis Zukofsky, and even James Joyce, who similarly sought to escape Anglocentric social, literary, and political values in their own countries. Like them, and like the other writers discussed in this book, he inhabits a geographical and cultural periphery, and was not without influence among them. Like Stein and like Zukofsky, he is a great neglected poet.

When Bunting died on 17 April 1985 Jonathan Williams, who knew that my wife and I had spent much of the previous winter in Hexham in order to be close to Bunting, asked "poets, writers and friends of BB to rise to the sad occasion and celebrate the man and his work," and properly insisted that "criticism is not wanted." The result, here gathered as Chapter 8, was "Six Plaints and a Lament for Basil Bunting," which appeared in *Conjunctions* 8 (Fall 1985): 165–79, and in *Line* 6 (Fall 1985): 59–71. Bunting believed that literary criticism is a waste of time, and my one venture into criticism of his work, " 'To Make Glad the Heart of Man': Bunting, Pound, and Whitman," suggests some of the ways in which Bunting contributes to the tradition the essays in this book address. It was written at the request of Carroll F. Terrell for his collection *Basil Bunting: Man and Poet* (Orono, Maine: National Poetry Foundation, 1981), 145–58.

The first published of these essays, "Recurrencies," was written for *Paideuma* (7.3 [Winter 1978]: 523–38), which sought (as Hugh Kenner put it) an essay defining the quality of Zukofsky's *un*likeness to other poets for its Zukofsky Memorial issue in 1978; I must record here my gratitude to Celia Zukofsky for her readiness to answer queries and for her encouragement in the preparation of this essay, as well as for her permission to quote from Louis Zukofsky's correspondence with Cid Corman. Similarly, I acknowledge with thanks her cooperation and encouragement in the writing of Chapter 3, which first appeared as a review of the one-volume California edition of *"A"* in *Paideuma* 9.1 (Spring 1980): 203–10, under the title "I Am Different, Let Not a Gloss Embroil You: Louis Zukofsky's *'A' 1–24*" – as well as for her permission to quote from Zukofsky's letters to Cid Corman and Carl Rakosi therein. I have substantially revised this review for its appearance here.

The first written of these essays, on Zukofsky's *The First Half of "A" – 9*, was an offspring of a seminar I conducted in 1966–7 on Williams and Zukofsky; I owe a great deal in its preparation to Louis Zukofsky, who from 1966 until his death in 1978 not only answered numerous questions but permitted me both to describe and to quote extensively from that work – a work that, he stated, should never be reprinted. At the insistence of Paul Zukofsky I have somewhat revised this chapter, which was first published in Carroll F. Terrell (editor), *Louis Zukofsky: Man and Poet* (Orono, Maine: National Poetry Foundation, 1980), 203–

25. The remaining chapters appear roughly in the order in which they were written, with the essays on Zukofsky (some of them slightly revised at the request of Paul Zukofsky) clustered together: There is inevitably slight overlap, especially of quotations and citations that are central to my view of Zukofsky. I owe many thanks to Louis Zukofsky and to Celia Zukofsky, with whose permission and encouragement much of the research for these essays was carried out between 1967 and 1978.

A condensed version of "'Actual Word Stuff, Not Thoughts for Thoughts': Williams and Zukofsky" was delivered at the special session of the William Carlos Williams Society, "William Carlos Williams and Louis Zukofsky," held at the MLA Convention in New York in December, 1981. I have removed many of the hallmarks of the lecture script from which it was first printed in *Credences,* new series 2.1 (Summer 1983): 104–22. "'Only Is Order Othered. Nought Is Nulled': *Finnegans Wake* and Middle and Late Zukofsky" has been more substantially revised from the form in which it was first delivered, at the Tenth International James Joyce Symposium, held in Copenhagen in June, 1986. It was first published in *ELH* 54.4 (Winter 1987): 957–78.

Of the remaining chapters in this book which have previously been published, "Robert Creeley What Counts" first appeared in the Creeley issue of *Boundary 2* 6.3/7.1 (Spring–Fall 1978): 329–34, and "Writing as Assemblage: Guy Davenport" as a review–essay in the inaugural issue of *Line: A Journal of the Contemporary Literature Collection at Simon Fraser University,* 1.1 (Spring 1983): 71–88. Milton Hindus requested "Exploring the Mere: A Note on Charles Reznikoff's Shorter Poems" for his *Charles Reznikoff: Man and Poet* (Orono, Maine: National Poetry Foundation 1984) 281–88, and Lee Bartlett called for an obituary notice for Robert Duncan in 1988; Chapter 11, "Go contrary, go sing: Robert Duncan" appears here in substantially the form it had in *American Poetry,* 6.1 (Fall 1988): 65–9.

The essay on Susan Howe with which this book closes was written following Howe's too brief visit to Vancouver in 1985, and was first published in the Susan Howe issue of Tom Beckett's (now lamentably defunct) journal *The Difficulties* 3.2 (1989): 71–83. I began Chapter 1, on Gertrude Stein, as an introduction to the book as a whole; it is designed (among other things) to explicate the reading strategies which generated the essays (it will be useful, reading these essays, to have texts of the poems discussed close to hand), and to balance the closing essay on Susan Howe, a woman writing at the end of the historical period the book considers. The section on "Lifting Belly" was read in my absence at the Thirteenth International James Joyce Symposium (Monaco, June 1990) as part of a session conducted by Bonnie Kyme Scott on "The Women's *Ulysses*"; it has not otherwise been published.

Writing the chapter on Stein as an introduction to the book emphasised the need for a historical context in which to place the whole book. The resulting Introduction, suggested by Albert Gelpi and the two anonymous readers for Cambridge University Press, has benefitted enormously from close and at times severe readings by Robin Blaser, David Bromige, Karen Mac Cormack, Steve McCaffery, and Marjorie Perloff. I thank all five warmly indeed.

I am indebted to the Social Science and Humanities Research Council of Canada for a Leave Fellowship for the year 1984–5, and to the University of British Columbia both for a year's leave from the English Department and for financial support from its Social Science and Humanities Research Committee. I benefitted far more than anyone has a right to expect from the signal help offered by a number of librarians: Ellen Dunlap, then of the Harry Ransom Humanities Research Center, The University of Texas at Austin, and her successor, Cathy Henderson; Saundra Taylor of the Lilly Library, Indiana University; Robert Bertholf of the Poetry Collection, SUNY Buffalo; and Erika Wilson. Station KQED, San Francisco, generously provided me in 1966 with a typed transcript of their NET film *U.S.A. Poetry: Robert Duncan and John Wieners.* I owe a great deal not only to my students in Vancouver who have borne with me as we worked out some of the analyses in these essays, but especially to the many individuals who gave so freely of their time and energy reading drafts of these essays and in conversation. I owe an especial debt to Guy Davenport and to Hugh Kenner, who both actively encouraged me in writing the earlier of these essays and offered invaluable friendly criticism – it is impossible to record how much their friendship and words helped me.

In addition to those I have already named I wish to thank especially Charles Bernstein, Robin Blaser, Ulla Dydo, Harry Gilonis, Susan Howe, Michele Leggott, Jo Powell, and especially Lorraine Weir for astonishing help and encouragement in various of these essays. They alone know how much I owe them. Above all, however, for her cool but friendly eye, constant discussion, ruthless blue-pencilling, support, and insight, I thank my wife, Meredith Yearsley Quartermain. The dedication of this book is but poor acknowledgement.

# *Acknowledgements of Copyright Material*

I thank authors, publishers, and other copyright holders for permission to quote copyright matter as follows:

Excerpts from letters and manuscripts by Basil Bunting, Lorine Niedecker, and William Carlos Williams are printed with permission of the holders – the Poetry/Rare Books Collection, University Libraries, State University of New York at Buffalo; Department of Special Collections, the University of Chicago Library; the Mountjoy Collection, the University of Durham Library; the Lilly Library, Indiana University, Bloomington, Indiana; the Headmaster, Leighton Park School, Reading; the Harry Ransom Humanities Research Center, University of Texas at Austin; and the Collection of American Literature, Beinecke Rare Book and Manuscript Library, Yale University.

Excerpts from letters and manuscripts by Basil Bunting, copyright © 1985 the Estate of Basil Bunting, are printed with the permission of the Executor of the Estate of Basil Bunting.

Excerpts from *The Collected Poems of Robert Creeley, 1945–1975,* "The Lover," copyright © 1983 the Regents of the University of California, are reprinted by permission of the University of California Press.

Excerpts from letters from Guy Davenport to Peter Quartermain, copyright © 1977, 1983 Guy Davenport, are printed with the permission of Guy Davenport.

Excerpts from letters from Robert Duncan to Peter Quartermain are printed with the permission of the Literary Estate of Robert Duncan.

Excerpts from Susan Howe, "Scattering as Behavior toward Risk," from *Singularities,* published by the University of New England Press for Wesleyan University Press, copyright © 1990 Susan Howe, are reprinted with the permission of Susan Howe.

Excerpts from *From This Condensery: The Complete Writings of Lorine Niedecker,* ed. Robert J. Bertholf, copyright © 1985 by the Estate of Lorine Niedecker, are reprinted with the permission of Cid Corman.

"The girls outshout the machines," from *Poems* (1920); "A dead gull in the road," from *Going To and Fro and Walking Up and Down,* and "Machine Age," by Charles Reznikoff, published in *The Complete Poems of Charles Reznikoff,* two volumes, copyright © 1977 the Charles Reznikoff Estate, printed with the permission of Black Sparrow Press.

Excerpts from William Carlos Williams, *Collected Poems 1909–1939,* Volume 1, copyright © 1938 by New Directions Publishing Corporation, are reprinted by permission of New Directions.

Excerpts from Louis Zukofsky, *"A",* copyright © 1979 Celia and Louis Zukofsky, are reprinted by permission of the University of California Press.

Excerpts from Louis Zukofsky, *Complete Short Poetry,* copyright © 1991 Paul Zukofsky, are reprinted with the permission of the Johns Hopkins University Press and Paul Zukofsky.

# *Introduction*

*When you realize that . . . the bible lives not by its stories but by its texts you see how inevitably one wants neither harmony, pictures stories nor portraits. You have to do something else to continue.*
Gertrude Stein. 1923.[1]

The essays in this book are about poets working in the "line" of American poetry running from Gertrude Stein through Louis Zukofsky and the Objectivists to the Language Writers. Writing of this sort characteristically takes an oppositional stance, continually insisting that reality is not a preconstituted world "out there" to be experienced, any more than a poem is a predetermined schematic of rhyme, organised rhythms, and identifiable themes. The central preoccupation of the writers discussed in this book is the recognition that in preconstituting the world we de-liberate our experience, thereby foreordaining the real; their central insistence is on the autonomous nature of the poem as part of an indeterminate physical and socioeconomic world. Objectivist writing, as historically labelled, is but one manifestation of this mode. William Carlos Williams said that Objectivist writing "recognises the poem, apart from its meaning, to be an object to be dealt with as such"; George Oppen, calling it "making an object of the poem," said that it "really means . . . the necessity . . . for achieving form."[2]

The difficulty with the Objectivist label is well known. Zukofsky claimed that he coined the term, in response to Harriet Monroe's demand for a literary movement with a name, to label the February 1931 issue of *Poetry* that he was editing. The interest of that issue, Zukofsky said, preparing *An "Objectivists" Anthology* six months later, was "in the few recent lines of poetry which could be found, and in the craft of poetry, NOT in the movement. The contributors did not get up one morning all over the land and say 'objectivists' between toothbrushes."[3]

Despite the amount of critical attention the Objectivists have received, theirs was an amorphous movement, for they had neither programme nor agenda. Originally consisting of Louis Zukofsky, George Oppen, Carl Rakosi, Charles Reznikoff, and Basil Bunting, writers who knew each other through Zukofsky or Williams and who, like the latter, found it extremely difficult to get published, the Objectivists have now somewhat loosely come to be identified with writers who remained in the United States when their compatriots chose to work in England or Europe. Michael Heller includes the too-often neglected Lorine Niedecker in their number; and if we adopt Michael Palmer's description of their work as characterised by "resistance, social awareness, and exploratory integrity"[4] then the Objectivists would include, in addition to all the writers discussed in this book from Stein to Howe, Robin Blaser, Robert Duncan, Charles Olson, Jack Spicer, and a host of others, including Palmer himself.

Nevertheless, calling the poem an object is extremely useful, though it has its shortcomings. The great virtue is in suggesting that poems share with physical objects an identity separable from those who make or perceive them, while the great drawback is the suggestion that they have the static quality we associate with nouns, semantically considered.[5] In a world whose certainties are as undermined as I suggest in the following pages, our sense of what constitutes an object has been radically problematised. To call a poem an object is not to see it in the traditional art sense of "masterpiece": aloof, irreproachable, transcendent, separate from our lives; but to see it as an autonomous object, an identifiable thing that we can look at out there in the world, and respond to – much, perhaps, as we might respond to a chair or a desk: something of use, but something whose existence is nevertheless independent of or goes beyond its use. By no means, then, "art for art's sake." Chairs and desks are so heavily contextualised in our culture that it is extremely difficult to see them.

The introduction of so-called primitive art into western Europe and North America in the closing years of the nineteenth century, through the studios of Braque, Picasso, and Brancusi for instance, was an act of such radical decontextualisation and rehistoricisation of that art as to give those artifacts the kind of status as object that I am talking about. Such objects are difficult to read, because they challenge our assumptions about the processes of reading, about what constitutes "value," about knowledge and about "knowing." A poem as a decontextualised object creates enormous problems for the reader, and it is the experience of these problems which constitutes that of the poems discussed in these essays. The kind of interaction that takes place between perceiver and object in this situation is such that the very term *object* begins to lose its identity as noun, becoming agency, or verb. Gertrude Stein wrote "a noun is the name of anything, why after a thing is named write about it"; she sought in poetry so to reconstitute the noun (the poem seeks to attain the condition of noun) that it embodies naming as a perceptual and cognitive *act*.[6] When William Carlos Williams began thinking about the poem as "a machine made out of words"[7] he seems to have been thinking of the poem as verb in addition to thinking of it as made thing. The *Century Dictionary* defines machine as "any organization by which power not mechanical is applied and made effective,"[8] – a means, that is, of transferring energy. In 1951 Olson called the poem "a high energy-construct," defining it as "energy transferred from where the poet got it . . . , by way of the poem itself to . . . the reader."[9]

One effect of rethinking writing in these terms is to open the poem to registering and attending to areas of experience hitherto deemed unworthy of literary attention. By denying traditional distinctions between poetry and "life," as well as between genres, and by dissolving or ignoring boundaries between "high" and "popular" art, the poem is thus free to incorporate what Jonathan Monroe reserved for the prose-poem: "the restoration of lost voices [of] prosaic speech and everyday struggles – the struggle, among other things, for the power of speech," and to absorb "the speech of the marginal and the oppressed."[10] The poem is free to be inarticulate. Even to stutter.

For these reasons I hesitate to call all this a tradition; that word usually refers to a set of beliefs informing social and political programmes, or even adherence to sets of formal proprieties. Nor is it a tradition in the sense writers and critics talk of a "Pound–Eliot" tradition or, as does the journal *Sagetrieb,* a "Pound–H.D.–Williams tradition."[11] The mode of writing these essays consider, radical though it is from a social and a political point of view, is hardly to be characterised as political in the sense that Pound's, Eliot's, or even Williams's work can be said to be political, for above all else it refuses to be programmatic. It is too conscious of the world as, in the long run, unknowable, impenetrable, and disobedient (or recalcitrant) to human orders; of the future as utterly unpredictable. Similarly, of the incapacity of language to describe or fix, and also of the blur, rather than the distinction, between the outer and inner world: Language is unreliable as a register of either, for what we say registers accurately neither our thought nor our feeling, our anguish nor our desire. Ordinary syntax is, like the language of classical mathematics, incapable of describing a world whose unity seems more often delusional than actual.

My discussion of Gertrude Stein, which opens this book, describes this sort of modernism as disjunctive writing, in flat and generally "abstract" language, recalcitrant to description, ambiguous, highly wrought, apparently disjointed and even vacant (which is to say, seemingly "about" nothing at all). Yet it is identifiably a passionate and extremely concentrated act of attention to a tangible (i.e., perceived) world whose most salient characteristics (multiplicity and uncertainty) are aspects of its inexplicableness. This sort of modernism is one response to a long series of shifts in epistemology and ontology which can most adequately be seen as linguistic, in that the kinds of certainties traditionally attached to linguistic statements were undermined and subverted, coming to a head around the close of the nineteenth century. In 1843, for instance, Sir William Rowan Hamilton "discovered" (his term) a revolutionary algebra ("Quaternions") in which the product of *ij* is not equal to *ji* but to *minus ji* – a topsy-turvy algebra Karl Marx seems to have adapted in *Das Kapital* (1867) when he argued that "*20 yards of linen = 1 coat*" is not necessarily the same as "*1 coat = 20 yards of linen*."[12] Such a redefinition of the notion of equivalence, part and parcel of an overall deracination of language, is symptomatic of a major breakdown of traditional hierarchic orders, an uprooting and ideological failure central to the subject of this book.

Darwin's proposal in 1859 that we are descended from apes was as much a threat to common sense and thus to linguistic assumptions as were Freud's proposals. Formulated and elaborated throughout a long career which began in 1885–6, these included the suggestions that we do not know why we do things, because the springs of our behaviour lie in our subconscious; that dreams have meaning; and that our casual or mistaken utterances are more meaningful than our deliberate (i.e., intended) ones. Our meaning is not what we meant to say, and mistakes are not (as Robert Duncan was fond of saying) to be thought of as mis-takes. When, in *Prolegomena to the Study of Greek Religion* (1903), Jane Ellen Harrison demonstrated that ancient Greek religion and mythology originated in dark and sometimes bloody rituals rather than in reasonable thought or in fiction; and that Dionysus, the principle of irrationality, is as important in Greek thought and life as is Apollo, the principle of reason; she demolished the comfortable notion of the Golden Age of classical Greece, changing the meaning of the word "classical" forever after, and radically questioning, with Freud as well as Sir James G. Frazer, the notion that we are the reasonable creatures of a rational culture. Frazer, in his comparative study of the beliefs and institutions of mankind, *The Golden Bough* (1890–1915), helped establish the idea that folklore and myth embody ways of looking at the world and ways of thinking about it. This gave impetus on one hand to anthropological studies which gradually dispelled the notion that certain societies and individuals are "primitive" or "savage" (thus questioning the very notion of "civilised"), and on the other to studies of language and symbolism. Similarly, investigations of Homer and of oral poetry began to undermine notions of orthodox grammar and conventional verbal logic by recognising paratactic syntax as a legitimate structure for the sentence. This undermined the predilection for hypotactic subordination and social hierarchy built into such linguistic proprieties as style, grammar, and spelling.

The pattern, in which hierarchies break down to be replaced by pluralities and polyvalencies, and certainty is supplanted (usurped) by indeterminacy, is repeated in all branches of human knowledge. Among the writers discussed in this book it takes the form of an oppositional poetics which embraces as energy source and material the very subversion and deracination which so distressed writers like T. S. Eliot. "Go / contrary," said Charles Olson, "go / sing."[13] For example, the discovery of paleolithic cave paintings at Altamira in 1879 and at Pair-non-pair and La Mouthe in the last decade of the nineteenth century, where such paintings (and thousands of them were discovered) gradually led to the recognition of archaic or paleolithic man as intelligent, artistic, and possessed of a culture. The study of these paintings and of aboriginal art from Africa, the Americas, and Australasia contributed at the turn of the century to fragmenting of perspective, breakdown of verisimilitude and the picture-plane in painting, and to the legitimation of alternative modes. Cézanne, in any case, showed that paintings are not pictures but *paint,* and Mallarmé told Degas that "poetry is not written with ideas but with words"[14] – a notion Williams would refine in the late 1950s to "*the spaces between the words,* in our modern understanding."[15] In the twentieth century Werner Heisenberg learned (through Willard Gibbs) how to use Hamilton's quaternions in quantum analysis. The world of quantum physics defies rationality, since light is *both* wave *and* particle, since (as Niels Bohr put it in a lecture in 1927) "an independent reality in the ordinary physical sense can neither be ascribed to the phenomena nor to the agencies of observation,"[16] since every observation of phenomena introduces uncontrollable elements, since space and time cannot be distinguished, and thus cause and effect cannot be discerned. "If we ask" (this is J. Robert Oppenheimer) "whether the position of the electron remains the same, we must say 'No'; if we ask whether the electron's position changes with time, we must say 'No'; if we ask whether the electron is at rest, we must say 'No'; if we ask whether it is in motion, we must say 'No'."[17] Citing, in "The Virgin and the Dynamo" (1905), Samuel Pierpont Langley's idea of "an indeterminable number of universes interwined," Henry Adams called this "supersensual world in which [man] could measure nothing except by chance collisions of movements imperceptible to his senses," a case of "physics stark mad in metaphysics."[18] Language can neither describe nor fix "reality" because reality itself is beyond both definition and knowledge, "a universe," as Marshall Berman put it, "in which all that is solid melts into air."[19]

In March, 1914, T. S. Eliot was a student at Harvard Graduate School, working on the philosophy of F. H. Bradley, and one of his teachers, Bertrand Russell, commented that faced with such a world "the *ordering* intellect grows weary, and becomes slovenly through despair."[20] Henry Adams's remark in the *Education of Henry Adams* (published in 1907), which Zukofsky was fond of quoting, that "the child born in 1900 would then be born into a new world which would not be a unity but a multiple" found its echo in Gertrude Stein's line in *Tender Buttons* (1911) that "The use of this is manifold," and in William Carlos Williams's impatient explanation to Harriet Monroe in 1913 that "life is above all things else at any moment subversive of life as it was the moment before – always new, irregular."[21] Writing can be no more definitive than can one's place in history.

Yet, John Seed has asked, "What else but the real history of his times – the determining conditions in which people live – should be the poet's concern?"[22] At best, as any historian knows, "determining conditions" can only be guessed at, though each of us, perhaps, can point to those apparently governing her or his daily life; guessed at *there,* they are real enough. And "the real history"? In 1930 Zukofsky called it "the attractions of living recorded,"[23] thus relocating "the real." Zukofsky insisted by that, as my second through fifth essays elaborate, on the particulars of the physical world, material daily living, and on the poem as *material* register of the poet's own registry of that world. Attentive to concrete particulars, the writer must avoid abstraction, or what Williams in 1919 called "an easy lateral sliding,"[24] and shun the personal, psychological narrative which attempts to display some form of "self-worth" or attain some kind of "self-realization." Writing of this sort has no therapeutic function whatsoever, and cannot accurately be termed "confessional." As Bob Perelman has pointed out, "real history" refuses to place the "I" in a privileged position, unaffected by the world, aloof from the reader. Rather, it "insists on the reader participating, which is reasonable, seeing that language is as much in the reader's head as the writer's."[25] In even the most difficult and resistant passages – say by Gertrude Stein, or in late work by Zukofsky – the writing springs from an event in the "real world": a glimpse of a book, a reflection of light, a public speech, a newspaper report, a word. Such pretexts of the writing may not be discernible to the reader, since the writing does not so much seek to encode a series of paraphraseable truths as to enact immediacies of perception.[26] As it happens, problematic, often unaccountable, such writing has epistemological, ontological, and indeed social and political import.

The act of writing, or rather of enunciating, making "sense," articulating (or not), in constituting the poem becomes part of its "content." In Zukofsky's and Davenport's work as in Stein's and Howe's, compositional procedures are part of the writing, and the reader has her or his part to do. When Williams said of "Objectivism" in 1963 that "the mind rather than the unsupported eye entered the picture" he was simply (!) rephrasing what he had said in 1930 in an essay on Gertrude Stein written with Zukofsky's help, that "the whole of writing . . . is an alertness not to let go of a possibility of movement. . . . The goal is to keep a beleaguered line of *understanding which has movement* from breaking down."[27] Basil Bunting seems to have had something very similar in mind when in the early 1930s he wrote of "the events that *make up* the world" (my italics): Facts are events, themselves "a single complex occurrence."[28]

In 1928, after reading Zukofsky's "Poem Beginning 'The'," William Carlos Williams commented that "It escapes me in its analysis (thank God) and strikes against me a thing (thank God). There are not so many things in the world as we commonly imagine. Plenty of debris, plenty of smudges."[29] With Zukofsky, Oppen asked that the poem meet "'a test of sincerity' – that there is a moment, an actual time, when you believe something to be true, and you construct a meaning from those moments of conviction."[30] This is not far removed from Williams's suggestion in 1925 that Poe's misplaced reputation as "a fault of nature" and "a find for French eyes" was the direct result of his rejection of "colonial imitation," and of his assertion that place "*must* be where he *was*."[31] Williams's italicising of *was* is signally revealing, for it suggests that Poe is, as Zukofsky and Oppen ask, bearing witness. The poem is to be testimony, taking its identity and function from a view of the world that dismisses, as largely irrelevant to the work of art, the notion of masterpiece. A concern for the latter rests on a consideration of the means by which something called "nature" becomes something called "art"; it rests on the notion that what constitutes "art" is necessarily preconditioned by a set of rules, stated or not, which exists prior to the work and to which the work must conform. The predilection for rules that the notion of masterpiece fosters separates the poem from the outside world, demands it conform to abstract criteria. In separating the work of art from the work of nature the artist separates the self from the work, and the work from the life: Art is seen as immutable, even absolute. Further, such a view fetishises and commoditises the work of art, so that it becomes subject to possession, and the act of "understanding" the poem is identified with the comprehensive act of taking something in order to put it away. This is what the writers discussed in this book eschew, virtually at any cost, for the poem must be true to itself. "I am in-bound to the event," Robert Duncan wrote in 1958; "I bore witness to the order of meanings that were there."[32] As an act of testimony the poem is anchored firmly in the compositional moment of the poet's life, including accidentals immediately to hand, and incorporates into itself its surrounding events. Susan Howe has argued persuasively that Emily Dickinson's poems are frequently shaped by the size of the paper on which they are written; a number of critics have remarked upon the relationship between Stein's writing and what was printed on the cover of the *cahier* in which she was writing.[33] If the poem is true to its own history (the history of its composition) then necessarily the poem is error free. Words, words, words. Where, as Zukofsky asked L. S. Dembo, are you going to get them? Where do they come from? Are words, as Basil Bunting once half-seriously suggested, "mouthfuls of air"? Sometimes, yes. But there is a physical and social world, already there.[34] Poems, that is to say, are usually about something, start somewhere. "A" – 13 seems to have started in a stroll and conversation with Zukofsky's son Paul, but the poem does not exist for the sake of that sort of subject matter. It exists for the complex of relationships apparent in its perception and cognitive reception.

All of this suggests, at least in part, why it is extremely difficult to talk of Stein's "disciples" or even of her "imitators."[35] If she attracted any literary followers in the 1920s, the only ones we can readily name are Edith Sitwell (whose work is extremely unlike Stein's) or the eccentric and largely forgotten Abraham Lincoln Gillespie. It is not even a tradition of forms, or of formal concerns. Even with the wisdom of hindsight, one cannot predict, say, a Susan Howe from a Gertrude Stein. Although in important respects both writers share a methodology and attitude towards their poetics, each is conditioned by a radically different ideology due to their necessarily discrepant histories. Yet Howe is very much a part of the "line" in poetry that these essays explore, as are, indeed, the confrontational poetics of Bruce Andrews ("Context needs a Contest")[36] and the subversive hilarity of Steve McCaffery's videos.

Louis Zukofsky is, after Gertrude Stein, the great central figure in this poetics, yet it is clear to even the most casual reader that they radically differ from one another. If Stein is an "inclusive" writer in that each piece in *Tender Buttons* has (as Oscar Cargill complained)[37] too much meaning rather than too little, she is not one in the sense that Zukofsky is, for her writing is notoriously devoid of immediately identifiable reference. Stein exploits strategies that enhance wide ranges of possible meaning, but the range is predominantly syntactic; Zukofsky, in some respects like Joyce, exploits allusion and reference only in the long run to disable them or (more frequently) to render them ancillary to the poem. Like Stephen Dedalus, he tends to "work in all he knows," yet, as he told Lorine Niedecker in 1935 about "A" – 8, the reader must juxtapose the statements to read them as music, and *never* read them as explanation.[38]

Meaning is problematic for each of the writers discussed in these essays, and it is precisely that problem which makes their work so intransigent and so attractive. Stein's writing foregrounds linguistic rather than thematic or narrative procedures and connections while demonstrating that coding is not the motive for writing, or rather, that decoding is not where it leads: Writing does not bend toward a singular Truth. This is not to say that her work is without themes, but that she eschews conventional discursive or narrative patterns just as she avoids normative, narrative, or discursive syntax. *Patriarchal Poetry* is not organized under a series of headings, like an essay, though it fiercely attacks patriarchy – a particular form of hierarchic ordering; *Lifting Belly* adheres to no readily recogniseable narrative structure, even though it records Stein's life with Alice Toklas from day to day. Characteristically narrative, Bunting's writing moves meaning to the periphery, as does Zukofsky's, giving primacy to sound: "the meaning is hardly ever of any importance," he said; and he once praised Persian music to Zukofsky because it is what he called "multilinear" rather than monolinear.[39]

It is the multilinearity that is crucial, and the recurrent collision in twentieth-century American poetics is between semantic singularity and multiplicity. Pound said that "the monotheistic temperament has been the curse of our time,"[40] yet he could not escape it himself, witness his fascism, which proves him the child of his age. The central crisis has been of hierarchic thought, in its sociopolitical, economic, and literal manifestations. Heterogeneous diversity has undermined authority, challenging and reconstituting the processes by which meaning comes to be, and discrediting traditional notions of authorship and reading which repeatedly accord the writers discussed in this book neglect if not outright hostility. Bruce Andrews speaks of the necessity to abandon the controls of hermeneutic for the multiplexity of behavioural reading.[41] The increasingly uncomfortable misalignment, which relegated certain writers to submerged, eruptive, and insurrectional activity within and beside accredited modes, was exacerbated in America by the linguistic disruption and even demolition of empowered cultural patterns through the agency of foreign immigration.

The same year Henry Adams was pointing to Samuel Pierpont Langley's "indeterminable number of universes intertwined" (1905), Henry James – in a speech to the graduating class at Bryn Mawr College – was pointing to multiplicities and contradictions much closer to home: a virtually indeterminable number of immigrants, bringing alternative cultures with them, disjoining the language from "the family, the ancestral circle."[42]

With a strictly English ancestral circle in mind, James, high-Victorian, Anglophile, and frankly "conservative" (47), in *The Question of Our Speech* flatly blamed what he called "the high modernism of the conditions now surrounding, on this continent, the practice of our language" (40) for the "mere helpless slobber of disconnected vowel noises" (25) which American language has become, "an easy and ignoble minimum" (16) barely distinguishable from "the grunting, the squealing, the barking, or the roaring of animals" (16). Embodied in its most virulent form as a "vast contingent of aliens" (44), the "disaster" (40) of high modernism threatens the very foundations of American culture. "The forces of looseness are in possession of the field," he warned (47), and they "dump their mountain of promiscuous material into the foundations" of the language itself (43).

Of the nearly 28 million immigrants to the continental United States in the period 1820–1910, 63.5% of them (i.e., nearly 18 million) arrived in the thirty-one years 1880–1910, and 31.5% (almost 8.9 million) in the first eleven years of the twentieth century. In 1905, when James was speaking at Bryn Mawr, immigrants were arriving on average 2,400 a day; two years later, at the peak of immigration, the rate was over 3,500 a day.[43] Few of them spoke English. In 1854, one of the peak immigration years, half of the 427,833 immigrants had been German speaking, and 37%, English; in 1882, 32% of 788,922 immigrants spoke German, and 22% English; in 1907, of 1,285,349 immigrants, 29% and 8.9% spoke German and English, respectively. The Census Bureau reported that in 1900 over 12 million (16.4%) of a total population of 76.3 million were foreign born, and roughly 16 million (21.4%) were native born of foreign parents; that is to say, 37.8% of the population were either foreign born or native born of foreign stock. The thirteenth Census (1910) reported that of the more than 32 million Americans in the continental United States enumerated as "Foreign White Stock" (i.e., 35% of a total population of nearly 92 million), well over 22 million of them – nearly 24% of the white population of the continental United States – came from non–English-speaking stock.[44] Since the Census only recorded statistics for the white population, the figures are conservative, but it seems reasonable to estimate that roughly one person in four in the continental United States in 1910 learned English as an additional language, or did not know it at all.

Four of the writers discussed in this book were "native born of non-English foreign-stock." Gertrude Stein, William Carlos Williams, Charles Reznikoff, and Louis Zukofsky either learned English as their second (or third) language or grew up bilingual. When she was eight months old, Gertrude Stein's German-speaking family moved to Vienna and stayed there until she was four and a half, when they moved to Paris (which they left when Stein was five). Spanish was the predominant language in the house when William Carlos Williams was a small child; his mother preferred French to her native Spanish and learned English only reluctantly and imperfectly. Zukofsky, like Reznikoff the child of Russian Jewish immigrants, according to his own testimony was first "exposed" to English when he went to school, the family language being Yiddish.[45] Reznikoff's family was bilingual, though he commented that "my mother's English was very limited" and "my Yiddish is very bad."[46] We are "loose, dissociated (linguistically), yawping speakers of a new language" said Williams in 1948, echoing the Whitman who almost a century earlier had steeped himself in the foreign or rustic tongues of stage drivers and teamsters overheard at Pfaff's bar on Broadway.[47]

Faced with the "unprecedented" and "uncontrolled assault" (40) on the language by "the American Dutchman and Dago, as the voice of the people describes them" (41), James called for the restoration of a "tone-standard" (12) to retrieve American culture from "the grimaces, the shouts, shrieks and yells, ranging over the whole gamut of ugliness, irrelevance, dissonance, of a mighty maniac who has broken loose and is running amuck through the spheres alike of sense and sound" (43). A tone-standard: "The French, the Germans, the Italians, the English perhaps in particular, and many other people, Occidental and Oriental, I surmise, not excluding the Turks and the Chinese, have for the symbol of education, of civility, a tone-standard; we alone flourish in undisturbed and . . . something like sublime unconsciousness of any such possibility" (12). Invoking as he was the authority of a koiné, "a common language, with its modes of employment, its usage, its authority, its beauty" (6), and the authority of a "coherent culture" (6) embodying "our admirable English tradition" (20), James was taking the position of the imperial governor faced with demands for colonial independence, pleading for canonical standards and norms, indeed the restoration of specific unitary cultural values and authority, for order. He is pleading for a world of stable forms, clear differentiations, propriety, and decorum; what Charles Bernstein has called "an imperial clarity for an imperial world."[48] In short, he is alarmist. "All the while we sleep," James said,

> the innumerable aliens are sitting up (*they* don't sleep!) to work their will on their new inheritance and prove to us that they are without any finer feeling or more conservative instinct of consideration for it, more fond, unutterable association with it, more hovering, caressing curiosity about it, than they may have on the subject of so many yards of freely figured oilcloth, from the shop,

> that they are preparing to lay down, for convenience, on kitchen floor or kitchen staircase . . . : durable, tough, cheap (45–6; James's italics).

In *The Question of Our Speech* James affords an almost textbook example demonstrating Jacques Attali's proposition that "subversion in musical production opposes a new syntax to the existing syntax, from the point of view of which it is noise."[49] The noise of immigrants mangling American English undoes the heart and soul of James's civilisation: the power to discriminate and order. James's argument rests not simply on notions of the "best," but on the notion of "intrinsic" value,[50] without which culture can be neither a unity nor monolithic, and certainly can no longer be thought so.

Faced with this loss of Culture, demolition of History, and break of Continuity, many writers turned away from such edicts. The situation of the American writer in the first thirty or forty years of this century bears distinct resemblances to the situation of the writer in the postcolonial world where the grand hegemonic authority of rule by imperial standard is giving way to a frequently bewildered and more often than not anarchic series of disagreements which threaten to render the social and political fabric utterly incoherent. Which tradesman was it, asks the little Baron Snorck in Zukofsky's novel *Little,* whose name was Einstein?[51] The withdrawal of ruling power is accompanied by an apparent loss of a shared world. It was with an air of faint surprise and even relief that George Oppen told L. S. Dembo in 1968 that "It turns out it's true that one can find common ground, provided only that the mind possesses that virtue, which is just to say provided people give a damn, really."[52]

But of course the imperial rule did not disappear all at once (and has not, indeed, disappeared yet). The non–English-speaking immigrants did not spread themselves evenly over the continental United States, but tended to cluster in New England, the Middle Atlantic States (New York, New Jersey, Pennsylvania, and Delaware) and the Midwest. They avoided the South. In 1900 only 7.9% of the white population of the South was foreign born or native born of foreign stock (as compared to 37.8% for the continental United States); fewer, that is to say, than in 1870, the earliest year in which such a count was made. In 1850, 45% of the population of the Middle Atlantic States was foreign born (655,929 of them in New York, the bulk of them presumably in New York City), while only 14% of the population of New England was foreign born (and many of them Irish).[53] It is hardly surprising that Southern writing should be linguistically and culturally distinct from that of the rest of the nation, and it is surely no accident that the New Criticism, essentially

Anglophile as it was, should have close ties with southern universities and colleges as well as with the Ivy League.

A Lorine Niedecker poem asks the carpenter "Homer / did you write that book?"[54] In such a muddled world what is a writer to do? Go to Europe, as Pound and Eliot (and Stein) did? Vigorously reject the English tradition, like Williams? Perhaps. In the opening poem of "Hugh Selwyn Mauberley," Pound affords virtually a classic instance of the postcolonial writer's dilemma. Invoking the peremptory English structure in order to undermine its monolithic authority, the poem ends up reinforcing what it seeks to dismiss, for the reader needs the cultural apparatus the poem questions in order to understand that the apparatus is being challenged. In inviting the reader to place the stuffy and self-satisfied voice of educated literary authority against the personal voice of the (imaginary?) poet and find it wanting, the poem ends up acculturating readers to the hegemonic standard. In demanding that readers recognise a culture they may not know, the poem is likely to be misunderstood by those whose experience of clubby cultivated London literary voices is too limited for nuances of tone to be significant, or to do other than baffle them. Similarly, much of the energy of Howe's poetry arises from the intensity of her desire for the security of nouns (defined, known) and the uncertainty of verbs (in process, unpredictable, incomplete). To disregard such tensions, or to dismiss them as inconsistencies and thus as "errors" is to dehistoricise these writers. The writers discussed in this book share a historical situation and position. This is why Basil Bunting (who as a Northumbrian poet sought to break the central authority of the London literary tradition, and found himself numbered among the Objectivists) talked of the need "to escape from the hampering measures imposed by our memory of several centuries of English verse written by models imported from other lands."[55] Williams learned to celebrate the immensity of the task facing the writer dealing with a deculturated language. "And what do I care," he asked in *Kora in Hell,* "if yellow and red are Spain's riches and Spain's good blood. Here yellow and red mean simply Autumn!"[56]

James was right to define high modernism in linguistic terms: The fragmentation of the language accelerates that of culture. The immigrant learning English "streetwise," while living and working with other immigrants, is hardly integrating into a literary or cultural tradition. Learning English through grammar books and by recourse to dictionaries and primers is not conducive to an absorption of the hegemonic culture. Small wonder that Zukofsky should write, from 1932 to 1934, a fiction titled *Thanks to the Dictionary*. A condensation of the story of David beginning in 1 Sam. 16, drawing on a vocabulary determined by (random?) page samplings from two dictionaries, it attempts to demonstrate that writing need not, indeed, be about any particular thing at all.[57] It is almost a commonplace amongst twentieth-century American writers to notice, as Stein did in her 1935 lectures on narration at the University of Chicago, that in American writing, words "began to detach themselves from the solidity of anything"; long before Barthes's floating of the signifier she said that American language exhibits a "lack of connection"[58] with material daily living. Small wonder that Laura Riding commented in 1927 that "None of the words Miss Stein uses . . . has ever had any history. . . . They contain no references, no meanings."[59] In *Kora in Hell* (1919) Williams defined the poem in terms of its linguistic immediacy, unmediated by (Anglophile) cultural presuppositions and prerequisites: "That which is heard from the lips of those to whom we are talking in our day's-affairs mingles with what we see in the streets and everywhere about us as it mingles also in our imaginations. By this chemistry is fabricated a language of the day which shifts and reveals its meaning as clouds shift and turn in the sky."[60]

Yeats in 1901 complained of Longfellow that "no words of his borrow their beauty from those that used them before, and one can get all that there is in story and idea without seeing them as if moving before a half-faded curtain embroidered with kings and queens, their loves and battles and days out hunting, or else with holy letters and images of so great antiquity that nobody can tell the god or goddess they would commend to an unfading memory."[61] It is not that Williams's language is without history, but that its history is not European; rather, it is local, polyglot, and as likely as not merely personal. It is not that those who learn a language through books rather than through speech rarely come to feel the kinship of words, so much as that the grounds of what I. A. Richards calls "the interinanimation of words" have radically shifted.[62] Much of the language Americans used, certainly, had no visible antecedents as they walked down the street, and the imperative, especially but not only in school, was to adopt an English overlay. Malcolm Cowley complained bitterly that "our studies were useless or misdirected, especially our studies in English literature: the authors we were forced to read, and Shakespeare most of all, were unpleasant to our palate; they had the taste of chlorinated water."[63] What landscapes did Charles Olson's father carry in his head as he walked his Post Office rounds in Worcester? What mythologies did he attach to them or find in them? When Williams calls *Paterson* "a reply to Greek and Latin with the bare hands" he is identifying his poem as an attempt to end the split between American writing, speech, and landscape by getting rid of the English and European lamination. In the context of the state of the American language, Malcolm Cowley and Slater Brown's remark in a 1924 issue of *Broom* that "Eliot believes in tradition, form, everything dead,"[64] is both poignant and urgent. Such cultural breakdown redefines ignorance as it redefines "education," and alters their value. "Memory," Bruce Andrews observes, "gives us a system of reference. And opacity gives us a system of amnesia, or a reminder of the mnemonic challenge."[65] And the challenge? To make "sense" – an act of great attentiveness, insisting as it does on the particular, the concrete, the present; resisting as it does abstraction and theory.

Little Baron Snorck's question about Einstein is central to the poetics discussed in this book. For if you have a fragmented culture in which the solid security of shared (and perhaps unspoken) assumptions and traditions is no longer available, then you can no longer depend upon implicit references. If in such a world there is so much information that you can no longer identify (let alone prescribe) "essential knowledge," then you can no longer assume your audience knows or cares for the same as you do: the ground of sharing and of care shifts. If you have a world in which masterpieces are no longer recognisable and works of art no longer identifiable, a world without authority, and, for the non–English-speaking immigrant to America, a world without any history except that which the immigrant carries, then the ground of recognition shifts, too. If the language you speak to all intents and purposes has no visible antecedents as you walk down the street, then in writing a poem the very language itself is at risk: In saying what we mean we do not necessarily mean what we say. "All the questions they ask," said George Oppen: "'What if red doesn't mean to him what it means to me?' Well, all those questions get answered."[66] But they get answered behaviourally, as cognitive response. John Berger comments that the effect of modern methods of reproduction has been "to destroy the authority of art and to remove it – or rather to remove its images which they reproduce – from any preserve. For the first time ever, images of art have become ephemeral, ubiquitous, insubstantial, available, valueless, free."[67] Pound, and after him Duncan and Olson, said repeatedly that we can only use what we've got, rather than what we long for. As Williams implicitly asked of Poe, where else can your place be, except where you *are*. His words from *Kora in Hell,* that the poem be made from "that which is heard from the lips of those to whom we are talking in our day's-affairs mingle[d] with what we see in the streets and everywhere about us," suggest a similar project. The poem is an act of attention for the reader as it is for the writer: an attendance on language.

In the Preface to *An "Objectivists" Anthology* (1931) Louis Zukofsky talked of poetry through the analogy of cabinet making, specifically comparing the poem to a desk as an *object,* an assemblage of irreducible parts, a piece of work which embodies (something to do with capillaries and veins) the process of its making, and thus incorporates something of its maker. Once you've built the desk you cannot control *X*'s response to it, although it's unlikely that *X* will try to eat it. *X* might burn it, or put it in a field, or paint it, or take it apart and make something else with it, or even sit at it. It's quite likely, of course, that *X* will recognise what it is – a desk is a fairly common object, after all – and will assess it, analyse it, in terms of its deskness. In thinking of poems as objects, not only does the writer have no control over what the poem might mean to its reader, but the ground of meaning is shifted from what perhaps had best be called a series of cultural imperatives (such as the use of symbolism to reinforce certain social attitudes and beliefs) to the very act of reading itself. Value is thus shifted from artifact to process. Hence Zukofsky can speak of the *Cantos,* despite their complexity, as meaning simply themselves, rendering love and hate to a chain of *poetic* fact. The point is not, then, what the *Cantos* might tell us about love and hate, any more than the point of a desk is what it might tell us about eighteenth-century Parisian economics. Looking for news about love and hate in poems is to read with a predatory intent and eye. It is the *form,* even the gestalt, of the desk that matters – someone unversed in economics or in the history of furniture design can still discern the *desk,* not the wood it's built of.[68] Cultural baggage seriously impedes the act of reading, whether we are reading poems or reading desks, by fostering confusion between historical (or economic or whatever) fact and "poetic fact."

The sort of ironic detail in films like Jim Jarmusch's *Mystery Train,* where the camera picks up the street name *Chaucer* in an utterly derelict part of Memphis through which two Japanese teenyboppers walk on their pilgrimage to Graceland, finds its parallels in Teenage Mutant Ninja Turtles named Michelangelo, Leonardo, Donatello, and Raphael, which may or may not, on the part of the scriptwriters,[69] be an elaborate joke designed to deculturate the audience. In deprivileging or perhaps reprivileging cultural icons, such a disturbance of settled hierarchies and authority is but an extension of Williams's refusal to let red and yellow mean anything but themselves, or autumn – signifying, that is, the local, what is immediately known, without exaggeration or overlay from elsewhere, in the here and now. Hence *Kora in Hell* or the birth-of-Venus passages at the opening of *White Mule* are written against a dominant cultural apparatus, in opposition to a cultural baggage that impedes observation by inferiorising immediacy, making it stand for something else and turning it into a transparent window that seeks to deny its own existence through self-effacement. He called it "crude symbolism."[70] Any other baggage attached to the text is up to the reader.

Works like *Kora in Hell* herald such activities as Steve McCaffery's radical assaults on what he calls the word as "postponed presence."[71] His video "An Intention to Be Wrong" films a series of encounters that starts with truth set as a verbivisual adequation between what the audience sees and what the audience hears ("the man sits down"). Through five restagings the commentary gets increasingly out of kilter with what appears on the screen, and the adequation collapses as the description and its enactment move from fact through metaphor to downright lie.[72] We cannot decode the speech in ordinary ways: and the astonishing gulf between what the eye hears and what the ear sees is utterly hilarious. The increasing dislocation of reference is a result of an increasing disconnection between the words and their anticipated meaning, between the filmed event and the anticipated verbal description. It finds its literary equivalent in works as different as Bruce Andrews's *Give Em Enough Rope* (1987) and McCaffery's *The Black Debt* (1989):[73] The increasing mismatch between such semantic elements as sentence pattern, repetition, voice, and context so undermines ordinary decoding procedures that the reader is forced to take account of both the individual particulars (each separate word) and the totality in which those words appear (the whole text). In effect, such work presents islands of localised meaning, promoting (in McCaffery's words) "forms based upon object-presence: the pleasure of graphic or phonic imprint, for instance, their value as sheer linguistic stimuli."[74]

The point is that the poem must exist in the world in the way that a desk does, and although the analogy is too simple, it is useful in reminding us that poems do not have a "point" any more than a desk does. In discursive or even in "referential" terms a desk is not making an argument; referentially speaking, it is culturally independent. Whatever argument the poem may make in the course of our reading is the lumber out of which it is built – it may or may not be recognisable and may or may not engage assent. Basil Bunting rather irritably told Alan Neame, who was asking him about meaning in the *Cantos,* that "I don't see why people should want to 'understand' everything in a poem."[75] In 1965 Jack Spicer said that "if you have an idea that you want to develop, don't write a poem about it," because the poem you write "will really have a meaning different from what you started out with the idea of."[76] Spicer, taking further than Bunting was prepared to the notion that the poet is not responsible for the meaning of the poem, stating flatly that the poet has little or no control over it, saw as crucial the necessity to "distinguish between you and the poem" (177): The poet, "something being transmitted into" (178), must obey the poem as it is dictated to her or him; the structure of the language (grammar, morphology, syntax, and so on) in resisting the poem interferes with it (205). For the structure of the language is normative; it sets patterns and presuppositions of correctness, meaning, and its constitution. "The more you know (in a university sense)," said Spicer, "the more the temptation is" to interfere with the poem (178–9). In 1942 Williams confessed to envying Eliot: "If only I had the sound and knowledge of the Greek in my head how I could put it to use today. But maybe I couldn't. I might become . . . helpless with it."[77]

Robert Duncan was fond of telling the story of Ezra Pound buying an Italian typewriter, with the slash mark (/) where the period was on his old one. Half-way through typing a canto for Harriet Monroe, Pound noticed that where his original had contained periods, his clean copy had a slash. Consequently, said Duncan, Pound rewrote the poem to incorporate the change as a necessity. Whether the story is true or not is less important than the fact that Duncan told it: In being obedient to the history of its own composition the poem is freed of all error, and the process of writing the poem becomes part of the poem's "subject matter." Zukofsky's regret that he had printed the early versions of "A" 1–7 in *An "Objectivists" Anthology* springs from his sense that the poet should not betray his poem by falsifying it: Errors (such as those revised out after 1931) should be incorporated into the poem as it evolves.[78] The essential difficulty is to break through patterns of expectation, desire, and preconception, even the preconception of what a poem is. Williams wondered more than once whether his interests were "pre-art" and whether he was a "barbarian."[79] Such independence of the poem from the poet is part and parcel of the necessity to break the mediation of language and pass through into the immediacy of experience by making language itself the experiential source.

The independence of writers from their productions has its corollary in the independence of the written from the reader – poets, after all, are readers too, even of their own poems. Gertrude Stein's words which stand at the head of this Introduction remind us of that independence, that writing is *text* not story, and remind us too that through such independence the writing and reading are acts:

> When you realize that . . . the bible lives not by its stories but by its texts you see how inevitably one wants neither harmony, pictures stories nor portraits. You have to do something else to continue.

That "something else" is the cognitive act, the verbalizing act, even (as Aristotelians might put it, in opposition perhaps to Spicer) a processual mimesis. To attend to the poem rather than to what is outside it (but the distinctions of inner and outer are blurred) is to engage in the interaction of perceiver / thinker / poet / reader with object / poem, and such interaction is always problematic. It is especially so if, in reading, we expect a more-or-less paraphraseable meaning to emerge. The works discussed in this book frequently include their own instructions on how to read them because, in the act of writing, the poet (like the reader in the act of reading) is learning how to see, register, and read. Olson's much-quoted insistence that "one perception must immediately and directly lead to a further perception,"[80] because springing from a shared historicality, has a common application to all of the writers discussed in these essays.

Transgressive of traditional and normative modes, reading and writing are social as well as cognitive acts. As we read, individual perceptions come together to compose an environment of individual and discrete perceptions, rather than a consciousness unified by some single criterion which, coming down from centuries before, bears the name of Truth. Writing of the sort discussed in these essays looks very much like the familiar lyric catalogue – even that of "Sumer is icumen in" – except that things stand in no clear relationship to one another save contiguity. Much of the syntax is paratactic, for parataxis forces the reader to build hierarchies on no authority other than her or his own. Hence the only firm thing to hold on to in the poem, that holds the writing together, is not *meaning* in the sense of an encapsulation which can be separated out, cashed in at the end of the reading in exchange for the knowledge-claim that "this is what the poem means," but *language,* the voices, the play in and of language, the dialogue with the poem taking place in the reader's consciousness, moving toward some sort of cognition and recognition of meaning and structure which cannot be separated from the decisions made within the writing/reading. In 1910 William James defined such consciousness as "a field composed at all times of a mass of present sensation, in a cloud of memories, emotions, concepts, etc. . . . Its form is that of a much-at-once."[81] Particulars, then, which "coalesce and are dissolved," according to James, in the much-at-once, but which are not placed one subordinate to another. A surplus of meaning, not a parsimony, and fecund.

The imperative to capture polyvalent clusters of associations and perceptions, and to preserve the simultaneity of field, requires abandoning normative syntax, and even intelligibility. The task of the writing, indeed, is to undo them, for our experience of the world undoes the rule of hierarchy and authority as set patterns. Yet, as Bruce Andrews cautions,

> However suspicious we are of the systems which generate the dead weight that pretends to make *X* "stand for" *Y*, there is no true naming, no original semantic openness or flows of energy to be

> recaptured innocently, no reason to take things "in themselves" apart from performative (communal) *use,* apart from socially grounded rhetoricity and artifice.[82]

The poem emerges in the act of composition, and reading is a compositional act. What is most striking, perhaps, about the writers discussed herein is their refusal to compromise their ways of seeing and registering the world. A moral imperative runs through their work, a kind of "methodism"[83] which seeks to liberate and clarify our sense of an object by revealing its characteristics as verb, as meaningful act. "It is difficult / to get the news from poems," Williams wrote in "Asphodel That Greeny Flower"; "yet men die miserably every day / for lack / of what is found there." Utopic or dystopic, the aesthetic, social, and political nature of the poem is, in its polysemousness, evidential of a faith in a world realisable through continual and unflinching attentiveness to the immediacies and the potentialities of meaning and experience, and the pleasure the interplay of presence and possibility affords.

# 1

# "A Narrative of Undermine"

## Gertrude Stein's Multiplicity

> *"I mean what IS all that out there which we CALL focus? . . . What IS focus, Brakhage? Hey?"*
>
> Charles Olson

> A sentence is this. (122)
>
> The which is an article. (129)
>
> A sentence is made of an article a noun and a verb. The time to come is a sentence. (155)
>
> What is the difference between words and a sentence and a sentence and sentences. (170)
>
> A wish is an article not followed by a noun. (193)
>
> A lake is an article followed by a noun a lake is an article followed by a noun a lake which is there. (196–7)
>
> What is a sentence. A sentence is something that is or is not followed. (200)
>
> Gertrude Stein, "Sentences" (1928).[1]

The sheer mischief of these scraps from "Sentences" destabilises the act of reading. The playfulness undermines our customary notions of meaning; in its continual disturbance of our expectations it subverts not only our sense of what we do when we read, but also our notions of how meaning is constituted. In its use of decontextualisation which may or may not lead to pun, in its careful undermining of conventional grammatical and syntactic strategies and orders, with perhaps the substitution for them of rhythmic, rhyming, or other patterns; and in its subversion of expectations through following a strategy of establishing and then renouncing linguistic patterns and/or literary conventions, Stein's writing perpetually destabilises itself (no easy accomplishment) by foregrounding linguistic (as opposed to referential or representational) concerns. Stein's writing assaults clarity by suggesting that clarity is itself an assault upon and hence a violation of the sheer complexity and richness of a sensory world whose "chaotic plenitude" (Jayne Walker's phrase)[2] cannot be verbally articulated or mapped.

In the sixth of the sentences I quote, the formulaic opening *A lake is* declares conventionally that the rest of the sentence will define a lake lexically for the reader; to continue the definition with *an article followed by a noun* transforms something called "definition" into something called "grammatical analysis," an activity conventionally indicated by placing the term to be analysed in quotation marks (" 'A lake' is . . . "). In being descriptive not of a feature of the physical landscape (lake) but, through its illustrative nature, of parts of speech and thus of a sentence, Stein's sentence violates the presumed contract set up with the reader by the opening three words (which declare a lexical and thus referential function for the sentence). It thus shows the reader that the generic differences between definition and grammatical analysis (and, by implication, other modes) are putative merely. The transformations in the sentence do not end there, of course, since the sentence goes on to repeat the opening nine words (such repetition itself violating the context which they themselves established for the sentence). It is only with the third repetition of *a lake* that we are afforded any clue as to how to read that repetition, since it is possible to read the sequence *a noun a lake* as a sequence in apposition (lake = noun; a lake = article + noun); we thus by a fairly simple process of parallelism might read the repeated *a lake is an article followed by a noun* appositionally. But *a noun a lake which is there?* Since *which* might well refer to either *noun* or *lake* we can read the deictic *there* either as referring to "there at the beginning of this sentence" or, indeed, "over there, in the landscape out *there*" – in which case the sentence doubles back on itself, that opening formula after all pointing to a feature of the physical landscape.[3] Indeed, this sequence of transformations, this double movement in the sentence, has been encouraged by the introduction of *lake* into the paragraph in the first place with "A sentence is why they will like a lake. A lake is really very nearly never frozen over it is very pretty. . . . " (196).

Viewed in isolation from the larger setting of "Sentences," Stein's strategies in this sentence look simpler than they are; they obviously have a great deal in common with the ambiguities proposed in "The which is an article" – does the sentence declare *the* or *which* to be the article? These ambiguities undermine the reader's control of meaning by violating grammatical convention, for if *the* is an article, then the sentence is fragmentary; if *which* is an article then the sentence redefines the parts of speech, provoking along the way a neat little word play in which we ask "which *which?*" The definiteness of the article begins to slide. "The which is an article" is a declarative sentence that undermines its own declarativeness, since we cannot, through reference to the external physical or social world, assign priority to either meaning. No amount of linguistic or even of cultural information will help settle the matter: declaring too much, the sentence declares nothing but enjoins serious play. No wonder that elsewhere in "Sentences" she can ask, "Supposing a sentence to be clear whose is it" (148).[4] The transformational strategies in which her writing abounds render impossible the reader's *possession* of meaning, for in rendering inaccessible to the reader the customary contract with the author as authority it undermines the reader's sense of his/her own certainty as arbiter of the meaning of the text. Stein's attack on notions of clarity radically undermines our notions of knowledge: It is difficult to know what we know, or even that we know, for we can only see clearly (and therefore "know") what is static. Her writing, completely antiauthoritarian, cultivates its own indeterminacy of meaning because it takes place in and is part of a world that is itself indeterminate.

This is as true of her work of 1912 as it is of that of 1928 and later – as, for instance, entries in *Tender Buttons* (1912) like "Roast Potatoes":

ROAST POTATOES
Roast potatoes for.[5]

Like other entries in the "Food" section of *Tender Buttons,* "Roast Potatoes" deals in transformations: In the title we are inclined (on the basis of our reading of the other titles in the sequence) to read *roast* as adjective and *potatoes* as noun; the inclusion of *for* at the end of the text, however, encourages us to read *roast* in that sentence as a verb (imperative) – in which case the grammatical transformation in turn transforms cooked into raw potatoes. Further readings suggest further possibilities: *potatoes* as a verb, for instance, or *for* as *four,* which is French for oven – and the writing circles within and among a plurality of semantic, syntactic, sonic, and referential fields, playfully moves in and out of referential and linguistic priorities.

All this is well known, as is the notion that Stein's work constitutes a more or less systematic investigation of the formal elements of language and of literature: parts of speech, syntax, morphemics, etymology, punctuation, the sentence, the paragraph; description, narration, poetry, prose, drama, and genre (my list is not exhaustive). In 1935 Hal Levy recorded Stein as saying: "The great thing about language is that we should forget it and begin over again."[6] I propose to look at a number of Stein's texts to see how, in the course of re-inventing literary signification, she radically redefines as pluralities both the act of reading and the role of the reader, in the process writing a veritable storehouse of technical resource. Such a linguistic/artistic enterprise, persistently and deliberately undermining certitude as it does, makes generalisation about her work a risky business indeed. What I offer is *one* reading of her work, and it is partial. There are many others.

## I

I begin with a piece from *Tender Buttons,* "Book," and in the course of my discussion will quote the work entire. It is five paragraphs long, plus title.[7] *Book.* Not only does the absence of the article leave *book* undifferentiated from other books, but it suggests that we are faced here with a text-intrinsic (i.e., nonreferential) system, for the definite article, when used deictically, points to the physical world; by itself, *book* does not, pointing rather to a notion.[8] Lacking the article, *book*'s grammatical ambiguity (at first sight noun, but possibly imperative or even, perhaps, a proper name) in any case undermines its referential aspect by drawing our attention to *book* as word, as evocation of a semantic field, rather than as object. The movement of the title, then, is towards linguistic as opposed to referential priorities, but this movement is somewhat modified by the first sentence, which begins to hint at the sort of circling I've already remarked on in the "lake" sentence and in "Roast Potatoes": *Book was there, it was there.* The repeated *was there* echoes the repeat of *Book* (from the title), and suggests that (the) book has been moved (the lack of an article as well as the repeat perhaps lending a note of agitation), and the dislocated deictic *there,* instead of presenting a problem because it is anaphoric (backward pointing), encourages us to read this sentence as the start of a fairly conventional narration/description, as a bit of speech perhaps. And this "illusion of reference"[9] is reinforced by the second sentence, which repeats *Book was there,* not only strengthening the focus on *book*'s placement, but also on *there*ness (thus emphasising relationship), pointing to presence/absence.

The opening is straightforward, then. But the imperative that begins the third sentence, *Stop it, stop it,* immediately problematises the text, for – radically dislocating the antecedent of *it* and thus violating the conventions implicit in the first sentence – it shifts this seeming narrative by shifting to the imperative – preserving a note of urgency but introducing apparent incoherence. To whom is it addressed? Some character in the story other than the speaker (if this is a story)? the reader? There is a small irony in the fact that the *it* of *Stop it* problematises the text precisely because syntactically anaphoric it echoes – syntactically rhymes with – the anaphoric *there* of the first sentence (regularity, then, offering disruption). Here is the whole of the first paragraph; of the five paragraphs, it is the only one in the past tense:

> Book was there, it was there. Book was there. Stop it, stop it, it was a cleaner, a wet cleaner and it was not where it was wet, it was not high, it was directly placed back, not back again, back it was returned, it was needless, it put a bank, a bank when, a bank care.

Fifty-seven words, eleven of them *it,* in three sentences. The difficulties we encounter assigning that second *it* (as the grammar might demand) to "book" encourage us probably to withhold meaning at least until the end of the repeated *stop it* (and these short clipped sentence units hurry the reader along), so that we tend as a result of the repetition to read the third *it* as referring to previous – and even current – repetition (*stop repeating!*), or as an act of deixis. But the fourth *it* further problematises the text since it shifts us to *cleaner* when what we expect is a continuation of *it*'s previous roles if not a clarification of *stop it,* and with the fifth occurrence, *it was not . . .* , although *it* could be "cleaner" it could equally well be "book" – a welcome act of recognition encouraged by the *where* (deictic) *it was wet.* The dynamics of this (the sixth) *it* are interesting, for this *it* might after all not be anaphoric (referring back to *book* or *cleaner*) but instead be what in traditional grammar is called an expletive: the neutrality of propositional discourse as in "it is raining" – a structure in which *it* is semantically empty (which is, then, yet another means of undermining meaning). Such a use of *it* is cataphoric (i.e., points forward in the sentence) and thus delays the statement of the grammatical subject. We now (through the possibility that book was not where wetness was) have something (however tenuous) to cling to in the way of stable meaning. And this is true whether the *it* of *where it was wet* is expletive (propositional), or refers to "book," or refers to "cleaner." In this particular disruption the shifts are mappable, and can be articulated. In a sort of reversal of an earlier syntactical rhyme, disruption offers regularity, briefly stabilising the text.

From this point on the fortunes of *it* in this paragraph are increasingly difficult to map. The seventh, *it was not high,* seems to echo exactly the ambiguities of the sixth occurrence. But there is another sort of shift going on, a syntactic move from "not where it was wet" to "not high"; the first using an adverb of place ("where") to indicate a condition (wetness, or rather, dryness); the second, avoiding an adverb of place ("where") to indicate place. The eighth offers another unsettling shift – are we talking about "book" or "cleaner" here? – but the whole sequence from the eighth to the ninth *it* ("it was directly placed back, not back again, back it was returned") registers the passage of time, if we read *it* as book, and if we read "it was returned" as repetition for emphasis of the action expressed by "it was directly placed back." But the ninth *it* is especially intractable, partly because of the difficulty of seeing the distinctions between the three actions ("directly placed back," "not back again," and "returned back"), and partly because of the inversion of "back it was returned." *It was needless.* What was? one of the objects? Or the action (putting it back)? Or the redundancy ("back" three times)? Or is *it* rather an echo of the expletive we saw in "it was wet"? The last two possibilities mark this clause as a major transitional point in the paragraph, moving the language away from any referent in the environment, increasing our sense of this text as self-referential, encouraging us to read this writing as a text-intrinsic system. This move culminates in the non-sensical proposition *it put a bank.*

The energy of this writing comes from the ways in which the tension between referentiality and its lack becomes a structural principle: Indeterminacy of meaning enables grammatical movement and pattern to become a principal means of coherence. Thus *it,* which early in the paragraph we learn to read deictically and/or anaphorically, is also used cataphorically as ground for the forward movement of the prose. Stein frequently, that is to say, selects one constituent in the anaphoric/deictic pattern and uses it as source and agent of the next forward movement. In conventional writing, the play of meaning (coherence) is a major formal principle; it is less important in this writing than cohesion (linking) of patterns and movements. Indeterminacy of meaning, that is, binds this writing together and at the same time engages the reader in a commentary on the text which the text, in its ambiguities, itself performs. If we ask, "Where did that *bank* come from?" Stein answers (or asks?), *When,* at what stage in the sequence? The sequence *book, back, bank* is a cohesion of phonological patterning (vowel infixes occurring inside consonantal lexemes [*b—k*]) involving withdrawal and deposit. And, appropriately, withdrawals and deposits (absences and presences – or the reverse) are banking activities. A complex punning sequence, then, in which the paragraph, ending with the punned *banker,* comments on its own activity.[10]

After the difficulties of that opening paragraph, the rest of "Book" is fairly straightforward, for we have now learned to read with an eye to the play of language and of meaning, rather than with an eye to referentiality and the communication of meaning. The present tense signals a shift from the complex introductory motions of the opening paragraph; and, with each of the remaining paragraphs beginning with an imperative (*suppose, suppose, cover up, please*), we settle down to a comparatively straightforward play of patterns. To note that *please* is possibly an exception in the sequence of imperatives is simply to note once again that in its shift away from referential language the writing plays an elaborate game with the reader's expectations. The nature of that game is suggested by the play between the opening clause of the second paragraph, which offers a conventional description of a banker, and the non-sequiturs that follow. Here is the second paragraph:

> Suppose a man a realistic expression of resolute reliability suggests pleasing itself white all white and no head does that mean soap. It does not so. It means kind wavers and little chance to beside beside rest. A plain.

Working on the edge of the paraphrasable, the paragraph includes minimal instructions to the reader on how to read it: *beside,* incontestably written as a verb, surely cautions us to pay close attention to parts of speech, and to notice the transformations in *kind wavers:* adjective + noun, or noun + verb. *Beside* as verb invites us to read the third sentence as commentary on the text, and we see (if we have not already done so) that *kind* indeed does waver in that opening clause. *A* (the indefiniteness of the article?) has been made plain? To be stuck with little chance to beside, beside rest, is pretty flat and plain? The language begins to bristle with possible significations, a move encouraged by the verbs of the opening sentence (*suppose, suggests,* and *does that mean*), which are the language of commentary. The paragraph as a whole, a mental/linguistic landscape rather than a verifiable description of a world outside the text, stands in marked contrast to the struggles the first paragraph gave us. The appositional phrase describing *man* plays a perfectly intelligible conventional sketch of a banker (with, perhaps, a sharp aside on the profit motive?) against non-sequiturs (*white all white does that mean soap*) and the next sentence, beginning with an *it* which lacks clear antecedence, comically refers to *reliability* and/or serves as an evocation of the multiplex *it* of the opening paragraph. If *that* does not mean soap then *white* means *white* and *that* is left hovering on the edge of a deictic gesture pointing outside the text – but this is only so if the *it* of *It does not so* refers to *that.* Such insistent deictic play joins multiple associations (between, for example, soap, whiteness, reliability) to invoke a range of semantic fields – whatever is going on here it is not *meaning* that is plain, and the reader begins to glimpse (among other things) latent puns. Which is to say that the activities of this writing are strongly reminiscent of a great deal of traditional poetry.

Such experience of language *qua* language characterises the rest of "Book," with repeats of syntactic and grammatical patterns as well as sound patterns (rhymes, words, phrases) working as the source of coherence. Here are the third and fourth paragraphs:

> Suppose ear rings that is one way to breed, breed that. Oh chance to say, oh nice old pole. Next best and nearest a pillar. Chest not valuable, be papered.

> Cover up cover up the two with a little piece of string and hope rose and green, green.

The initial *that* tends to transform *rings* from noun into verb, but refers anyway to what was *suggested* in the second paragraph? But the suggestion was only words, so it only breeds *that* (i.e., the preceding), which is a ringing ear (which hears the words, perhaps, that the eye reads on the page). The repeated interjection (authorial?) *Oh* is commanded and then exemplified (said) in a quite complicated little play which goes on to rhyme *oh* in *old* (and there is a pleasing consonantal play in "chance" and "nice"), while *pole* leads to *pillar.* That authorial interjection brought to the page those new objects that had come to her attention – and those new objects include the page, for *papered* is what words are, in writing, and in our reading. So the next paragraph picks up *papering* in its *cover up* which, doubled, varies the usual repeat-pattern and leads to a more-or-less unassigned *two* which itself might refer to the repeat itself (*cover up*), leading in turn to the repeated *green* which closes the paragraph in a symmetry with the repeated *cover up*, a symmetry that is echoed in the pattern *rose* (holds *oh*s, rhymes *suppose*) affords, in its ambiguity (noun? verb?) providing a symmetry with the previous paragraph's *rings.* Quite dense aural plays, then, in which new "information" enters the data of the paragraph to give impetus to the vocabulary, breaking the pattern while furthering it.

So the final paragraph begins with a break, in that the repetition at its opening is alliterative rather than verbal:

> Please a plate, put a match to the seam and really then really then, really then it is a remark that joins many many lead games. It is a sister and sister and a flower and a flower and a dog and a colored sky a sky colored grey and nearly that nearly that let.

The triple repeat of *really then* removes/subtracts meaning, in part because *then* so repeated not only shifts its own sense from occurrence to recurrence but also shifts the sense of its companion *really.* The opening two clauses play with cause and effect and in so doing seriously undermine our understanding of *it:* please a plate? put a match? much more likely *it* refers to *really then,* especially when we get to *lead games,* for philosophy is one of *many many-lead games* which rely heavily on the kind of logic remark *really then* is. But then so is this writing a *lead game,* though it is light rather than leaden – unlike, perhaps, the (rainy?) *sky colored grey.* And so we come to our old friend *it* for the last time in a sentence that repeats another old friend, *that,* here rounding the poem out to a sense of ending if not conclusion. The list of objects reads like the summing up that *it* thereby becomes: everything heretofore in this writing? everything that follows? book? what sort of day *it* is today? It is a grey sort of day and I am indoors (this is a domestic scene) reading/ writing book, another woman (two?) with me, and a dog, and a flower or two (one of them a rose?) providing a single splash of colour (other than white and grey). Confined? Freed? *Nearly that nearly that let.* Which *let* is *that* – obstruction? or permission? Noun, or verb? Both. This writing arises from a felt particular world that includes but is not confined exclusively to the act of writing itself. So through a series of astonishing turns and plays "Book" circles between the referential and the linguistic, and what we do in reading it is not only watch the words composing, working, but join in. It affords a narrative of our own unfolding perceptions of language as it unfolds before us, and it is thus the reader's story as well as Stein's. It is not a "representation" of Stein's life. The writing is the result of intense concentration on what is before the writer's eye, and that includes the words the writer has put and is putting on the page.

If I have devoted a great deal of space to thus sketching the processes of reading/writing "Book" that is because I want to get at the *sort* as well as the *intensity* of attention Stein's writing demands. It always keeps the reader on edge, just off balance; faced with the unpredictable, with the apparent random, the reader is forced to pay attention to *how* to make sense. And it is with the processes of "Book" in mind that I want to turn to two larger works, *Lifting Belly* (written in 1915, 1916, and 1917 in Mallorca, Paris, Perpignan, and Nîmes, where Stein spent those years of the war) and *Patriarchal Poetry* (written ten years later, in 1927), to get at the dynamics of Stein's demands on the reader.[11]

## II

A great love poem, a celebratory hymn to domesticity, *Lifting Belly* is one of the great referential poems of this century, yet, paradoxically, it draws much of its energy, beauty, and humour from its strategy of almost completely withholding reference from the reader. Profoundly transgressive in that it records a relationship that is "illicit" (hence not to be written), the poem assaults the standard interpretive notion of meaning as an "essence" that must be extracted just as it assaults the standard interpretive practice of peeling away "layers" of signification through abstracting and then explicating "key" words and phrases which will "unlock" the text. *Lifting Belly* is predicated on the paradoxical desire to write out the humour and affection of sexual and domestic love while at the same time preserving and protecting it through a cryptic style that, on one hand, encodes certain references and thus withholds them from the reader, and on the other records in a more-or-less daily journal the events of the day. The poem refers, that is to say, to a preexistent narrative already known to the lovers, whose voices are registered throughout the poem.

The poem early declares a narrative/descriptive base, moving rapidly from "I" to "we," only to begin undermining that base with the puns of the third paragraph. "I saw a star which was low. . . . I want to tell about fire. Fire is that which we have when we have olive. Olive is a wood. . . . All belly belly well." That punning invocation of the title, almost discursive commentary on what came before, is the only virtual anomaly in a sequence plainly addressed to a reader, and the security and predictability that address seems to afford is reinforced by a series of strong narrative markers: "I have been . . . ; Sometimes . . . ; When . . . ; We quarreled with him then . . . ; The next time . . . "; and so forth. But the implicit promise, that this writing has the sort of security and coherence that plot, description, and character conventionally afford, is undermined with the sixth paragraph's inclusion of a "you" who clearly cannot be the reader, and it is almost completely withdrawn by the irruptive "I don't pardon him. I find him objectionable" of the ninth. The main function of this new unassigned voice is to privilege the pre-existent narrative – that is to say, to make it inaccessible to the reader without destroying its integrity and hence coherence as a sequence of events. Strictly speaking, it is not a pre-existent narrative, but a day-by-day unfolding to the lovers whose story it is (where, after all, did that interruptive voice come from?). The reader is never told who the "objectionable" *he* is, and the many obvious extratextual references – like "Lifting belly or Dora" (25) for instance – are left unexplained, thereby enhancing their personal nature. Only occasionally and in the most fragmentary or speculative way is the reader privy to the "events" referred to in the poem, and then it is usually because some other reader/critic has explained the code. The strategies of *Lifting Belly* force the reader to trust the situation of the telling, and thus to trust language patterns, the recurrences and variations, as manifesting the poem's coherence. Yet, at the same time, the uniformity and predictability of those patterns is continually undermined. Stein's strategy thus radically emphasises the reader's sense of the poem's referentiality while rendering the precise nature of the reference irrelevant (the poem exacts no demands on the reader's cultural knowledge). The poem makes no concession to the reader, and the concomitant dislocated referentiality of the work in its severity intensifies the personal erotic charge implicit in the title. But at the same time it makes it difficult of access, protecting from readerly intrusion the privacy of the sexual and domestic world the poem celebrates. The strategy of concealment, that is to say, protects the texts from the hostile reader and in enhancing the poem's intimacy reveals it to the sympathetic eye and ear. That the intimacy celebrated is unmistakably lesbian is incidental and even insignificant; the power of the text is in the unabashed quality of the highly personal world the speakers in it share.

The unabashed nature of the text is achieved by an astonishing series of repetitions (the phrase "lifting belly," for example, occurs 483 times in the course of the poem's 1,812 paragraphs)[12] and by the poem's refusal to sort out the "I" and the "you" of the dialogue. It is difficult to distinguish inner from audible speech, and it is impossible definitively to determine the boundaries of any given utterance. Stein deliberately obscures the source of speech through an arbitrary and inconsistent notation of speech in which paragraphing, punctuation, and line breaks serve to blur rather than clarify the identity of the speaker,[13] and thus the individuality of one speaker is subsumed in and absorbed by the individuality of the other, interweaving the beloved into the text as participant rather than as object external to it. The reader tries to figure out who is who through careful reading along patterns of expectation closely similar to those exploited in "Book," the patterns perpetually being thrown off balance. With the identity of the speaker thus protected, there overarches the poem a sense of shelteredness, of a quotidian private sequestered world intensely shared by those who dwell therein, self-sufficient and self-sustaining, impervious to outside prurience or curiosity. In this astonishing erotic and comic idyll the text offers the beloved – and hence the (sympathetic) reader – privilege and delight, protection and blandishment; "we" floats through the text defining and redefining the shared pleasure lifting belly affords, whether title, phrase, or act.

It is this blur of indeterminacy that both defamiliarises the title phrase as we repeatedly meet it, and at the same time exploits it as a principal agent of revelation in the text. Thus the sentence "lifting belly is so . . . " runs through the poem (but especially in Section 1) as a series of propositions, statements, descriptions, affirmations, definitions, illustrations, rejoinders (my list is not exhaustive). In its long career of some eighty-seven repetitions it is almost impossible to pin down: "lifting belly is so strong" eleven times in the poem, and "so kind" at least twenty-eight times.[14] It is also (and I cite almost at random, page numbers in parentheses) so exact (18, 32), satisfying (13, 15), judicious (14), sweet (13, 51), consecutive (13), seen (16), long (15), high (9), round (22), careful (13), erroneous (7), accurate (8), droll (16), readily watchful (27), able to be praised (12), a measure of it all (12), cold (8), and warm (13). The contradictions are not simply semantic or lexical; they are also functional and syntactic, since to be "so recherché" (25) is to have a quality of a quite different order from being "so pleased" (49), which is in turn a long way from being "so necessary" (11), or "so strange" (20, 47).

Presented in its formulaic expression, such a sequence of qualities, abilities, and characteristics, that is to say, can be as easily read as an exploration of "is so" as it can of "lifting belly." Indeed, at times the text brings us up short with a variation of the formula that demands we redefine its terms, and hence reread and redefine its elements and even role, as in, "Lifting belly is so" (16). Period. Or, "Lifting belly so meaningly" (51). Such shifts draw the reader's attention (sometimes, not necessarily at every reading) to such expressions as "You don't say so" (23) or "I don't wish it to be said so" (9), which in turn forces reconsideration of the formulaic "lifting belly is so. . . ."

Such practice works to destabilise meanings to which we are likely to get habituated by sheer repetition, and *Lifting Belly* abounds in so many instances that it would be silly to try to list them. Stein's techniques of destabilisation run from fairly simple substitution (like "bouncing" [16] or "mixing" [12, 13] for "lifting") to subtler syntactic and grammatical shifts in which "lifting" is used in a great variety of grammatical ways, through the addition of an adverb, for example (lifting belly phlegmatically [25], fairly [36], magnetically [27], and so forth); through the addition of a verb (lifting belly means me [17], adjoins [20], asks [24], captures [25], and so forth); or through the addition of an indeterminate part of speech (lifting belly pencils [27]). Gerund, participle, pet name, verb phrase, noun phrase, adjectival phrase, the isolated "lifting belly" followed by a period and taking a paragraph all by itself (twenty-one times in the poem), is remarkably unstable. Stein's strategies deliberately frustrate all attempts to fix "lifting belly" into a static syntactic or denotative meaning, and the fact that this is the poem's title is further transformative; the repetition of "lifting belly" on one hand lends the poem coherence, an air of unity, while its ambiguous status as a phrase means that the work discusses itself as a multiplicity, thereby giving us permission to read it *variorum,* as in a state of constant redefinition. "Lifting belly," the poem tells us, "is a name" (7), "an expression" (16), "a repetition" (17), "a language" (17), "a quotation" (35), and "not very interesting" (8). Ordinary language is transformed into extraordinary suggestiveness (what are the parts of speech in a sentence like "Excitement sisters" [18]?). Similarly, words like "caesar" and "cow" become charged but impossible to fix, even if we happen to know the code. It may be, indeed, that a knowledge of the code is actually a hindrance to our reading of the text, for it narrows the multiplicity of transformations. "Lifting belly in the mind" (34).

The fluidity thus achieved has much in common with *Patriarchal Poetry,* which in its extensive use of lists draws on techniques closely similar to those of *Lifting Belly*. Part of one list, for instance, drawing on conventional and nonconventional grammatical uses of *and,* reads:

Patriarchal Poetry at best.
Best and Most.
Long and Short.
Left and Right.
There and More.
Near and Far.
Gone and Come.
Light and Fair.
Here and There.
This and Now.
Felt and How
Next and Near.
In and On.
New and Try
In and This.
Which and Felt.
Come and Leave.
By and Well.
Returned.
Patriarchal Poetry indeed. (139–40)

Opaque indeed, and covertly if not blatantly inviting the reader to skip, since the eye running down a list tends to hurry along, inattentive, expecting more of the same, expecting tedium. The strategy here is to play transformations against the convention of the list, that is, against the reader's expectation of uniformity. For this list is a curious series of pairs, each member of which matches its partner differently. *Best* and *most* might but need not be contrasting terms – the decision is qualitative; *long* and *short* (like *left* and *right?* hardly!) are quantitative contrasts. It is difficult to see what the relationship is between *there* and *more* (though there's a more-or-less vague gesture toward rhyme). Position contrasted with quantity? But *near* and *far* are familiar, and perhaps afford us a relief that is reinforced by the equally familiar (but a reversal of the cliché) *gone* and *come:* Of course, the fact that we associate *gone* with *far*ness and *come* with *near*ness means there's another reversal going on here, too. Most of these pairs are irreversible binomial idioms; Stein shows that reversing them does not indeed produce nonsense but, by breaking the conventional (patriarchal?) semantic construct, produces meaning. The next pair, *light* and *fair,* is conventionally of synonyms, but by now the reader no doubt suspects the conventional meaning, and, as Ulla E. Dydo remarks of Stein's language as a whole, "the bonds that tie words to things are loosened and names split off from objects."[15] This notion has been strongly reinforced by the time we reach *Felt and How,* a line that radically departs from the conventions this list seems to have established: It pairs a participle (or is it a noun?) with an adverb (invoking the colloquialism "and how!" in the process?) in one of two unpunctuated lines in the list. Dropping the punctuation draws our attention to the aptness of the run-on pair *How Next,* and the writing begins to comment on its own procedures. So as we proceed through this list we turn more and more to the linguistic and not the referential relationships between the words in the list, only to be brought up short, perhaps, by the sequence of the last three lines I quote. For here *Returned* (playing puns, perhaps, on *Leave* and *By/e*) marks a return to the first line I quoted (*Patriarchal Poetry at best*), and leads to the utterly ambiguous *Patriarchal Poetry indeed.* Is this ironic or not? How can we possibly tell? To reflect that the uppercase version of "Patriarchal Poetry" is only one of several in this text and *might* refer to the poem's title simply complicates the matter. What we have is a list that establishes its own rules only to change them as it goes along; it also exhibits, however, the sort of movement I already commented upon in the sentence about "A lake" and in "Book." The list doubles back on itself, pointing perhaps to a generic patriarchal poetry "out there" in the (physical/social) world as well as to the poem of which these words are the title, as well as to the words themselves – which, by this stage of the poem repeated a very great number of times (I have not counted them), have begun to lose whatever precise lexical meaning they might have had.

To the extent that it is an attack on the authoritarian power of conventional, Anglocentric, and male literary values *Patriarchal Poetry* is a referential work. "Patriarchal poetry," says Stein,

> makes it incumbent to know on what day races will take place and where otherwise there would be much inconvenience everywhere.
>
> Patriarchal poetry erases what is eventually their purpose and their inclination and their reception and their without their being beset. Patriarchal poetry an entity. (142–3)

"Patriarchal poetry," Stein says, "makes a land a lamb" (138); is "obtained with seize" (139); "Patriarchal Poetry connected with mean" (139) – which in context means meanness as well as meaning; "Patriarchal Poetry deny why" (139) – because "Patriarchal Poetry is the same" (139). In this forty-page work containing a wonderful parodic eighteen-line verse entitled "Sonnet"; containing innumerable lists of phrases marching down the page; containing permutations and repetitions; containing seemingly endless sequences of non-sequiturs; the phrase "Patriarchal Poetry" comes to act as a kind of stabilising rhythmic force, a steady beat of recurrence, in a linguistic context notable for its multiplicity and unpredictability of meaning and suggestiveness. The repeated phrase

"Patriarchal Poetry" virtually loses all meaning and comes to serve as a functional cypher: The whole poem is a form of deconstruction, then, in which the discourse demolishes the term – and the authority and stability of the cypher – embedded within it and shaping it, acting out as it does *non*patriarchal modes of writing. Here is a short passage:

> Patriarchal Poetry to be filled to be filled to be filled to be filled to method method who hears method method who hears who hears who hears method method method who hears who hears who hears and method and method and method and who hears and who who hears and method method is delightful and who and who who hears method is method is method is delightful is who hears is delightful who hears method is who hears method is method is method is delightful is delightful who hears who hears of of delightful who hears of method of delightful who of whom of whom of of who hears of method method is delightful. (138–9)

This sentence is remarkable, among other things, for its method: a series of phrases repeated in threes, a series of grammatical patterns repeated in threes and fours, a variation from the pattern "who hears" to the pattern "who hears of," so that the preposition "of" comes to dominate a pattern earlier dominated by the pronoun "who," while at the same time the initial preponderance of the verb "hears" gives way to the conspicuous verb "is," and then reasserts itself. A cumulative pattern, gradually enlarging its field as the vocabulary expands.

What I find most interesting in this passage, however, is the syntax: The word "who" appears twenty times (and "whom" twice) in this sentence of 114 words.[16] Do *any* of them introduce a relative clause (or are they interrogatives)? In order to make sense the mind seeks to subordinate elements, as in the sequence "and who who hears and method method is delightful and who and who who hears method is method is method is delightful," but the subordination won't hold, not simply because that "who" is anaphoric (like the "it" in the opening of "Book"), but because, waiting as we are (or would be in more conventional writing) for a verb signalling the main clause, faced with phrase after phrase and clause after clause, whose boundaries are so indistinct that we cannot easily or clearly differentiate one from its neighbour (like the identity of the speakers in *Lifting Belly*), we simply cannot assign priority – save in the most tentative way – to any given sequence of words: Are we to read "whom of of who," for example, the way we might read "among / of green" in William Carlos Williams's poem "The Locust Tree in Flower"? The syntactic data in the sentence are held in the mind virtually in an equivalence of value, since each moment of syntactic lucidity is immediately displaced by a subsequent word (often but by no means always a repetition). In such intense localisation of meaning we find ourselves rescanning the words to discern alternatives to the syntactic pattern we hit upon, and we are left sorting through a variety of reading strategies: Are these words in apposition, or are they subordinate to one another? What part of speech is this? And we find ourselves holding more than one reading in mind at once. The net result is that the hierarchies are ironed out, and we read the language paratactically, nonpatriarchally.

The question of pronouns is crucial. "I can't say it too often" runs a line in *Lifting Belly* (11), and in calling on the anaphoric use of pronouns Stein emphasises their linguistic nature as shifters: The shift in meaning that personal pronouns undergo as they are used by different speakers talking together is an index of the nature of all pronouns as shifters, and thus to the point that anaphora is essentially deictic.[17] It also reminds us that all utterance is context sensitive. The opening of Section 3 of *Lifting Belly,* "Lifting belly in here" (38), operates similarly, since the adverb *here* is a shifter, and this sentence, suggesting as it does someone calling to a visitor, performs a context transformation: The sentence becomes direct address to the reader, who thereby becomes hearer, and *here* deictic. Stein's use of anaphora and deixis to foreground language as language rather than as reference enables her to recreate in her writing the canonical situation of utterance, face-to-face, by putting us in a special condition of utterance, page-to-face, in the process suppressing page-to-face's conventional markers. This being so, then in the sort of doubling from referential to linguistic concerns and back again that's going on in the sentence about the lake and in "Book," her writing circles through transformations of the situational context of utterance, dissolving the boundaries traditionally observed between spoken and written language, and rendering inaccessible to the reader the customary contract with the author as authority. This technique, one means of achieving what I called a blur of indeterminacy, enables her through that indeterminacy to write with great precision, as in "Four Dishonest Ones" (1911), and with great compression, as in "A Little Novel" (1927).

## III

Here is the opening of "Four Dishonest Ones" (1911); as published in *Portraits and Prayers* it is six pages long.

FOUR DISHONEST ONES
Told By A Description Of What They Do.

They are what they are. They have not been changing. They are what they are.

> Each one is what one is. Each is what each is. They are not needing to be changing.
>
> One is what she is. She does not need to be changing. She is what she is. She is not changing. She is what she is.
>
> She is not changing. She is knowing nothing of not changing. She is not needing to be changing.
>
> What is she doing. She is working. She is not needing to be changing. She is working very well, she is not needing to be changing. She has been working very hard. She has been suffering. She is not needing to be changing.
>
> She has been living and working, she has been quiet and working, she has been suffering and working, she has been watching and working, she has been waiting, she has been working, she has been waiting and working, she is not needing to be changing.
>
> She has been working, she is not needing to be changing. She has been one working and every one was knowing that she was not needing to be changing. She is what she is, she is not needing to be changing.[18]

That it is impossible to decode suggests that decoding is inappropriate. The neat little syntactic pun in the subtitle, "told by a description" where we might expect "told by Gertrude Stein," though indicative perhaps of some high-jinks to come, does not point to the main source of difficulty in this writing. *That* lies in the pronouns. For what we have here is a passage entirely devoid of proper names, utterly reliant on a series of pronouns of which none has an antecedent (unless it is another pronoun), of which none points – as names do – to something outside the text. And while it is perhaps quite obvious to treat "they are what they are" as tautological, as, on reading the first sentence, we might be inclined to do, we do not get very far into the second paragraph before we begin to reconsider: If each one is what "that one" is, is each one the same as "that one over there," or is each different from all the others? Is this a passage describing the singularity of each member of a group, or the uniformity of the group? It is impossible to decide. By the time we get to the third paragraph, we cannot tell whether its five sentences "describe" one, two, three, or four different people. And so on. Four dishonest "ones," precisely encountered. And the verbs tell us how habitually dishonest they are: All of these verbs express action as continuous and not completed (i.e., they are durative, not perfective, in meaning) without, however, implying any futurity. That is to say, the grammatical aspect of the verbs allows for some possibility of change. The writing refuses conclusions, even about dishonesty.

It works by putting all the immediacy of spoken language on the page, with all the immediacy of person-to-person contact. But as a piece of face-to-face speech it is of course inadequate, precisely because it is not accompanied with those gestures that would render the deixis meaningful. It's a bit like walking along the beach and finding a bottle with a message in it that says "meet me here a week from now with a stick about this big."[19] The deixis is devoid of useful context and, devoid of references because there are no names, this is a wholly text-intrinsic system; all the pronouns are anaphoric (backward pointing) or cataphoric (forward pointing) within the passage; unable to move outside the limits of the text we are faced with an exercise in structural semantics, in which pronominalisation has to carry the weight of what nouns customarily do. Hence there is a great deal of repetition, for through that repetition the pronouns begin to acquire concreteness. What we have here, then, is a linguistic instance in which repetition enhances rather than diminishes meaning or detaches the word from its meaning. For a semantician this sort of language has a theoretical existence only, for it is a quasi-language.[20] In deliberately choosing a form of utterance that is on one hand highly deictic and the other entirely devoid of nouns, Stein is declaring that she is conducting an empirical investigation into the language: Lacking nouns, what happens to the prose? What sorts of words besides pronouns come to take on the concreteness of nouns? In part, perhaps, it is an attempt to discover whether the actual immediacy of the spoken word can ever be on the page. The "*told* by" of the subtitle, then, plays semantic fields against one another, and thus undermines and enlarges the conventional sense, playing with the expectations "told" and "description" provoke. The reader ends up doing many things at once.

Such multiplicity does not make for certainty. The blur of pronominal reference and thus of identities that "Four Dishonest Ones" exhibits delineates the tentative nature of perception; the multiplicity generates great concentration and compression. A more refined version of the strategies of "Four Dishonest Ones" is Stein's "A Little Novel" (1926), which exhibits remarkable and characteristic Steinian compression with almost textbook clarity. Including the title, it is 301 words long. Here are the first two paragraphs.

> Fourteen people have been known to come again. One came. They asked her name. One after one another. Fourteen is not very many and fourteen came. One after another. Six were known to be at once. Welcomed. How do you do. Who is pleasant. How often do they think kindly. May they be earnest.
>
> What is the wish.[21]

Narrative, obviously. The title led us to expect that, and novelty (which is *perhaps* slight). The curious choice of tense in the opening sentence problematises what is a fairly clear paragraph; to explicate the ramifications suggested by *have been known* might well take several pages (an opening chapter?), since it suggests a time sequence that is immediately undermined by the next sentence, and at the same time it *might* (since its tone and sentence structure suggest the aloofness of commentary) be attitudinising. I simply cannot tell. Is the *one* who *came* one who is coming *again?* That seems possible, but if *they asked her name,* then presumably not (unless those who *have been known to come again* have not been known to do so by those who asked her name [in which case "she" is returning to a place rather than to a host or hostess]).

Rather than endlessly parenthesise the possibilities, the reader is tempted, indeed obliged, to hold the implications of the first sentence in abeyance, and to turn to the spots of clarity in the narrative. The clarity is localised and multiple, and the net effect is to reinforce an aspect of the first sentence I have yet to mention: Whose is the narrative voice? Where is this narrative voice coming from? Indeed the narrative voice shifts, as the paragraph progresses, and by the end of it we realise that the voice of the opening sentence is itself multiple.

For the paragraph is notable for the way in which almost every statement becomes a shifter. *One after another* did what? asked her name? or came? Presumably both. *Fourteen came* at once? unlikely – one after another? presumably; but *six were known to be at once.* Does that mean they arrived together? Not if they came one after another, though since they are unlikely to have jammed through the door in a solid phalanx they would indeed have come one after another, "at once." The sentence does not, of course, say that the six came, but that they were *known to be at once.* Everybody already present heard about their presence at the same time? or did they arrive noisily, so that they were known to be (arriving) immediately (at once – as soon as they arrived). When in the third paragraph we read that "It is very often a habit in mentioning a name to mention his name," we begin to suspect that some of the people present are quite well known (though this is only one reading of this sentence, since one character is named Benjamin Charles and another[?] Benjamin James). So perhaps *six were known to be at once* because of their reputations? Or perhaps they became well known (i.e., known to be) at the same time, but long before the party started (if this is a party; it's probably a social rather than a business or political occasion) – or even share the same birthday? There is no way in which we can assign priority to any one of these (or any other) interpretations with any certainty, so all are equally true. The kinds of guesses we make, some later confirmed, some later denied, some left unconfirmed, are precisely the sorts of guesses we make at social gatherings, or in those "realistic" sorts of novels which, assuming a preexistent narrative, refuse to explain the background to the reader.[22]

The rest of the paragraph is equally dense, equally rich in possibilities and multiplicities of meaning. The guests are greeted by the host(s), greet each other, but not necessarily pleasantly, and even if pleasantly the pleasantness is simply a cover up for hostility and/or suspicion (or is it), and oh dear let's hope they're all earnest (honest? sincere? without pretence?). That last sentence seems to be an unspoken thought, though it need not be. It certainly suggests that the narrator is a participant in these proceedings (perhaps an early arrival?), and that this writing is reportage. The opening sentence does not suggest this anything like so strongly, and the second paragraph completely dislocates the source and role of the narrative voice. *What is the wish.* Are we to read this even as a question? It does not help us to decide when we recall that Gertrude Stein disliked question marks, believing that "anybody can know that a question is a question and so why add to it the question mark."[23] But if it is a question, to whom is it addressed? And where does that deictic *the* point? And so on.

There is an astonishing wealth of data in "A Little Novel," and our experience reading it is analogous to the experience of "being there." We piece the narrative together ourselves, sorting out what the plot is, or even whether there is one, as we go along. But what is particularly interesting about it is the ways in which, drawing on devices we have already seen at work in "Book" or in *Lifting Belly,* playing with phrases like "at once," it attacks the conventional notion of literal meaning by demonstrating its plurality (how can anyone, after reading this work, think "at once" has *a* literal meaning?), while at the same time it has an identifiable referential quotient and thus assaults our notion of fiction. Dismantling familiar models of constructing narrative meaning, "A Little Novel" forces the reader to examine or question reading procedures and to examine or question the assumptions behind writing conventions. Ending "And they" (unpunctuated) the work suggests that the completeness of this narrative – if it is to be completed at all – is a matter for the reader, who is thus enjoined to participate in the writing of this prose. Reportage? Perhaps. To read "A Little Novel" is to experience *words* – and once again we see a Stein title playing semantic fields against each other. The novelty is not so slight after all, and the work offers a world only slightly novelised.

## IV

Blurs of indeterminacy, then, in which the writing circles round between writer and reader, between syntactic and referential signification, between genres, between modes of verification and modes of knowing, between writing and speech. Stein achieves her astonishing multiplicity of meaning and suggestion by withdrawing her language from lexical and referential signification while at the same time gesturing towards it. What is remarkable about it is its play with shifters, and its extension of shift to include whole ranges of syntactic and grammatical structure conventionally regarded as fixed. It constitutes, then, a radical attack on certainty, and in the long run posits an unknowable world if "knowing" means fixity means control. Yet the writing is remarkably accessible. To figure out what's going on in works like "A Little Novel" the only thing you need besides a knowledge of the language (as you might have got it from learning to speak it) is to have been to a social gathering of some sort. The writing, that is to say, demands very little acculturation of its readers. This stands in marked contrast to the practice of Stein's contemporaries like Joyce, say, or Eliot. For when Joyce writes a phrase like "spittinspite on Dora O'Huggins" in *Finnegans Wake*[24] it is very much to his purpose that the reader sooner or later know that Dora is an acronym for the Defence of the Realm Act, for that recognition will enable the reader to discern interpretive patterns that themselves function to undermine the possibility of textual referentiality in *Finnegans Wake* – like Stein's work, a radical assault on the ways meaning conventionally takes place. Such knowledge is of little help to the reader who comes across "Lifting Belly or Dora" in *Lifting Belly* (25). Joyce achieves his illusion of reference by emphasising and complexly playing with the exophoric tendencies of words on the page. Characteristically Joyce's writing acquires its astonishing multiplicity and range of meaning through referring more or less explicitly to materials outside the text, only to use that range of reference to undermine the referential aspects of the writing. Like Stein's, Joyce's is a text-intrinsic system, a complex play of stabilising and destabilising activities and patterns against each other, incorporating lexical and semantic referential patterns which Stein suppresses.[25] The great writers of what is called International High Modernism – Yeats, Eliot, Pound, Valéry and even Joyce – in their attack on conventions and norms load their writing with cultural information, and are Eurocentric where they are not Anglocentric in ways in which Stein is not. Stein deliberately excludes such cultural apparatus. Hence Laura Riding could observe in 1927 that "None of the words Miss Stein uses have ever had any experience. They are no older than her use of them. . . . None of these words . . . has ever had any history. . . . They contain no references, no meanings, no jokes, no despairs,"[26] and Eliot could see Stein as a threat. "There is something precisely *ominous* about Miss Stein. . . . Her work . . . is not good for one's mind," he wrote of "Composition as Explanation" in 1927. "If this is of the future, then the future is, as it very likely is, of the barbarians. But this is the future in which we ought not to be interested."[27]

Stein was fond of saying that America was the first country to enter the twentieth century, because it "found out that the cheapest articles should be made out of the very best materials." Her delight in her Ford cars is but one aspect of her delight in "series manufacture": mass production makes goods of the very best materials accessible to all. The matter of being American, and the question of what constitutes American writing, pervades all of Stein's work. As an American who learned English as a second language, and acutely insistent that "Americans in their nature their habits their feelings their pleasures and their pains" have "nothing to do with England" she nevertheless saw that the American language "instead of changing remained English."[28] Her strategy in writing, of taking language further and further away from customary and paraphrasable referentiality, from its lexical and denotative functions, derives, like her strategy of dissolving conventional linguistic and literary boundaries and genres, from her profound and persistent opposition to the authoritative and authoritarian dominance of English models, from her opposition to Anglocentric literary standards, conventions, and procedures which in poems like *Patriarchal Poetry* she identifies as patriarchal and indeed elitist.

Joyce once told Arthur Power that he did not think America "is going to produce much literature of importance as yet, for to produce a literature a country must first be vintaged."[29] W. B. Yeats, in 1905 wondering "why America has not produced more beautiful art," queried whether it was "because America has to assimilate with herself millions of immigrants who not only come with alien traditions but speak English coldly and unimaginatively because it is still a foreign tongue."[30] Yeats speaks the voice of Cultural Authority, of education, and of civilisation. Stein wants her writing to be available to *any* speaker or reader of English no matter how "alien" she or he may be, no matter how ignorant of cultural matters and conventions. Those millions of immigrants who crossed the Atlantic in the last quarter of the nineteenth century (and before) fled from Europe to escape what Americans had learned to define as its "feudal" society in order to start again. With a new beginning came a new language, and a new but more often than not an intensely localised culture. In the words of William Carlos Williams, another American who like Stein learned English as a second language, "The rose is obsolete."

For the American immigrant learning (American) English as a second language, the history in that language is the history the immigrant finds there, puts there, is *individual,* and its verification, its reality, will be authenticated in the dictionary. What was it Yeats said about good writing? That it cannot be done by those "ignorant of any meaning in words finer than the dictionary meaning."[31] That word "finer" needs in Stein's view to be recast, for if the work of art, the writing, is to be of the twentieth century and American, available to everyone in that land of immigrants, no matter what their education, culture, origin, or acculturation, then the work must carry within it its own history, and there can be no hierarchies of meaning except for those that reside within the text itself, no privileged series of values redolent of English or European cultures or religions or of male patterns and dominions. By this logic there cannot be a single meaning of the text, for to provide that is to empower the author over the reader, and to falsify experience. When the film maker Stan Brakhage visited Charles Olson in May, 1963, following Olson's instructions he held his hand in front of his face to find out exactly where all the lines of that hand were most sharply visible. "I tried it," he wrote to his wife, "and found FOCUS somewhere between four and six inches" in front of his face. Whereupon Olson leaned over: "And, Brakhage, what is all the rest beyond that point – I mean what IS all that out there which we CALL focus?. . . What IS focus, Brakhage? Hey?"[32] Stein asks the same question, holding the language, as opaque as Brakhage's hand, before the reader's eye. What is all the rest, beyond that language? She problematises her texts to undo the reader's preconceptions and to render cultural baggage inappropriate, for what is heard/read is not a paraphrasable meaning (language is not transparent) but a variety of processes by which meaning is achieved.

So the work is to be accessible, but not, by that, easy.

> Reading.
> Is reading painful.
> When one has not the habit of reading reading is not painful. One can read hands. One cannot compare that with reading a book. Either the one or the other is useful and both are so pleasing to the ear and eye.[33]

A book is a made thing, made of words. Its language must be anaphoric or cataphoric, pointing backwards or forwards in the text, and its extratextual gestures are only that, gestures which forward the linguistic play and call into question the truth-value of exophoric certainty. Her language, then, is notably and deliberately deracinated. Thoroughly democratic, resistant to institutionalised power and meaning, it is indeed what Yeats called for, art.

# 2

# *Recurrencies*

## *No. 12 of Louis Zukofsky's* Anew

> *The great difficulty of these works is to know how to listen to them. Perhaps our Occidental tradition does not predispose us in that direction as much as is necessary; the Occident always has needed a largely explicit gesture in order to understand what is being told to it.*
>
> Pierre Boulez, "Webern"[1]

In the following pages I quote, intermittently but *in toto,* a poem taken almost at random from Louis Zukofsky's shorter work, the twelfth of *Anew* (1946).[2] It is a difficult, even a baffling poem, and I do not explicate it fully. Like much of the work that is in the *Complete Short Poems,* it has beauty and grace but is slight seeming. It is because of that apparent slightness that in the pages that follow I at times risk overexplaining, in an attempt to open (especially in the opening lines of the poem) the subtle pressures and speeds of the poem's movement and thought. At the same time I think to myself that I am not explaining enough, a charge, surely, that many readers or would-be readers would level at Zukofsky. The beauty of the poem I leave to speak for itself.

The poem has no title. Marcella Booth (117) gives a very precise date for its composition: 16–17 January 1944, one week before the poet's fortieth birthday, when Zukofsky was working for the Hazeltine Electronics Corporation writing instruction manuals for radios, submarines (according to Paul Zukofsky), bombsights, and the like.[3] The first two lines make a sentence, a slightly puzzling one:

> It's hard to see but think of a sea
> Condensed into a speck.

The first line seems to be generated by a fairly simple pun in which the "see" of *understand* (rather than of *sight*) becomes the *seen* body of water through the word "think," which here means *imagine* or *picture*. And the second line through the imperative of the first points us firmly to the realm the word customarily points to in other contexts, that of ideas and concepts, by changing the picture in the mind's eye, by *making* us think (thinking is a changing, a transforming): "condensed," reduced in size, perhaps even concentrated; "speck," a minute particle, so small that it might catch the eye. Concentrated: intensified. The *seen* idea, then, the mote in the mind's eye, is accessible to the understanding, and the abstract has been made concrete. Yet we do not know what "it" is. *It* is hard to see.

Viewed thus closely, this reflective pedagogical voice is the voice of wit bordering on whimsy. But the rhythm of the verse, pushing forward by sounding almost like doggerel (the first line tends, in the ear, to resolve into two, because of the rhyme and the short iambic clip of it), discourages such reflection, at least at a first reading. There is an element of risk: skirting doggerel, skirting whimsy, and even, perhaps, skirting incomprehensibility. Zukofsky's verse is always at an edge; the verse is not allowed (nor is the reader) to settle down into stable patterns or clear lines of secured thought: There is a turbulent edge. As William Carlos Williams noticed during the continuing crisis of a flu epidemic, "values stood out in all fineness."[4] Such a sense, that the uncertainty brought on by the urgency of crisis strips us of inessentials and brings us down to particulars, is not uncommon and is fundamental to Zukofsky's poetics. He continually throws the reader off balance, encouraging alertness, demanding attention to detail. So lest the ear (or foot) too comfortably settle into an iambic jingle, the third line of the poem breaks the rhythm by being visually shorter (only four syllables, where the first two were nine and six) and quantitatively longer than the second (it slows down through long vowels, consonant clusters, and the emphatic pause conveyed by the dash). And in line four, which (appropriately) mentions light, the verse speeds up again:

> And there are waves –
> Frequencies of light,
> Others that may be heard.

This is speech, pared to essentials. Condensed.

It is tempting to think, as the waves of the "sea" of the first line become waves of light and then of sound, that these essentials reflect associations only, that the poem is proceeding by mere associative thought – mere in the sense that the occasions arise, arbitrarily, in the poet's mind, in his understanding, in his private rather than his public life. It is tempting, but it is also mistaken, to do so. For while these lines serve, perhaps, to identify "it" a little more closely, we must remember that the link between sight and sound is never associative merely, whether in Shakespeare (where Bottom, bethinking himself of his translation into an ass, says "The eye of man hath not heard, nor the ear of man hath not seen") or in Zukofsky (for whom poetry is "sight, sound, and intellection" – *A Test, vii*), or in physics (where problems in high-frequency sound and in light can be solved with the same or similar equations). They tend to coalesce. Yet the next sentence of the poem, which has line six all to itself, apparently identifies the poem's thought as associative:

The one is one sea, the other a second.

Such counting is measure, and sorts differences (and it might, too, suggest light and sound, measured by time).

Allen Ginsberg has called poems timebombs; sooner or later they go off. With this line it would seem that Zukofsky is almost afraid that the poem might not go off at all, and so he explicates his text. The repetition of one in "the one is one," coming as it does hard on the heels of "heard" and occurring as it does in the idiomatic speech pattern of "the one/the other" (itself, notice, a pattern suggesting discriminating thought), points to the sound of that "sea," points to the alphabet. C. Once again wit bordering on whimsy? Perhaps. But also, in the use of sound to demonstrate sense, a case not of Zukofsky explicating the text so much as of the poem explicating itself, with the poet maybe just along for the ride. Those who are blind, who cannot see, turn after all to the ear.

Which is why the sixth line only *apparently* identifies the poem's thought as associative. The line points to the language in which the thought occurs, and begins to suggest how the language itself is generating the poem. For with the poem enjoining us to listen to it with the attentive ear as well as look at it with the reflective eye, it begins to make sense. In addition to "see" as to perceive light waves with the eyes, and to "sea" as a large body of salt water, there is also the symbol, in its various written forms (C, C., c, c., etc.): the musical note (i.e., "the key note of the normal or 'natural' major scale, which has neither flats nor sharps, in its signature"); a cathode; an (electric) current; the speed of light; capacitance (i.e., "the ability to store a charge of electricity"). They share the identical sound, and the manner of the poem's thought has been announced, we now realise, in the pun of line four's "frequent c's" (in a line, note, speeded up, and mentioning light). The thought of the poem proceeds through associations that arise in the dictionary, through identities that occur in language. There is a lot of interweaving going on, sight and sound. (The alert reader, indeed, might notice that "second" is, in music, an interval.)

The "it" of line one now begins to be clear: forms of energy – light, sound, electricity, the physical tangible world of the sea; energy, that is to say, in the form of waves. The opening sentence of the poem, indeed, appears to be in response to a remark that Zukofsky slightly misquotes in a note (*CSP* 104) to a poem written 22 November 1938, *Anew* 29 "Glad they were there" (*CSP* 93). Hendrik Antoon Lorentz, 1902 Nobel Prize in Physics, is explaining his notion of the electron to an audience at Columbia University early in 1906. Zukofsky himself was just over two years old. In restoring his words to their context I have italicised those that Zukofsky quotes:

> As to its physical basis, the theory of electrons is an offspring of the great theory of electricity to which the names Faraday and Maxwell will be forever attached.
>
> You all know of this theory of Maxwell, which we may call the *general theory of the electromagnetic field, and in which we constantly have in view the state of* the *matter or the medium by which the field is occupied. While speaking of this state, I must immediately call your attention to the curious fact that, although we never lose sight of it, we need by no means go far in attempting to form an image of it and, in fact, we cannot say much about it.* It is true that we may represent to ourselves internal stresses existing in the medium surrounding an electrified body or a magnet, that we may think of electricity as some substance or fluid, free to move in a conductor and bound to positions of equilibrium in a dielectric, and that we may also conceive a magnetic field as the seat of certain invisible motions, rotations for example around the lines of force. All this has been done by many physicists and Maxwell himself has set the example. Yet it must not be considered as really necessary.[5]

It is hard to see? Not according to Lorentz, who says it may be preferable *not* to. The pedagogical voice, in the opening lines of the poem, is explaining things to us. It is teaching particle physics:

> It's hard to see but think of a sea
> Condensed into a speck.
> And there are waves –
> Frequencies of light,
> Others that may be heard.
> The one is one sea, the other a second.

And the next lines (the fourth sentence of the poem) narrow the subject further: electricity, as it behaves in a condenser (i.e., a *container* for electrical energy – it is an arrangement of conductors separated by a dielectric – i.e., by a nonconductor). The condenser (nowadays called a capacitor, but not when Zukofsky wrote the poem)[6] is the brainchild, in its more developed forms, of Michael Faraday, mentioned by Lorentz. And Faraday, whose researches were "intimately associated with electrical discovery, and who also carried out fundamental work" on the dielectric of the condenser,[7] is well known to Zukofsky: His words are quoted three times in *A Test of Poetry,* completed some three years before this poem was written, in 1940. Here is the fourth sentence of the poem:

> There are electric stresses across condensers
> That wear them down until they can stand no strain,
> Are of no force and as unreclaimed
>   as the bottom of the sea

(The bottom of the sea? *Thump!* brings us back to the tangible tactile physical world, the root of it, the *nature* of it, lest we forget the injunction: think of a *sea. Think* of a sea.)

> Unless the space the stresses cross be air,
>   that can be patched.

It is a mark of Zukofsky's inclusiveness as a poet that he should speak of "electric stresses across condensers," that the fourth (and fifth) sentence of the poem should be an account of the breakdown of a condenser, probably as a result of overloading its capacitance, $C$ (at "breakdown voltage"). Here is how a textbook describes it:

> The energy expended in charging-up a condenser is stored in the dielectric in the form of the electric field of force, which is established between the plates of the condenser. This field stresses the dielectric to a greater or lesser extent, depending upon its magnitude and also upon the nature of the dielectric between the plates of the condenser. . . . for all materials there is an ultimate limiting stress which, if exceeded, will bring about failure of the dielectric. This failure usually takes the form of a puncture, an electric spark passing through the fracture so made, . . . resulting in the dissipation in heat of some or all of the energy stored up in the dielectric. In gases or liquids the rupture is temporary, and the insulation is restored as soon as the electric force is reduced. In the case of solids, however, the rupture punctures the material and usually completely destroys its insulating properties.[8]

Energy that cannot be fully contained. (Or understood.) Elsewhere in the same book we learn that a discharge current ($c$) from a condenser dissipates "mainly as heat, partly causing a rise in the temperature of the connecting wire, and partly producing the heat, light, and sound given off by the spark that always occurs just as the wire makes connection with the two plates. . . . If the voltage is at all high, a very bright and loud spark will occur."[9] In *Bottom: On Shakespeare* Zukofsky quotes

Faraday's characterisation of *spark* in his *Experimental Researches in Electricity* as "that brilliant star of light produced by the discharge of a voltaic battery . . . known to all as the most beautiful light that man can produce by art" (*Bottom* 206).

Heat, sound, light. These properties of condensers are pertinent to the next (long) sentence of the poem, which in its opening clauses refers to the energy loss that occurs in a condenser hooked into an alternating current, "alternations that escape." This is a hard sentence to follow, and I am not at all sure that I follow it. As though, having given me instructions for "understanding" the poem, it must not be too easy. Something is being withheld, so that the reader will have something to work against, so that in its difficulty the poem will engage the reader. Zukofsky thus risks, of course, making the poem so difficult that the reader will give up – it is almost, indeed, as though, placing his trust in the melody rather than in the reader's decoding abilities, he wants the reader to give up. But in any case, this, the longest and syntactically the most complex sentence of the poem, serves to remind the reader that "condenser" has other meanings than the electrical. With the transformations that occur in the syntax of this sentence (parallelling, perhaps, the transformation of electrical into radio waves, which the sentence seems at least in part to be about), and with the transformations possible in the meaning of "condenser," it would be a mistake to conclude that the poem, or even the first half of it (which ends with this sentence), is "about" physics or electricity. There is a lot of interweaving going on. The language is beginning to resonate with possibilities of meaning, many of them withheld (and that resonance was itself declared by the anaphoric "it" of the opening line).

> Large and small condensers,
> Passing in the one instance frequencies
>     that can be turned to sound,
> And in the other, alternations that escape,

(Frequencies, then, moving in waves. Sound, but also electricity, an alternating current.)

> So many waves of a speck of sea or what,
> Or a graph the curve of a wave beyond all sound,

(Escape, beyond all sound. Does he have radio transmission in mind? The next two lines of this difficult sentence, proceeding as it does by phrases and clauses interrupted by dashes, suggest that he may.)

> An open circuit where no action –
> Like that of the retina made human by light –

(Sound, electricity, radio, and light. Waves, but not contained. This is *organic* physics, if we regard that retina. The syntax is difficult, perhaps itself a circuit where no action:)

> Is recorded otherwise
> Than having taken a desired path a little way
> And tho infinitely a mote to be uncontained for
> ever.

The 1935 *Webster's Unabridged,* standard when Zukofsky wrote this poem, defines an electric current as "of especial practical importance as a convenient means of transferring energy to a distance and for the transformation of energy" (which may suggest to the reader Charles Olson's 1951 definition of a poem as "energy transferred from where the poet got it . . . , by way of the poem itself to, all the way over to, the reader").[10] And the Fourteenth Edition of the *Encyclopaedia Britannica* (1939) defines a condenser as "an instrument for compressing air, gas, or steam, or a device for concentrating electricity." The Eleventh Edition tells us that a condenser has as its object "the concentration of matter, . . . with intensification of energy." *Dichten,* Basil Bunting showed Ezra Pound in a German–Latin dictionary, "= *condensare.*" Sound, travelling in longitudinal waves, alternately crowds together (condenses) and thins out (rarefies) molecules of air. Light, travelling in transverse waves, can be intensified and brought to a focus by passing it through a condenser. As the Fourteenth *Britannica* puts it, a condenser "is used in photography to produce powerful illumination of a slide or other object which is being used. A lantern condenser causes light rays to converge after passing through the slide, so that they may also pass through the remaining lenses, which focus the picture on the screen." The screen at the back of the eye is called the retina.

Retina reminds us not only of light, but of sight: "an open circuit . . . / Like that of the retina made human by light," while the "graph the curve of a wave beyond all sound" reminds us of hearing. The sentence ends noting the existence of the unseeable which cannot be contained, which, in an open circuit, follows only a desired path: In the first direct comparison of the poem, this is likened to what makes perception human, what transforms or shapes the retina as human – what makes us see *how* we see. (In the theory of electrons, the only movement in an open circuit is random; electrically speaking, there is no action.) What then are we to make of "This science" in the next line?

"This science" might indeed be physics, for much of the vocabulary of the poem is drawn from it: waves, frequencies, electric, stresses, strain, force, condenser, space, light, sound, open circuit, graph, alternation (as of current), hard (radiation), infinite(ly), second, and so forth. To say nothing of *C*. But two things are worth noting. First, that the last nineteen lines of the poem (the second half, that is, from "this science" on) are notable for the complete absence of such language – *none* of the vocabulary is scientific. And second, that, of the scientific vocabulary of the first half, none of it is exclusively the jargon of physics. It could just as well, for example, be drawn from music (second, C), or from aesthetics.

The next sentence of the poem, in fact, begins to develop the notion of aesthetics.

> This science is then

(What are we to make of "then"? Is it a term in logic, or is it sequential time? Or both?)

> This science is then like gathering flowers of the
> weed

(This is a taxonomic science, then? Gathering *weeds?*)

> One who works with me calls birdseed
> That are tiny and many on one stem

(Multiplicity, then, and hard to see. Fragile, delicate, they have beauty:)

> They shed to the touch tho on a par
> with the large flower
> That picked will find a vase.

These lines could just as well be about poetry. In a famous and often-quoted passage in "A" – 6, written in 1930 (some thirteen years before this poem, then), Zukofsky claimed two voices: one in which melody is prime, and all else accessory; the other, an objective – a lens bringing the rays of the object to focus, and at the same time (*natura naturans*) the desire for what is perfect.[11] The noun, and the verb; the object, and the action. Sound. Light. Brought to a focus. By a condenser: a poem. Or a poet.

There is a lot of interweaving going on: sight and sound. When Zukofsky wrote in *A Test of Poetry* (*vii*) that "The test of poetry is the range of pleasure it affords as sight, sound, and intellection," he was echoing Pound; much of *Bottom: On Shakespeare* (written 1947–60), however, is a tightly focussed consideration of the relation of sight to sound in poetry, and discrimination between various kinds of seeing (the index entry for "eye(s)" reads "*passim*, 9–443" – i.e., the whole book). Wondering "whether visible is better than audible and how much wiser must ear be than eye to avoid harm" (*Bottom* 24), Zukofsky notices on one hand that print preserves words "for the eye to fathom but not see" (18) and on the other that a violinist keeps the sound together by touch ("his *orderly* fingering" – my emphasis) and by sight: the fingering "at which he looks while playing." The violinist's skill combines the three, the eyes, "exercised to effortless fleetness," echoing the exercise of the fingers and of the ear (424); "but he limits his looking as he listens not to outrun tangibly the critically fleeting visible order, so that no wrong twisting of fingers can effect a frightened look that the sound may not come clear" (424).

The eyes, then, must not anticipate and so must take nothing for granted: The erring brain can beguile the eye into seeing what it wishes to see, what it intends, what is desired, what may not actually be there. (And "an open circuit where no action"? There is latency, potential, at the very least.) Shakespeare's art, says *Bottom,* is an art of recurrences, and this poem, *Anew* no. 12, with the letter *C* sounding some thirteen times, *see,* is then to be fathomed by the reflective eye which is at the same time, like the eye of the violinist, fleet. And the recurring *C* instructs us to listen to the sound of the poem (wit, once more, bordering on whimsy) just as the opening line urges us to *think*. Since the poem is in print, "a graph . . . recorded," there is no danger that we will not look at it (though we may not see it). Shakespeare's plays, Zukofsky tells us, "are always resolving tensions of *melody* and *sight*" (424, his emphases): Notice, again, how line three of the poem is audibly longer but visually shorter than the lines around it.

"This science," then, is what? The poem does not tell us, any more than it explicitly identifies the "it" of line one. In the second direct comparison of the poem, we are told what it is *like:* not the delicate and ephemeral flowers, but the "gathering" of them. To gather is to bring together, rather than to pick (which can also mean choose). The picked flower goes to the vase; the birdseed (what plant is it, anyway? umbelliferous? like caraway? teasel? a *weed,* at any rate) equals it in beauty but cannot be contained (the attempt to contain – to bring it to use, as birdseed presumably – mars the beauty: no longer "many on one stem"). Like gathering what will not last, but changes in the picking. How tempting, to see this as a theme for the poem; to see this as a metaphor for "science," where – as Bertrand Russell once described it – we see "the discovery of more and more facts, each in turn the death-blow to some cherished theory."[12] How tempting to see it as an analogy for the scientist–observer, who interferes with the phenomena he or she would observe, simply by looking at them – an idea known in particle physics as the "principle of indeterminacy." How tempting, and how wrong. The next sentence of the poem specifically instructs us *not* to treat the poem thematically.

I see many things at one time
    the harder the concepts get

Which is to let the flower, "tiny and many on one stem," mirror forth something other than *these* themes, to the reflective eye. Perhaps it mirrors all themes? Perhaps. But like any good instruction book, the poem tells us, not what is to be said, not what is meant, but how, the process of it:

> I see many things at one time
>     the harder the concepts get,
> Or nothing
> Which is a forever become me over forty years.

Which *is,* not which is like. Many upon one stem. Many things at one time. The poem is moving towards multiplicity of meaning, not the single theme which disposes a hierarchy. This is not the art that Pierre Boulez calls "a series of refusals in the midst of so many possibilities."[13]

William Carlos Williams, Zukofsky's friend and at times mentor, chose the Stuart Davis drawing as frontispiece for *Kora in Hell* (1920) "because it was, . . . graphically, exactly what I was trying to do in words . . . – an impressionistic view of the simultaneous."[14] Davis's drawing is notable for its lack of perspective; it would be an exaggeration to say that everything in the picture occupies the foreground, but it would not be one to say that everything in the picture is of equal importance. The eye, progressing round the page, seeks an ordering principle but finds linkages, interconnectedness, and concludes (which is not conclusion) that everything is going on at once, there is no progression. "I see many things at one time." And the words in the poem say more than one thing at once. Then. Condenser. Recorded. *C.* Part of Zukofsky's admiration for Shakespeare rests on his recognition that Shakespeare could do so many things at once, and *hold* the understanding. In this century, however, it is hard to see how to do so: John Cage has remarked that "our experiences, gotten as they are *all at once,* pass beyond our understanding."[15] We expect of the understanding, not that it "explain" things to us (*vide* the voice "explaining" physics at the beginning of the poem) so much as that it make them "cohere" in a single unified vision, that "understanding" articulate the world. But the "weed" in the poem cannot be contained: The attempt to use it, to give it single purpose (birdseed) mars the beauty/multiplicity of "many on one stem."

As a teenager, Zukofsky read Henry Adams (the first draft of his monograph on Adams is dated 7 May 1924 [Booth 199]), Henry Adams who, in his *Education,* noted that "the child born in 1900 would then be born into a new world which would not be a unity but a multiple."[16] A multiple: "The difference between Aristotelian unities and the concentrated locus which is the mind acting creatively upon the facts," Lorine Niedecker quotes Zukofsky as saying, is that "three or four things occur at a time."[17] A multiple: "I see many things at one time / . . . / Or nothing / Which is a forever become me over forty years." The simultaneous, one childhood reaching out to another: the child, the two-year-old Zukofsky who – unlike his own son, born 22 October 1943 and almost three months old when this poem was written – lived in a polyglot world. On the Chrystie Street of his childhood "all Zukofsky had to do to become immersed in a welter of foreign tongues," Barry Ahearn reminds us, "was to step outside his door."[18] A simultaneity of sounds. A multiplicity. In *Bottom,* Zukofsky quotes Henry Adams – words that might almost be a description of this poem – recording the impact of Samuel Pierpont Langley's work in physics and astronomy, and its effect on Adams between 1893 and 1900:

> In these seven years man had translated himself into a new universe which had no common scale of measurement with the old. He had entered a supersensual world in which he could measure nothing except by chance collisions of movements imperceptible to his senses, perhaps even imperceptible to his instruments, but perceptible to each other, and so to some known ray at the end of the scale. Langley seemed prepared for anything, even for an indeterminable number of universes intertwined – physics stark mad in metaphysics. (*Education* 381–2; quoted partially in *Bottom* 345.)

(Elsewhere, Zukofsky quotes Plato: "If number, measure and weighing be taken away from any art, that which remains will not be much" – *Prep.* 6.) Many things at one time. Or nothing. Either way, it is "a forever become me." *A* forever. The world of the simultaneous is the world of the instant, and of one possibility out of many – or all possibilities, caught in the complex movement. And hence:

> I am like another, and another, who has
> finished learning
> And has just begun to learn.

"Like," for the last time in the poem. "The simile," Zukofsky wrote in 1931, "can be not a wandering ornament, but a confirmation of the objects or acts which the writer is setting down."[19] These lines confirm a world where everything shifts.

In Stuart Davis's picture the eye looks at the greyhounds, at the washing on the line, at the priests, at the building, at. . . . The eye does not finally come to rest on a particular point. The objects in the picture are bound together in the first place by the landscape in which (presumably) they occurred, and in the second by the blank white paper that encloses them in a frame. If the mind clings to its own constructs, it clings blindly, and interferes then with the picture, and does not see it; puts something first, and thereby places something last. So, too, with this poem, save that the things in it are bound together by the sight and more particularly the sound of the words, by the language, in which they occur, and by the poet who records them. And the poet does not himself presume to gloss either what gave rise to the poem, or the poem itself. For to do so would be to say what it "means," and one sense of "mean," we should recall, is to intend, to have intentions. Instead, the poem enjoins us to stare in wonder, as well as to stare, wondering:

> If I turn pages back
> A child may as well be staring with me
> Wondering at the meaning
> I turn to last
> Perhaps.

And so the poem ends. Is the child there? It does not matter – for "it may be, as well"; as well as "it may as well be." Such discrimination is possible, but the poem rejects any necessity to choose between them.

There has been a lot of shifting and turning, much pressure and shift of thought, through the poem's progress, and the multiplicity of meaning, of possibility, of language – almost, one might say, the duplicity of it – persists. "Wonder": not to know, to feel doubt or curiosity. Not, then, knowing what the poem "means"? Like a child, not to "know"? The "it" of line one is still unnamed. "Wonder": to be astonished, to marvel, "at the meaning." Yet, like a child, to "know" – as a song, when heard, "by inexplainable proof of its own has that sense of the substantial known rather like the seeing of the eye than the idiom of the brain" (*Bottom* 424).

Energy can never be fully contained or understood. Neither can knowing, the life of the perceptions. And the poet can never carry the reader all the way in, to the poem: There must be a resistance, for the act of knowing occurs only in the doing – and it is only then that meaning, or its possibility, can arise. So the line breaks (the *sound,* then) increase the multiplicity of this language. Where, syntactically, does the "perhaps" belong? To "a child may as well be staring, perhaps wondering . . . "? Or is it "Wondering at the meaning, I take refuge/solace in a final 'perhaps' "? (The "then" of "This science is then" acquires, by this, a hesitant tone; the curious, wondering voice, no longer explaining so firmly as we thought.) And, "last": Is it "to endure"? or "finally"? One must answer: all of these things, and more.

The "it" of line one is still unnamed. Is it "science"? "physics"? "poetry"? All of these? or none of them? On Christmas Eve, 1943 (Booth 205), less than a month before he wrote this poem, Zukofsky completed a report for the Hazeltine Electronics Corporation. In it, he discusses language:

> As for the pictures in Larousse, there are also Walt Disney's, and they *move*. Animated every split second they can perhaps never be absorbed as any stationary picture. They do not *tend* to confine thought like a name. (*Prep.* 156)

In his *ABC of Reading* (1934) Ezra Pound insisted on "the moving image."[20] Lorine Niedecker, choosing her words with care, has spoken of Zukofsky's "calculus of thought."[21] In 1964, writing about Bach in "A" – 14, Zukofsky would curiously pun (his italics):

> French music then
> as *current,* "ornament"
> hid calculus of
>
> Leibniz, . . . (*"A"* 342–3)

Currents *move;* calculus is a mathematics that deals with moving objects, not fixities, and it deals with more than one at once, by determining the area under the graph of a given mathematical function (called the "curve") plotted over the span of one of the coordinates (called the "interval" – which is also a term in music); it gives a (very precise) approximation. "A graph the curve of a wave," says the poem in its longest and most complex sentence, rejecting the idiom of the brain for the substantiality of song. In 1931, anticipating his comment to the Hazeltine Electronics Corporation that the moving picture is valuable for its "multiple suggestion" (*Prep.* 156), Zukofsky had said that a poem is made of "words more variable than variables, and used outside as well as within the context" (Preface to *An "Objectivists" Anthology, Prep.* 16). The language must resonate with possibilities of meaning; many of them may be withheld.

Multiples. Variables. Yet tending to a unity nevertheless: Unity is always a possibility in or behind a work where the poet seeks multiple meanings in one word, where meanings are permitted to accrete to words, to proliferate, where the poem is a deliberate remembering of possible meanings, rather than, by choice, a forgetting: "like gathering flowers." There is, then, no "picked" meaning that can be stuck in a vase, held up for our admiration; no choice bloom. There is, then, no "theme" to the poem in the way in which there might be a theme to a freshman essay or *Paradise Lost* – what Pierre Boulez calls "particularities *already* integrated."[22] The poem is not "about" anything; for it to be so would be for it to voice what Bertrand Russell called "dogmatism as regards the universe at large."[23] The hallmark of this poem is its inclusiveness. It is willing to let the universe in, if it will. There is a holding together, in the language.

So the "it" of line one is precisely that: "it." The word. The word without antecedent; without preconception. Let the language in, hear and see the word without predatory intent and the mind can be drawn to multiplicity not caged by thought, and the form of utterance becomes a weaving rather than an architecture, where, in the words of Pierre Boulez, "there is no distributive hierarchy in the organisation . . . , but there are successive distributions in the course of which the various constituting elements assume larger or smaller functional importance."[24] (He might almost be describing the structure of *"A"*.) This is hard to see, if our linguistic habit is that habit of "metaphor" which uses one thing to explain another, if language is for us only a vehicle.

Lorentz, in fact, warned against such pictorialisation of language and concepts in *The Theory of Electrons*. If there is a mote in the mind's eye, then that mote interferes with the seeing: All we can observe, he says in his chapter on the propagation of light, is *effects*.[25] "It's hard to see." And as for "*content,*" Zukofsky wrote to Cid Corman in 1960 about *"A"*, "the sooner I can get that out of the way & buried in the music of *the whole thing* the better."[26] The music of the whole thing: The test of poetry is the range of pleasure it affords as sight, sound, and intellection. Thinking, not thought, is the dynamic; the verb, not the noun; what Pound called "a dance of the intelligence among words and ideas." It is this activity which the reader must share, which holds the multiples together. The poem is not so much an object-which-means as it is a "practice" of meaning.[27]

Which is why this is a difficult poem, a "tough" poem Lorine Niedecker says. Yet it is a tantalising poem, because while it seems to tell us a great deal about how to read it – it has plenty of instructions in it, as I have suggested – much is withheld. It is almost as though, when Zukofsky wrote in *A Test of Poetry* (99) that "the forms of a particular communication . . . may never, in any society, be absorbed as automatically as air," he had decided therefore to make the poem as difficult of access as he could. So the poem, or the poet, seems perverse, aloof, withholding.

The intense deliberation of the poem, the dense concentration of thought and word, the refusal to hang the poem's movement on a fairly simple identifiable or paraphrasable "theme" or "meaning," all these make for an astringency in the poem that demands that the reader, to be a reader at all, trust the poem – and the poet – implicitly and absolutely. Just as the poet himself must trust the poem, the process of its writing. These things make for obscurity – yet Ezra Pound noted that a new language is always said to be obscure,[28] even (one might add) to the speaker who is trying it out. The poet must not be putting forward in the poem a "case," a personal case which shapes the writing by enclosing it within the frame of preconceived intentions, predilections, thought moving around what another idiom calls a closed circuit, to predictable ends. "Modern verse," says Williams, "forces belief";[29] forces belief here because the rest of the poem is not foreseen in the first line or sentence. Which is why Williams could say, reviewing *Anew,* "the *line* is the meat, not what it says."[30]

And, add to this, the poem's propensity to do what it cannot do fully: explain itself. The dynamics of the poem arise, in part at least, from the tension between a desire to let the reader into the poem, and an urge to keep the reader out lest in its ease of entrance the poem disappear. And both feelings border on necessity, for the poem's existence. The pressures thus generated shape the rhythm of the poem, as well as compress the syntax. What results is a tough knotty Grace; read the poem aloud, and notice the transformations – sight, sound, and sense. Grace, which derives from Greek Χάρις: a favour received, a delight. Did not Theocritus call his *Idylls* Χάριτες (16.6)? One authority, expounding Grace, calls it "loveliness and charm. Beauty in motion is very much the sense."[31] And it is *given,* if the reader will trust.

# 3

# *"Instant Entirety"*

## *Zukofsky's* "A"

*– – – Each writer writes*
*one long work whose beat he cannot*
*entirely be aware of.*

Louis Zukofsky, *"A"*[1]

One problem facing anyone writing a long poem is simply how long it takes to write. Either the world changes so radically that the original design for the poem no longer fits, or the poet does. It is a problem of form. Zukofsky's friend Basil Bunting was fond of citing Spenser's wisdom in abandoning the *Faerie Queene* after finishing only six of the poem's projected twelve books. "Things have changed since then," he said. "There's too much occurring too fast. A poem has to be written quickly, you see, if events aren't to ruin it." It took him two years to write *Briggflatts,* and he thought he'd pushed his luck.[2] *"A"* occupied Zukofsky for some forty-eight years, fall–winter 1926 to September, 1974, and events played their part. There's virtually a ten-year gap between the writing of "A" – 12 in 1950–1 and "A" – 13 in 1960, for instance, most of those years occupied with the writing of *Bottom: on Shakespeare* (1947–60). That gap has been highly visible in the composition of *"A"* because it has been reflected in the poem's publishing history, *"A" 1–12* appearing in 1959 (in Japan), *"A" 13–21* ten years later in 1969.[3] But there was a similar though shorter gap earlier in the poem's composition, between the completion of "A" – 7 (1930) and the start of "A" – 8 in 1935.[4] During those five years Zukofsky completed *An "Objectivists" Anthology* (1930); an early draft of *Thanks to the Dictionary* (1932); *The Writing of Guillaume Apollinaire* (1932); and a number of shorter poems, including "Mantis" and "Mantis: An Interpretation" (1934).[5] But "A" – 6 and "A" – 8 balance nicely around the complexities of "A" – 7's sonnets.

There are other intervals too. What is most interesting about the one-volume edition of *"A"* is the way it radically alters our sense of the poem's shape (the perspective of the poem), and in so doing makes especially clear the ways in which Zukofsky's poetics build on and part company with Pound's (the perspective of the poet). The breaks made inescapably conspicuous by the circumstances of publication virtually disappear, and other apparent discontinuities become visible. The move from "A" – 12 to "A" – 13 is remarkably smooth, for instance, and small shifts, parallels, and echoes ("recurrencies") obscured by earlier volume divisions are now clear. What is most immediately evident, however, is that Zukofsky tackles the formal problems time poses in the composition of a long poem by deliberately building discontinuity into its structure. He could not have predicted in 1926–7 that reading Gibbon would so temper his reading of Marx that *Das Kapital* would disappear from the poem after eight-and-a-half movements, supplanted by the family and by Spinoza, any more than he could have predicted his own marriage a dozen years before it occurred. He could, of course, predict that events would overtake the design of the poem if he did not build that uncertainty into the design itself, and he could expect that his poetics might undergo seemingly radical transformations (the unwary reader turning from "A" – 1 directly to "A" – 22 or even "A" – 14 might well wonder whether they were written by the same poet, let alone part of the same poem).

The major discontinuity in *"A"* occurs somewhere round the two halves of "A" – 9; – I say "somewhere round" partly because of the chronology of the poem's composition (the two halves of "A" – 9 completed ten years apart, in 1940 and 1950, and with "A" – 10 written immediately after the first part, and the intensely meditative "A" – 11 immediately after the second). The poem accommodates to this shift through a formal strategy conspicuously absent elsewhere in the poem: the second half of "A" – 9 matching the first; the form of "A" – 11 inverting the close of "A" – 8. The smoothness of form that marks "A" – 9 as a whole covers a radical shift in Zukofsky's own thought: the break from Marx, hereon absent, and the entrance of family, hereon central. And, with this, a major and formal shift in language, from the propositional to the meditative. But Zukofsky had (perhaps willy-nilly) in his thought allowed for such contingency, for from the very beginning the matter of relation has been primary in his aesthetics. So in 1933 he had defended *An "Objectivists" Anthology* against the charge of cultural elitism by citing Lenin's *Left: Communism, an Infantile Disorder:*

> This party rejected Marxism, stubbornly refused to understand (it would be more correct to say that it could not understand) *the*

> *necessity of a strictly objective estimate of all the class forces and their interrelation in every political action.* (Emphasis added.)[6]

From the very first line *"A"* presents complexities of interrelationship, and his aim is to achieve a simultaneity of multiples, political, aesthetic, historical, economic, linguistic. Marx's great gift to Zukofsky, embedded in Lenin's words I italicised, lasts through the whole of *"A,"* and Zukofsky's insistence, first, that it is "*impossible* to communicate anything but particulars – historic and contemporary – things, human beings as things their instrumentalities of capillaries and veins binding up and bound up with events as contingencies," and, second, that "the revolutionary word if it must revolve cannot escape having a reference"[7] are as applicable to the complexities of "A" – 22 as they are to those of, say, "A" – 7, whose opening sonnet can be read as an exploration of the "out of" of its second line. It is a shift in emphasis, not so much away from referentiality (the poem has themes, is about something, throughout) as toward the foregrounding of language.

Zukofsky tackled the formal problem of the poem partly by the simple act of faith that (any) relationship is necessarily meaningful once perceived, and partly by exploiting (any) poem's propensity to modify its own poetic as it proceeds. The mind finds order in the space the apparently random occupies whether that space be temporal, physical, intellectual, emotional – shared context makes relationship visible. As he put it in his 1929 essay on Pound's *Cantos,* the poet can move from one subject matter to another "comprehended in an instant entirety because all new subject matter is ineluctably simultaneous with 'what has gone before.' Postulate beings and there is breathing between them and yet maybe no closer relation than the common air which irresistibly includes them" (*Prep.* 77). To meet Bunting's world in which "there's too much occurring too fast," Zukofsky proposes the strategy of "instant entirety," a strategy he saw Chaplin exploit in *Modern Times* in 1936:

> World interaction of events today forces peoples to think in relation instead of discretely, and the speed of interaction on the part of an audience with the facts conveyed in a film is more immediate than whatever quibbling as to the director's 'real' intention. (*Prep.* 62)

The "facts conveyed" *within* the work are primary; thematic significance, "truth-value," are ancillary. In this, perhaps, the poem imitates "life"; certainly, insofar as it means the writer relinquishes a preset schematic "control," then the order the work exhibits or the reader finds is not necessarily "intended." In the words of "A" – 13, "the years make their order" (277). This is not to say, of course, that the poem is without themes, but that to attend primarily to them is to retreat from the poem. "A" – 8 has already been variously/mistakenly read as a proletarian epic, as Marxist/Stalinist, as failed sentimental Marxism; there are themes in the poem, to be sure (there are eight of them, indeed, in "A" – 8), but the poem lies in their interplay. The point of *"A"* (if there is one) is that there *be* no point; like any object, the text is self-sufficient.

This strategy of the "instant entirety" has its prosodic implications, for conventional views of formal coherence as a consistency of formal repetitions, architecturally or musically predictable, are not available to a poet whose prosody and form, like Zukofsky's, are so closely linked to his ideas about music. Recognizing that "each poem has its own laws" (*Prep.* 17) – that any poem, that is to say, inevitably (be it ever so slightly) modifies its own formal principles as it proceeds – Zukofsky took as structural principle for *"A"* the notion of prosodic variety. Basil Bunting told Hugh Kenner that Zukofsky's initial plan of the form included "a sequential table of difficulties to be overcome."[8] I take this to mean prosodic rather than thematic difficulties: Each section of the poem instructs the reader how to read its successor; each section modifies or breaks the prosodic "rules" that governed its predecessor. For example, "A" – 7 makes prosodic sense only if you have first read the first six sections. The prosody, that is to say, must *move,* and must always accommodate the unexpected.

Hence the poem meets a series of formal challenges. In "A" – 8 the question "For labor who will sing?" (48) is followed not only by a "Proletarian Song" (48–9) but by bits of an anthology, single lines from folksong and worksong (50) culled mainly from Zukofsky's textbook–anthology *A Test of Poetry* and his never-completed *Workers' Anthology;* "A" – 9 is a double-canzone in which "made things" *sing* – proletarian song with a vengeance. Zukofsky told Pound in 1930 that "A" – 7, planned to "justify the attack on sonneteers" in "A" – 1, ended up through an act of opportunist invention enacting and parodying the history of the English sonnet as "a direct outcome (an acceptance of your challenge) in The Dial for July 1928" (Pound's essay on Cavalcanti) that "the sonnet occurred automatically when some chap got stuck in the effort to make a canzone."[9] It also makes a nice filling for the sandwich of "A" – 6 and "A" – 8. "A" – 11 is almost exactly a mirror image of the "Ballade" that closes "A" – 8, and frees the poem into the prosodic range of "A" – 12. And so on.

*"A"* is a compendium and exemplum and even investigation of various traditional forms familiar (and some not familiar) to an English ear; like *The Cantos* it is a technical treasure house; unlike *The Cantos,* including prose and drama and indeed virtually the full range of the human voice, where the lower limit is speech (or even grunt – as on pages 359 or 519)

and the upper is music ("A" – 24). Writing about "A" – 9 on 11 July 1960, Zukofsky cautioned Cid Corman that "it's still LZ & not a prosody book,"[10] but one effect of reading the complete *"A"* is the realisation that one is witnessing or even participating in what might well be called a Drama of Prosody, one form addressing another, attending another. The formal range of *"A"* is truly immense, what with tercets, iambs, ballads, folksongs, elegies, hilarious Roman comedy, translations from Middle English and Welsh, and so on. "Akin jabber," there is English making noises like Greek (370), like Latin (393), like Hebrew (359–60), and even like Ojibway (539). As the poem progresses, so the poet's voice loses its individuation, till by the last two movements to be written, "A" – 22 and "A" – 23, the person of the poet is virtually effaced. Like a textbook, then. The notion of a prosody book is a strong element in *"A"* – it is as though Zukofsky had determined to write a work that would, if it was the only book you ever read, tell you all you need to know if you want to write poetry. In its technical richness and range it rivals the *Cantos*.

Once and for all, reading *"A"* in one volume effectively disposes of the *canard* that Zukofsky is a lesser Pound, and *"A"* a lesser *Cantos*. Or it should. That notion arose, perhaps, simply because academics (whose influence upon publishers' poetry lists is inestimable) first came across Zukofsky if they knew of him at all through Charles Norman's careful life of Pound, published in 1960, which did not address influence but traced a friendship. Add to that circumstance the academic custom of accommodating itself to anything new in literature by reading it in terms of "influences" rather than struggling with the writing in its own terms. That Pound was friend and mentor, that Pound encouraged Zukofsky, and gave him the fourth issue of *The Exile* to edit and some three or four years later sought his help in choosing writers to include in *Active Anthology* (parts of which Pound gave to Basil Bunting to edit) is well known.[11] As are their acerbic disagreements. Among papers in the Pound Center at Yale University are the first forty-nine lines of "A" – 1 corrected by Pound (the corrections are, mainly, cuts), and Pound is quoted (along with William Carlos Williams and E. E. Cummings) on Page 4 of that poem. Zukofsky's views in *A Test of Poetry*, where he talks of the pleasure poetry "affords as sight, sound, and intellection," look to the casual reader like a rehash of Pound, and Zukofsky himself in a letter to Pound (12 December 1930) felt the need to deny the charge that he was too much under Pound's influence (*Pound/Zuk* 78–9). Pound is not a major source for Zukofsky's *"A"* in the sense that say Bach, Marx, or Spinoza are, and Zukofsky himself was exasperated by those who never read either him or Pound carefully and then yoked his name to Pound's.

When Zukofsky finished "Poem Beginning 'The'" in the autumn

and winter of 1926, he began planning *"A"*. Pound first wrote to Zukofsky in August 1927 in response to "Poem Beginning 'The'"; "A" 1–4 was completed in 1928, save for minor cuts made in 1940, and the whole of *"A"* up to and including "A" – 7 by 1930. But Zukofsky read the *Cantos* (i.e., *A Draft of XVI Cantos* and *A Draft of the Cantos 17–27*) for the first time in 1929–30 in the New York Public Library when he was working up his essay on Pound which appeared in *Echanges* in 1930 and in Eliot's *Criterion* in April, 1931. And so, as Zukofsky explained in a 26 March 1953 letter that rehearses these facts to Lorine Niedecker (the letter is fragmentary), it is not a question of direct influence, but a matter of what was in the air at the time, which made young and elder alike make the same shapes, with the first to do so getting the recognition.[12] He had written much the same definition of influence at greater length in the *New Review* in May 1931,[13] but without the caustic note. In the fragment of a letter he subsequently dated "ca. 1941" but which is probably earlier, he rehearsed much of what he had written to Pound on 12 December 1930 in telling Niedecker that he had known some of Pound (especially *Cathay,* and especially "The Return" and "Exile's Letter") since he was fifteen, but had thought him somewhat precious. Coming across the prose and reading Pound's work in the *Dial* around 1925 radically changed Zukofsky's view, and he sent Pound "Poem Beginning 'The'" pretty well as soon as he'd got it written.[14]

The experience of reading *"A"* is so *un*like that of reading *The Cantos* that those who come to it expecting a mini-Pound will turn away baffled and disappointed, declaring its inferiority to Pound's (by page count slightly shorter) work. Zukofsky sketched the crucial distinction between his work and Pound's in his Foreward to the 1967 American edition of *"A" 1–12,* quoted on the dustjacket of the one-volume edition:

> The intent of the poet is not to fathom time but literally to sound it as on an instrument and so to hear again as much of what was and is together, as one breathes without pointing to it before and after. The story must exist in each word or it cannot go on. The words written down – or even inferred as written over, crossed out – must live, not merely seem to glance at a watch.

Writing a poem, Zukofsky often worked in pencil. As he reworked the text earlier versions would be erased, new versions written over the old, labyrinthine additions inserted. "A / child learns on blank paper," says "A" – 22; "the old man writes palimpsest" (524–5), an earlier text at the edge of the visible, teasing the reader, lurking under the new. But it is nevertheless a final text. It is hard if not impossible to construct the compositional history of Zukofsky's poem, for he wants that text to be singular.

And the poetics of the "instant entirety" demand that the text incorporate its own history, recording and incorporating its own errors as they occur over time in order that it be error free. For only by such means can it escape being overtaken by events. Alas!, he told Niedecker in a 1953 fragment, *An "Objectivists" Anthology* printed all the 1930 version of "A" – 1 to "A" – 7, rather than the revised.[15] Almost from the very beginning, Zukofsky is working toward a text of *"A"* that will, unlike Pound's, be indisputably *complete* in that it comes to an end, toward a text that will, unlike Pound's, be unique. Hence he usually destroyed the densely packed spiral-bound notebooks from which he drew his materials for the later movements of *"A"*,[16] just as he destroyed the notebooks on which the first version of *Bottom* was based. Hence his "Alas!" The text is carefully jointed (in 1932 Zukofsky spoke of writing in terms of cabinet making)[17] and thus articulate; transitions are carefully handled, and overall the impression is of a careful dovetailing rather than of weaving, the building of a structure rather than the weaving of a tapestry – again, then, unlike Pound, whose text is *variorum* and discontinues (as does Olson's; Olson is close to Pound in ways in which Zukofsky obviously is not).

With "A" – 24 the poem ends fittingly with a compilation by Celia Zukofsky, four voices, speaking to Handel's music suggested by Paul Zukofsky. A family affair: four simultaneous overlapping voices of four kinds: criticism, play, fiction, verse – or, as the text labels them, Thought, Drama, Story, Poem. And "A" – 24 begins (567), *loud:* "To the ear / Noises." And immediately adds, *soft,* hard to hear: "Or harmony." "A" – 24 is a set piece, a staged performance, a drama, in which the poem acts out its prosodic crises, and we are forced (if we heed at all) to discern: The background, the hard-to-hear, the half-hidden, the trace on the palimpsest, claims our attention, only to have the attention move on, instanter. Instant-er. It is thrown into the reader's lap. The Dedication of "A" – 24 to Celia, almost the last words before the Index (what other poem indexed by its poet can we name?)[18] enjoins the reader to hear "the work / in its recurrence." Complex, dense, an interplay of many voices at once, sounding together. "It is in the nature of music," Giorgio di Santillana reminds us, talking in *Hamlet's Mill* about fugue, "that the notes cannot all be played at once."[19]

Zukofsky would argue that in the poem they can, and are. It is a condition to which *"A"* aspires ("The story must exist in each word") and he has chosen particular means whereby to attain it. Overtly from the first lines of "A" – 1, Bach is declared one of those means: His music (and his life) runs through the whole text (*"A"* is also a history of western music: "A" – 11 is based on an Italian song Bach used; "A" – 24 literally sounds Handel [indebted to Bach] in performance). The poem early declares such antecedents as Spinoza, Marx (after "A" – 9, replaced by the family, Celia and Paul) and Aristotle, and it affirms in its behaviour the kinship, the family, of words: In each word can the family be seen, just as in each drop of water can the ocean be found. Here are some lines, from "A" – 13 (274–5). Zukofsky is quoting, but in the context they become his own:

> Why hop ye so, ye little, little hills?
> And wherefore do ye hop?
> It is because to us today, there
> Comes the lord bis*hop*.
> Why skip ye so, ye little, little hills?
> And wherefore do ye skip?
> It is because to us today, there
> Comes the lord bis*hip*.
> Why jump ye so, ye little, little hills?
> And wherefore jump ye up?
> It is because to us today, there
> Comes the lord bis*hup*.[20]

In its sheer playfulness this is the language of the nursery, of the child. There is an extraordinary freshness about the language of *"A"*, it is utterly limpid, and if it reflects in part the quality of the palimpsest, nevertheless the principal means of the poem come from four or possibly five antecedents – sources, if you like – who by their example gave Zukofsky permission to play. And they are largely, though whether by Zukofsky's design or by the accidents of publishing or of history, more or less concealed. Of them all, only Lewis Carroll figures as the subject of an essay in *Prepositions,* and only Gertrude Stein is mentioned in *"A"*. The other three are Laurence Sterne, Guillaume Apollinaire, and James Joyce, all quoted or mentioned in *Bottom: On Shakespeare* (Joyce's *Ulysses* is mentioned in "A" – 8).

Laurence Sterne, in that most mischievous of English novels *Tristram Shandy,* ends Book 1 with these words:

> I set no small store by myself on this very account, that my reader has never yet been able to guess at anything. And in this, Sir, I am of so nice and singular a humour, that if I thought you was able to form the least judgment or probable conjecture to yourself, of what was to come in the next page, – I would tear it out of my book.

*Tristram Shandy* is the masterpiece of indirection and digression, of apparent nonsense, punning humour, and seeming pointlessness. What other writer would put his Preface in the middle of Book 3? It cultivates, more than any other novel in the language, the art of delay: Like Don Quixote, the reader seems to be on a journey that is always getting sidetracked by enemies to be fought off and things to be explained before the story can get anywhere – and in getting nowhere, the story eventually gets everywhere. In "A" – 22, a geological history of the world, are concealed, in alphabetical order, the names of eight American cities; "A" – 23 is a political history that retells the epic of Gilgamesh and mentions no names. Sterne, the inclusive novelist par excellence, would have delighted in such mischief – and that Zukofsky knew *Tristram Shandy* can be adduced from William Carlos Williams's "The Work of Gertrude Stein," an essay that was largely written in collaboration with Zukofsky in the summer and fall of 1929.[21] That essay is instructive because it points to elements in Sterne and in Stein – their play of "sight, sense and sound contrast among the words themselves" and "their grammatical play"[22] – which Zukofsky also found in Joyce and Apollinaire: the play of the syllable, and of syntax.

Zukofsky wrote a film script, with Jerry Reisman, of Joyce's *Ulysses.* It has never been published, though Joyce – who said he liked it – suggested John Ford direct it. In the Preface to *An "Objectivists" Anthology* Zukofsky rejected "the streaming consciousness"; yet he felt close to Joyce, he told Cid Corman on 12 July 1963, not as a writer to imitate, but because, like Stein and Apollinaire, he worked with syllables, utterly without pedantry, pedagogy, and dogmatism.[23] Hence, as "A" – 12 puts it, "Let not a gloss embroil you" (129). Let the words *tell.* And, again like Apollinaire (and Sterne) Joyce is an inclusive writer: Stephen Dedalus, Zukofsky noted in *Bottom,* "works *in* all he knows."[24] The inclusive impulse in writing lends itself to more and more detail, more and more digressiveness, more and more insertion and addition of data in apposition to the main stream of thought or narrative, so that the writing tends less and less to subordinate itself to an avowed or even an implicit purpose (to be summarised as *point* or *plot* of story or poem). Such writing is quite in the tradition of English epic poetry (witness the lack of subordination in the syntax of *Beowulf*), and it leads the writer more and more to insist that the story must exist in each word. The *whole* story, that is. Gertrude Stein's *The Making of Americans,* long as it is, is astonishing for the way in which she uses the cumulation of repetition: Each new page summarises and draws on virtually a total recall of what has gone before. It is a highly concentrated book.

As such, it would have appealed to a writer like Apollinaire, who in a one-line poem like "Chantre" compresses, through the use of multiple puns and slippery syntax, a complex of at least three, call them "meanings," for the sheer play of it. In 1931 and 1932 Zukofsky wrote a long essay on Apollinaire (translated into French by Rene Taupin and published in Paris; the edition was mostly destroyed by a warehouse fire) that celebrates Apollinaire's attainment of "simultaneity." Apollinaire, in *Calligrammes,* uses not only syntax and pun but also the graphic to combine sight, sound, and intellection (painting, music, word) into a simultaneous complex of meanings: another means, then, of working everything in. The publication of *The Writing of Guillaume Apollinaire,* Zukofsky exuberantly told Carl Rakosi on 7 December 1932, should push Valéry and the rest into the back seat.[25]

These writers are to be thought of not as influences, not as models, but as instructive kin, offering the poet syntactic and thematic simultaneity, discontinuity, and multiplicity; each exhibiting the essential quality of the child, playfulness, and each, like the child, frequently breaking the rules. Play lies at the centre of *"A";* it is the particular means by which inclusiveness can be achieved, the intent of the poet realised, all the notes played at once. "The intent of the poet is not to fathom time but literally to sound it" – the play of words here, of "fathom" and "sound" and "time," is typical of Zukofsky and tells us (by calling "intent" and "literally" into question) a great deal. It attacks conventional notions of literal meaning by demonstrating its plurality and hence its uncertainty and hence its inclusiveness; it dislocates referentiality while at the same time asserting it, and it undermines "intent" while furthering it. Which is what Joyce and Stein do. Such simultaneity of possibilities, then, in which "the story must exist in each word," is what Williams and Zukofsky called for in their essay on Stein:

> Either, the mind has been taught to think, the mind moves in a logical sequence to a definite end which is its goal, or it will embrace movement without goal other than movement itself for an end and hail "transition" only as supreme.

But neither will do, alone, for "both movements are an improper description of the mind in fullest play" (*SE* 117). The demand that the whole story be present, in the word, is a notion that derives, most immediately, from Emerson's "Every word was once a poem. Every new relation is a new word,"[26] and Zukofsky's desire for inclusiveness is not indeed all that far removed from Whitman's. It demands of the writer an inventive opportunism that exploits and amplifies the possibilities the instant offers. The desire to include the whole poem in each word demands great and intense concentration on the part of the reader, demands a concentrated attentiveness to system/s as they emerge from the poem as it progresses, to relations and interrelations within the poem as they recur and change. Utterly devoid of symbolism as say Valéry or Eliot would use it, *"A"* is intensely a meditative poem demanding that the reader *dwell* on the syllables of the work as they occur, and find instruction. "The intent of the poet is not to fathom time but *literally* to sound it" – the mischief there! Dense, concentrated, baffling in the playfulness of its syntax and its puns, beautiful in its music, and in its sheer lyric passages, it will, if we have the patience, change the way we think, for such is the effect of mischief and play.

# 4

# "Not at All Surprised by Science"

## *Louis Zukofsky's* First Half of "A" – 9

*A man should be learn'd in severall Sciences, and should have a reasonable* Philosophicall, *and in some measure a* Mathematicall *head; to be a compleat and excellent Poet.*

John Dryden[1]

In November, 1940, Louis Zukofsky published in a mimeograph edition of fifty-five copies (forty of them for sale) his *First Half of "A" – 9*.[2] It sold slowly: He could send a copy to Edward Dahlberg in 1951, and he still had one left to send to Cid Corman in December 1958.[3] The poem opens:

An impulse to action sings of a semblance
Of things related as equated values,
The measure all use is time congealed labor
In which abstraction things keep no resemblance
To goods created; integrated all hues
Hide their natural use to one or one's neighbor.

Forty-four words; six different rhymes (action, sings, semblance, related, values, labor), sounding between them seventeen echoes (sixteen, if you discount "natural use"). The density continues throughout the stanza (and indeed throughout the whole poem):

So that were the things words they could say: Light is
Like night is like us when we meet our mentors
Use hardly enters into their exchanges,
10 Bought to be sold things, our value arranges;
We flee people who made us as a right is
Whose sight is quick to choose us as frequenters,
But see our centers do not show the changes
Of human labor our value estranges.

Fourteen lines, an upside-down sonnet, revolving round the "sold" of line ten, where the difficult syntax, in its compression, brings the voice up short amidst mellifluous lines whose tune lulls the attention, where rhymes sound changes almost like English church bells. If you read it aloud without paying much attention to the sense it sounds gorgeous, unlike any other poem in the English language. But the ear seduces you into figuring out what it says, and you pause, and consider. Should the voice pause for breath, for example, at the "when" in line eight, and then run on into line nine? Or do we run over the "when" to take a breath between the two lines? Is "sold" in line ten an adjective or the passive verb, "to be sold" – or is that not a distinction? The antecedents, in any case, are elusive, and our confusion over these apparently muddled parts of speech is reflected in the broken rhythms of the last four lines of the strophe. The language is very abstract, and it looks something like Marx, contrasting "sold things" with "made things," talking (after Aristotle) about proper use and unnatural use, about value, good, and labour. And in fact the sense of the strophe is fairly straightforward.

When he published *First Half of "A" – 9* in 1940, Zukofsky included a prose "Restatement" of the poem which summarised the first strophe as singing about things "embodying" a "common denominator of past work." Such an abstract evaluation, he said, conceals their nature as goods made to be used by people.[4] Voicing the sense, we fight against the tune: The syntax is so compressed, so difficult, that – drawn into thought by the demands of the ear – we are forced continually to shift tone, and we discover, tracking the complicated second sentence through, paying attention to the verse, that our thought is – like the syntax – perpetually shifting from one perspective to another: Ideas and thoughts come and go the way the sound comes and goes, the way parts of speech in this language modulate into one another. Not only do these lines bring voice to crisis, they bring thought to crisis too: We tend to bewilderment, for we are (as is customary in Zukofsky's poetry) left off balance, with only the music of the verse to hold us steady, and we are forced into a state of perpetual alertness and concentration where we remain open to possibilities of meaning and relationship.

In his 1946 essay, "Poetry," Zukofsky describes rhetoricians as responsible for arbitrary and absurd rules governing the use of commas before relative clauses. One wonders what they would make of the unpunctuated eighth line, no comma before "when." Zukofsky accuses them of existing "entirely in *that frozen realm without crisis* that Dante called the 'secondary speech'" (*Prep.* 10; emphasis added). Crisis, which might arise in syntax, or punctuation, or rhythm. Or there is the crisis of repetition, recurrence, as in "Julia's Wild" (*Bottom* 393). In Henry

Adams, about whom Zukofsky wrote a book by the time he was twenty,[5] *this* is crisis:

> Of all the elaborate symbolism which has been suggested for the Gothic cathedral, the most vital and most perfect may be that slender nervure, the springing motion of the broken arch, the leap downwards of the flying buttress – *the visible effort to throw off a visible strain* – never let us forget that Faith alone supports it, and that, if Faith fails, Heaven is lost. The equilibrium is visibly delicate beyond the line of safety; danger lurks in every stone. The peril of the heavy tower, of the restless vault, of the vagrant buttress; the uncertainty of logic, the inequalities of syllogism, the irregularities of the mental mirror – all these haunting nightmares of the Church are expressed as strongly by the Gothic cathedral as though it had been the cry of human suffering, and as no emotion had ever been expressed before or is likely to find expression again. The delight of its aspiration is flung up to the sky. The pathos of its self-distrust and anguish of doubt is buried in the earth as its last secret.[6]

Zukofsky quotes this paragraph in his work on Adams (*Prep.* 116), and omits what I omit: the opening sentence, which talks of "*apparent* instability" (my emphasis). The omission is interesting, for it points to what that crisis might be.

Michel Foucault locates that crisis in *thought,* which he calls "a perilous act";[7] Robert Duncan, in an essay on Olson, has spoken of *language* as risk, "the conquest of babble by the ear."[8] And Henry Adams, in *Mont-Saint-Michel and Chartres,* finds that crisis expressed in *structure,* in architecture, in building. "Look with delight," he enjoins us, "at the theatrical stage-decoration of the Gothic vault":

> the astonishing feat of building up a skeleton of stone ribs and vertebrae, on which every pound of weight is adjusted, divided, and carried down from level to level till it touches ground at a distance as a bird would alight. If any stone in any part, from apex to foundation, weathers or gives way, the whole must yield. . . . (*MSM* 109–10)

An *apparent* instability: the Cathedral at Chartres, a twelfth- and thirteenth-century building, "as solid," Adams notes, "as when it was built." Contemporary with Cavalcanti's precursor, Arnaut Daniel, whom Dante called *il miglior fabbro.* As airy, aerated, as light. An apparent instability.

And crisis? To record and elate for all time. Such crisis, that the line should bound from the page (yet still, perhaps, be the "bounding line" Blake wrote of in *A Descriptive Catalogue,* "distinct, sharp and wiry"): like a spring, wound, wound up. "A mason will tap a pillar to make its stress audible," says W. R. Lethaby. "We may think of a cathedral as so 'high strung' that if struck it would give a musical note."[9] In "A" – 6, written in 1930, Zukofsky talks of

> Forms only in snatches,
> Words rangeless, melody forced by writing, . . .
> ("*A*" 22)

These are difficult lines, and I shall come back to them. From their context I take them to signify a breakdown of a larger system from which the writer once drew. Words rangeless, I take as words with nowhere to go – like lost cattle – or unable to go, like penned ones. I take Form to be intermittent, and melody to arise from thought rather than from song or felt impulse. A breakdown of forms and a loss of resource.

In his essay on Adams, Zukofsky wrote that "Adams had not the faith which makes of its thoughts a system to be put forward as text" (*Prep.* 117). He might be talking of himself, for whatever the text *"A"* might be, it is no system: As indefinite article, *a* witholds completeness, is inevitably partial. *"A"* might be *rangeless:* "*adj. rare* . . . That has no range or limit" (*OED*). Words rangeless might be words that can go anywhere, then, making forms only in snatches, such forms being songs (snatches), melody forced by writing: an intermittency, perhaps, but hardly a system. Hugh Kenner reports, of *"A"*:

> Zukofsky began about 1927 with a formal plan, a plan of the form, which means in practice (1) an intuition of the poem without any words in it, a silent structural eloquence; and (2) a sequential table of difficulties to be overcome. I picked up this information from Basil Bunting, who doesn't know, nor do I, how closely the plan has been stuck to.[10]

Melody, *forced* by writing. There is no single thematic content of *"A"*, though there are intermittent themes; there is an *intended* structure, "a table of difficulties," a sequence, no matter how loosely one might think of it.

Such sequence has some coincidences – or rather, some elements that are hardly likely to have been planned from the beginning in 1926 (the last movement of the poem, after all, was finished in 1974).[11] There is for example the matter of dates: "A" – 7, written in 1928–30; *First Half of "A" – 9* in 1938–40, and the second half in 1948–50 – at ten-year intervals. *First Half of "A" – 9* is a canzone (which Dante, according to Ezra Pound in an essay Zukofsky read, set as "the grand bogey of technical mastery")[12] about "labour" and "value." The second half is, as any reader can see, a "reply" to the first half, "love" replying to "value." Each half copies exactly the rhyme scheme and form of Cavalcanti's

*Donna mi Priegha;* each half is seventy-five lines long: five strophes of fourteen lines each (but hardly sonnets) and a Coda of five lines. The whole of "A" – 9, then, is a *double* canzone, the second half as antiphon to the first extending and elaborating the (less successful) antiphonal contrast of chorus and solo voice in Zukofsky's earlier (1934) attempt at proletarian song, "Mantis" and "Mantis: An Interpretation"; echoing, too, Bach's double choirs in the *St. Matthew Passion.*

And "A" – 7? In 1928–30, at the beginning of those ten-year intervals, Zukofsky wrote this cycle of seven sonnets (that is, *half* a sonnet cycle, if ideally the sonnet cycle consists of fourteen sonnets). And in his essay on Cavalcanti, written by 1931 and in its final form published after Zukofsky had written "A" – 7, Pound says this:

> The sonnet was not a great poetic *invention.* The sonnet occurred automatically when some chap got stuck in the effort to make a canzone. His 'genius' consisted in the recognition that he had come to the end of his subject matter. (*LE* 168)

The sequence is of difficulties for the *writer,* and the compositional methods are opportunist; that is, Zukofsky seizes the difficulty when and as it presents itself. In "A" – 9, for example, the letters *r* and *n* are distributed in the first five strophes according to a mathematical formula, a poetic analog. When asked why, Zukofsky replied that the formula for a conic section was Jerry Reisman's suggestion; he used it with his usual impulse to overcome something, as a resistance for work or a working out – which is write by impulse: a push against, a counterthrust. During the writing, he commented, it may get easy after a while, but it must in any case look that way to the reader – for such is to sing. And when the poem's finished, it can be scrapped, made invisible.[13] It is also a means of getting another kind of thought and language – the mathematical and formulaic – into the poem to reinforce and support the vocabulary of an alternative discourse.

"A" – 7 is a sonnet cycle which, as it progresses, gradually breaks down: The predetermined form slowly collapses. The lines are almost uniformly decasyllabic (though the syntax breaks up the iambs early in the sequence), and there are are some notable exceptions which mainly cluster toward the end of the final sonnet (one line is a thirteener). The octets are in their rhyme scheme perfectly regular, but the sestets vary considerably, playing variations on a basic Shakespearean pattern until, in the final more-or-less Miltonic sonnet (which is itself a run-on from the sixth so that the two sonnets make a single rhythmic statement) the rhyme scheme collapses (rhyming "words" with "came" as it does) in lines of ten and eleven syllables respectively. At the same time, the decasyllabics of the sonnets move, in the final one, toward hendecasyllabics (i.e., toward the line of the canzone in "A" – 9, Arnaut Daniel toward Cavalcanti). Through the turbulent rhythms of "A" – 7, where quantity comes gradually to dominate, the form slowly collapses until the writing is scarcely recognizable as sonnets, is perhaps *sirventes*. "A" – 7, that is to say, is responsive to something other than its predetermined form, its overt plan. Its form is subject to outside interference which generates crisis: It might even, indeed, be seen as anticipating Pound's proposition that the sonnet "marks the beginning of the divorce of words and music" (*LE* 170).

At any rate, in "A" – 7 the sonnet-cycle form slowly collapses, and such collapse is followed by "A" – 8, whose burden is "For Labor, who will sing . . . ?" (and labour surely includes writing), and "A" – 8 slowly and labouriously, through stops and starts, works towards song. Quoting extensively from the correspondence of Marx and Engels, and from Henry and Brooks Adams, on the problem of "value," occasionally parodying Spinoza, breaking forth sporadically into more-or-less crude Proletarian Song (such as "March Comrades"),[14] quoting snatches – odd lines and phrases – from poems that Zukofsky was gathering for both *A Test of Poetry* (which once again suggests that *"A"* is, amongst other things, a textbook of poetry) and his *Workers' Anthology*,[15] quoting bits of interviews, newspaper reports, and "history," the ragbag collage of "A" – 8 struggles through its disorders, at the last, into song: the "Ballade" of thirty-eight lines with which it ends (*"A"* 104–5). In that struggle, "A" – 8 has recourse to formulaic elements: Among Zukofsky's papers at the Harry Ransom Humanities Research Center at the University of Texas at Austin there is Zukofsky's chart of the *r* and *n* patterns in what he calls the "Calculus Section" of "A" – 8, which immediately follows the crude Proletarian Song of "March Comrades" (*"A"* 49–53). Here the number of *r* and *n* sounds accelerates or decelerates in varying ratios in each stanza, treated in groups of three lines.[16] The "Ballade" itself, with its three ten-line stanzas followed by a six-line Coda, draws heavily on formulaic elements with its careful sequence of rhymes (which are the same for each stanza), its varied refrain (which in the Coda reads "Labor light lights in earth, in air, on earth"), and a scrupulous distribution of *r* and *n* according to formula.

In the mid–1930s Zukofsky had, with Jerry Reisman, been discussing and experimenting with the possibility of writing poetry according to various mathematical formulae (the manuscript notes on "A" – 8 illustrated on Booth 88 are largely in Reisman's hand), and after he had worked out his plans for "A" – 9, Zukofsky rewrote the "Ballade" to conform to "the analogy to the calculus," in which the number of *r* sounds may increase (or decrease) in a given section of seven lines while the number of *n* sounds remains constant (or vice versa) (Booth 53, 88).

However, the full complexity of song toward which "A" – 8 struggles is achieved not in the "Ballade" which brings it to a close, but in the complex formulaic double-canzone of "A" – 9, where the form of the canzone, although hendecasyllabic, reflects both the sonnets of "A" – 7 and the stanzas of "A" – 8's close. "A" – 9 is followed, after the seeming hiatus of "A" – 10's elegy (an inverted Mass) on the fall of Paris in 1940, by "A" – 11, whose stanzaic form is an almost exact mirror image of the closing thirty-six lines of "A" – 8 (an inverted "Ballade," then), though the writing is no longer formulaic, and which is devoted to the domestic life of the Zukofsky family.[17] In "A" – 11 the more or less turbulent surface of "A" – 9 is smoothed out into the clarity of Bach's music, into an intensely meditative lyric voice, more subdued, less overtly virtuoso, less public. The whole sequence of *"A" 1–12* enacts a theme declared in "A" – 4; it is progressively a more and more urgently felt struggle toward *form* and toward *song,* in which traditional forms break down, somehow to recur, recognisable, broken, crabbed, but nevertheless lurching towards music until, the music of "A" – 11 clear and firm, "A" – 12 is freed to go its own way, speech into song. "A noble structure is not a thing of will, of design, of scholarship," writes W. R. Lethaby. "A true architecture is the discovery of the nature of things in building" (*Architecture,* 159).

So, let us go back to Henry Adams. For as I read Louis Zukofsky, I see more and more of Adams's presence. Adams is discussing twelfth-century stained glass:

> The French held then that the first point in colour-decoration was colour, and they never hesitated to put their colour where they wanted it, or cared whether a green camel or a pink lion looked like a dog or a donkey provided they got their harmony or value. Everything except colour was sacrificed to line in the large sense, but details of drawings were conventional and subordinate. So we laugh to see a knight with a blue face, on a green horse, that looks as though drawn by a four-year-old child, and probably the artist laughed, too; but he was a colourist, and never sacrificed his colour for a laugh. (*MSM* 138)

Henry Adams is discussing an art that is close indeed to Zukofsky's, though I do not think that the details in Zukofsky are conventional – or, if they are, they are not conventionally treated. Whether or not they are subordinate is another matter. Adams's point is that the artists never hesitated to put their colour where *they* wanted it – yet the whole tenor of his argument is that the artist was subservient to the Muse (who, at Chartres, was the Virgin): Everything is done to please Her. The work, the worker, the artist, is without intention – or rather, the intention is to please the Muse, not the World or the Self. "Value," says Karl Marx, "does not wear an explanatory label."[18] I shall have occasion later to quote a story Guy Davenport tells, about "mg. dancer." It is hard to believe "mg. dancer" exists to please anyone but the Muse.

Secondly, Adams says in his passage that *content* is subordinate to *form:* or rather, that whatever it is that the stained glass does, it does not seek primarily to state propositions about the world, though it may seek to celebrate them. It seeks rather to have an *effect.*[19] It is also implicit in Adams's argument that the artists *may* not have known what the effect would be, ahead of time: We cannot know, for as Adams says "we have lost many senses" (*MSM* 128). Whether the artist knew or not, one thing is clear: *Form* is, as Adams discusses it, something to be *felt.* And one's feelings, though they may be intent, are hardly to be spoken of as having intentions. As Adams described it, or as I have talked about it in terms of crisis, form is a *force,* itself generative. Somewhere around A.D. 1300 Lawrence of Aquilegia, presenting a collection of letters to be used as models in writing (formulae, then) asserted that "it is better to work from form rather than from material."[20] Robert Creeley commented in 1966 that Zukofsky "feels form as an intimate presence, whether or not that form be the use or issue of other feelings in other times, or the immediate apprehension of a *way* felt in the moment of its occurrence."[21] That apprehension is a force which makes its own form or takes it as it finds it, ready made.

"Probably the artist laughed, too: but he . . . never sacrificed his colour for a laugh," Adams says. The poetry is not – any more than is a stained-glass window at Chartres – a proposition about the world. It is a play, a play of words, a play of content, where play becomes song, becomes colour. Melody, *forced* by writing.

> Forced: "*ppl. adj.* . . . Compelled, imposed, or exacted by force; enforced, compulsory; not spontaneous, voluntary, or optional. . . . Produced or maintained with effort. Strained. . . . In literary usage: strained, distorted. . . . Of actions, affected, artificial, constrained, unnatural. . . . Of plants, made to bear, or produced, out of the proper season." (*OED*)

The *Oxford English Dictionary (OED)* tells us, too, that "to force" is "to put a strained sense upon (words). Also, to force (words) into a sense." And a forced march is "one in which the marching power of the troops is forced or exerted beyond the ordinary limits." Guy Davenport once asked Louis Zukofsky what the "mg. dancer" is who dances in "A" – 21, "a milligram sprite, a magnesium elf, a margin dancer, or Aurora, as the dictionary allows for all of these meanings." "All," Zukofsky replied.[22]

Hence – or thus! – the lines from "A" – 6, a visible strain:

> Forms only in snatches,
> Words rangeless, melody forced by writing, . . .

"I take form to be intermittent," I wrote earlier, but there I had in mind "form" as a noun, when it could be verb. A "snatch" is a short space of time; it is a song or tune – or part of one; it is a sudden grab. "In snatches": by fits and starts, in hasty unsustained efforts. And "snatch" is also slang for what, in another poem ("The Translation"), Zukofsky calls "*malakos leimown,*" a soft grassy meadow, *pudenda muliebra.* Zukofsky's *Thanks to the Dictionary* gives us a clue: Go to the dictionary and these lines from "A" – 6 come to reveal what William Blake found: "Grecian is Mathematic Form," he wrote; "Gothic is Living Form."[23] Words rangeless, conveying not one meaning, but a play of meanings; the form not a system but a *way*. Words slip and slide in their syntactic bounds. Rangeless, words strain and threaten to crack, but the delicate balance holds.

"Writing," both as an *object* (the writing on the page) and as an *act* (the person writing), becomes *a* force: shaping, pressuring, bringing to *crisis* (the point, the dictionary reminds us, in the course of events which is decisive of recovery or death), bringing to crisis the *language,* forcing *melody,* perhaps as a plant might be forced. A range is a limit while it is at the same time an extent (a range of mountains), but "in order to draw a limit," Wittgenstein reminds us, "we should have to be able think both sides of this limit."[24] It is through boundary that we can imagine a beyond, a sense of further. And "strain" is an air is a tune. "To throw off" is to produce, or can be. And I come back to the by now inevitable Henry Adams, talking of "the visible effort to throw off visible strain." Which is to say, "melody forced by writing." And if this is the nature of the content, then how can the poet have intentions about what the poem will *say?* How can *"A"* remain, as James Laughlin called it in 1938, "an epic of the class struggle"?[25] Or, what may be more to the "point," how can one know what the poem will say until it says it? What kind of content might such a poem have? No predatory intent will serve: No theory or presupposition can account for the poem, or bring the poem to account; there can be no expectations of *that* sort. The poem is, as Robert Duncan asks, adventure, or discovery, or both: an act of crisis. And it is the outcome of a great deal of concentrated thought, like "the great cathedral" as W. R. Lethaby described it in a book Zukofsky read:

> a balanced structure of stone which found its perfected form at the limits where men could do no more. Thus it was said that a cathedral was not designed, but discovered, or "revealed." (*Architecture,* 159)

## II

"We have lost many senses," said Henry Adams. Ezra Pound, in his essay on Cavalcanti, provides an instance: "We appear to have lost the radiant world where one thought cuts through another with a clean edge, a world of moving energies" (*LE* 154), which is Adams's world of the Gothic, almost contemporary with what Pound calls Cavalcanti's "scholastic definition in form" (*LE* 161). One thought cuts through another; concentrated thought. Of the forty-one pages of *First Half of "A" – 9,* only two are taken up by the poem. The rest, as Zukofsky carefully tells us in the one-page foreword, consists of the materials that went into the writing of the poem. They are as follows:

> Cavalcanti's *Donna mi priegha* (2 pages)
> extracts from Karl Marx's *Capital* (Everyman's Library edition), chapters 1–13, and *Value Price and Profit* (22 pages)
> extracts from Herbert Stanley Allen's *Electrons and Waves: An Introduction to Atomic Physics* (3 pages)
> four translations of Cavalcanti's canzone: two by Ezra Pound, and two in slang, by Jerry Reisman (first two strophes only) and Louis Zukofsky (8 pages altogether)
> and a note on "The 'Form'" (1 page).[26]

The poem itself, titled *"A" – 9 (First Half),* is followed by a prose "Restatement" of the poem's "argument" (two pages). The note on the form quotes Pound's analysis/description of the rhyme scheme and structure of Cavalcanti's poem (*LE* 168), and describes the mathematical procedure by which in the second strophe, for example, there are thirteen *n* and thirteen *r* sounds in the first seven lines, and fourteen *n* and thirteen *r* in the second (*ng* combinations are not included in the count): *n* thus has an "infinite" acceleration over *r,* which does not increase frequency at all in this strophe. (Zukofsky explains that Jerry Reisman is responsible for the mathematical part of the form, and that the coda is "free.")

All this sounds like – and is – very complicated formulaic writing. The formulaic element of the poem is increased by the fact that the poem itself is a version if not exactly a translation of *Donna mi priegha* (which means that the "content" or "material" of the poem is provided) written under the formidable constraints imposed by specific vocabularies (Marx and Allen). By providing the matter of the poem, the formula can be said to guarantee coherence of thought, just as by providing letter frequencies and rhythms (to say nothing of complex rhyme patterns) it guarantees a coherent sound pattern: The occurrence of a similar sequence of sounds in each strophe unifies into a coherent structure: a complex song. "That's Herrick," Zukofsky said on the *U. S. A.: Poetry* television film about him, "I want to *deduce* something as good as that" (my emphasis).[27]

"For Labor, who will sing . . . ?" asked "A" – 8. And the coda to this poem provides the answer: no one. *Labour* can sing – as it does here – of its own accord. For, inspired by the abstraction "time-congealed labor" (line 3), the poem has in the course of its writing been *forced* to turn from the abstraction to the actual and specific labour the words themselves, in the song, embody:

song's exaction
Forces abstraction to turn from equated
Values to labor we have approximated (lines 73–5).

That is what the coda tells us, and it tells the truth, for in the course of the poem the writing works against so much, the formula demands so much; it is only through song's *exaction* in this way that the poem can work at all. Thus the abstract (like the word "value," for instance) becomes concrete, specific, in the activity – the action – the labour, which the form of the song embodies, and which the form of the song calls forth in the reader: concentrated thought. And the poem itself, *"A" – 9 (First Half),* becomes what Robert Duncan has called all great poetry, an act of incarnation, where the abstract is *bodily* put forth.[28] On Page 79 of *Bottom: On Shakespeare,* Zukofsky talks of the three terms "sense (the *universal* term for *singular* feeling), essence (the *universal* for singular *being*), and nonsense (i.e., non-sense, the *universal* for universal being unconcerned with singular *feeling*)" as having "always made up the arguments of logic and metaphysics." The language of "A" – 9, abstract (the first six lines, after all, summarise the opening chapters of *Capital*), *essence,* is converted into the *singularity* of sense, singular feeling, by the very act of writing the poem, or by the very act of reading it – by the act, that is, of *attending* it. The intense concentration of the poem demands much the same of the reader as it did of the writer: The method of composition forces labour, and the poem offers a kind of proof-by-experiment. In the act of understanding the poem, wound-in as it is, the abstractions of language, the things that are words, become singular, turn to the particulars of their existence – something that Spinoza always insisted upon. They act out, one might say, the Revolution they call for, and the reader participates in the activity of their incarnation. An idea is thus experienced, *felt*, and the words of the poem are immediate to our senses. "Were the things words," says line 7. By the time we reach the coda, they are – or rather, the words are things.

And we should not forget that the poem is a version/translation of Cavalcanti's poem, which Ezra Pound called "a struggle for definition" (*LE* 177). The poem begins with a question, and then seeks to answer it, in rational and philosophical terms, as well as in a densely musical form. And Zukofsky's stage-Irish/Brooklynese version dismisses the question, almost, by beginning "A foin lass bodders me I gotta tell her," reminding us of the sound, the *speech* of it, and forcing our attention on the patterns that emerge, the rhymes and echoes. It is a careful and comic debunking of the literary or "pretty," like Jerry Reisman's, whose first stanza insists on the flat matter-of-fact nature of the question the poem treats, with fine irreverence. It's called "A Dame Ast Me":

> It's so hot an' proud comin' so often, dough
> A natural freak, I'm itchin to speak becuz
> A dame ast what wuz love. Wut is it? I t'ink
> A heel in a crowd is not too dumb to know –
> It may be all greek, a lot of cheek or fuzz
> To wise guys – it does no good to teach a gink
> Who'll never ever be high's a Georgia pie
> Yet git by fine widout no experiments.
> I don't wanna, gents, nor am I apt a' prove
> Where it wuz born, how it begun to move,
> What its good points are an' how it gits in high
> An' how by an' large it is its own movements
> An' de pleasin' sense of what it feels "to love"
> An' if guys see it clear's a t'ing in a groove.
>
> (*First Half* 34)[29]

Cavalcanti's answer, says Pound, "shows leanings toward . . . the proof by experiment" (*LE*, 149). Zukofsky's answer ("A" – 9, that is), sticking to Cavalcanti's form, drawing on a mathematical formula for a conic section, takes a vocabulary drawn from Karl Marx and from modern physics as well as from Cavalcanti so that, concentrated, one thought may indeed cut through another, Marx through Cavalcanti through physics. In 1936, Zukofsky talked of Chaplin's great intelligence in *Modern Times,* interacting with others' in all its and their physical and sensory constituents (sight, sound, and so forth), to produce new because felt ideas (*Prep.* 60); and in his Foreword to *First Half* he says he intends the poem, figuratively speaking, to fluoresce in the eight of seven hundred years of correlated thought." Fluorescence occurs, says the *OED,* "when a substance is excited to fluoresce" by radiation or impulse, and is of course itself a source of light. Ezra Pound talks of a "radiant world" which we itself a source of light. Ezra Pound talks of a "radiant world" which we have lost, talks of "magnetisms that take form, that are seen, or that border the visible, the matter of Dante's *paradiso*" (*LE* 154). In 1896 Edison, "by coating the interior substance of a Crooke's tube with crystals of a new fluorescing substance," caused X-rays to change to light (*OED* 1933 Supp., "Fluorescing"). Later in his essay Pound remarks of Cavalcanti's poem that it is "quite possible that the whole of it is a sort of metaphor on the generation of light" (*LE* 161). "Light is / Like night is like us," things sing in lines 7 and 8 of *First Half of "A" – 9*. Things *sing*. "Labor, light lights in air, on earth, in earth," sings the ballade refrain at the close of "A" – 8.

The formula for a conic section Zukofsky uses to determine the distribution of *r* and *n* is a second-degree equation derived from Descartian or Analytical Geometry, in which, says Pound, "space is conceived as separated by two or three axes (depending on whether one is treating form in one or more planes)" (*G-B* 91). In his 1921 essay on Brancusi, Pound talked of "form as free in its own life as the form of the analytic geometers,"[30] while seven years earlier, in his essay on "Vorticism," he had written that "the difference between art and analytical geometry is the difference of subject-matter only" (*G-B* 91). Pound is talking about sculpture, but it sounds remarkably like a discussion of formulaic art (the music of Bach was especially attractive to those who would find mathematical procedures for composition during these years) and later in his essay Pound applies his geometrical analogy to writing. It is quite clear that in *First Half of "A" – 9* the three vocabularies, Cavalcanti, Marx, and physics, are to be treated as planes which intersect. As the documents in that publication show, the poem has a base in mathematics, and in "A" – 12 Zukofsky states emphatically that "A poet is not at all surprised by science" (*"A"* 186).

"Everyone who has lived since the sixteenth century," says Henry Adams, "has felt deep distrust of everyone who lived before it" (*MSM* 139). Which is to say, somewhere in the sixteenth century something happened which most clearly separates the thirteenth century (Cavalcanti) from the twentieth (modern physics). That Marx found it necessary to remark that "*value* does not wear an explanatory label" (*Capital* 47) reflects a world that has departed from *felt* ethical forms, that has lost the *singular* feeling, the particularity, of value; it instead finds its surety in empirical observation and verification: the proof by reason and the proof by experiment – value is an abstraction. The shift between Cavalcanti and Marx is more than a shift in language, it is a shift in thought, in the *forms* of thought, a shift, if you like, from the divine to the secular, where ethical authority has moved from Church to legal fiction of State, and has perhaps lost Author. To ask "Wut is it?" in 1290 is not to ask the same question in 1939. For one thing, Bishop Thomas Sprat, who published his *History of the Royal Society* in 1667, stands in between, as does Marx, whose thought Sprat (or what he reports) informs, and Sprat's answer (and Marx's) to the question would be in a language designed to register observation, to convey verification. Sprat's is not a language of affirmation so much as it is a language of counters, approximating mathematics. The members of the Royal Society, he wrote, have

> a constant Resolution, to reject all the amplifications, digressions, and swellings of style: to return back to the primitive purity, and shortness, when men delivered so many *things,* almost in an equal number of *words.* They have exacted from all their members, a close, naked, natural way of speaking; positive expressions; clear senses; a native easiness: bringing all things as near the Mathematical plainness as they can: and preferring the language of Artizans, Countrymen, and Merchants, before that of Wits, or Scholars.[31]

"Were the things words," says line 7 of "A" – 9. And, Zukofsky reminds us in *Bottom,* in Hebrew "the word for *word* is also the word for *thing*" (104). The seventeenth century dreamed of establishing an identity, in men's minds and in the world, between language and things. "Though we cannot comprehend the *Arts* of men without many praevious *studies,*" Sprat wrote, with such an identity in mind,

> yet such is the indulgence of *Nature,* that it has from the beginning, out of its own store, sufficiently provided every man, with all things, that are needful for the understanding of itself. (*History* 344)

The world Sprat proposes is a world subject to analysis, and capable of being understood, accounted for, controlled, in terms and in ways scarcely recognisable to Cavalcanti, to whom for example the word "impulse" might, Pound guesses, rest on "a Neoplatonic gradation of the assumption of faculties as the mind descends into matter through the seven spheres, *via* the gate of Cancer" (*LE* 184). Yet to Clerk Maxwell, the great nineteenth-century physicist, "impulse" is "the product of the average value of any force multiplied by the time during which it acts" (*OED,* "Impulse"). Maxwell's notion of it is a long way indeed from the Latin from which the word derives: a "push against." With the Latin in mind it becomes easy to see how "impulsive behaviour" might be the result of "a force or influence exerted upon the mind by good or evil spirits." Whatever the language of Maxwell does, it does not remind the reader of the mysteriousness (or of the mysteries) of the universe, for Maxwell's world, like that of his near-contemporary Marx, is subject to exegesis and explanation in terms that are verifiable, *measurable.*

"A" – 9 begins:

> An impulse to action sings of a semblance
> Of things related as equated values.

The material from Marx that Zukofsky quotes as one source of the poem's vocabulary is, in part, concerned with the *Value* of a *Product*. Both of these terms occur in Maxwell's definition of *impulse*. "An impulse to *action*." Pound ascribes "impulse" in the second strophe of *Donna mi priegha* to Mars, "spirited"; he does not use the word "action" at all in either of his translations of the poem, though anyone answering or thinking about the question "what is love?" might well begin by calling it "an impulse to action." For "action" is another word from Latin, from the participular stem of *agere: to do*. An action is a doing. Spinoza, the great seventeenth-century philosopher, lens grinder, and opponent to Descartes, whose presence and words march and sing through nearly all of Zukofsky's work (and, notably, through the vocabulary of the *second* half of "A" – 9), Spinoza, writing in Latin his geometric propositions to prove the existence of God, affirms that "*esse* = *agere*," to be is to act or to do; and he discovers, deduces, proves – what-you-will – that God is a verb (a notion argued somewhat forcibly some centuries before by Thomas Aquinas). Action, then, "sb.," is a verb, retains its verbal residue; it is a *doing*, a *process*. Yet on the other hand there is H. Stanley Allen, whose *Electrons and Waves* is another of the sources for Zukofsky's vocabulary in this poem. Allen calls the quantum "an atom of action,"[32] and defines "action" as "the product of energy and time" (a definition quoted in the coda of the poem; the "Restatement" [*First Half* 41] ascribes that definition to "applied mathematics") so that "if we consider the action during one complete period of vibration we find it equal to *h* [i.e., Planck's constant]" (*E&W* 45). Here an action is a *done;* action is a noun, measured. Its verbal residue has vanished, absorbed into *product*. In 1879 action was defined in a physics textbook as "proportional to the average kinetic energy which the system has possessed during the time from any convenient epoch of reckoning, multiplied by the time" (*OED*).

One might conclude that definition – at least, the kind of definition that assumes, as Hugh Kenner has put it,[33] that "the natural operation of the Mind" is "a sequence of assertions" entirely devoid of figuration – arises out of a world of appearance, and can find value *only* in appearance. Thomas Sprat found it a praiseworthy endeavour "to separate the knowledge of *Nature,* from the colours of *Rhetorick,* the devices of *Fancy,* or the delightful deceit of *Fables*" (*History* 62), but he failed as as result to see that he was pinning his faith on *semblance:* "a person's appearance or demeanour, expressive of his thoughts, feelings, etc., or feigned in order to hide them" (*OED*). An impulse to action sings of a semblance. *Semblance:* "a likeness, image, or copy of." Not, then, necessarily the "real" thing. The difficulty of definitions of the sort given by empiricists is that they freeze the world into a closed system of *nouns,* locked as they are into a world of appearance known only to the senses. Known only to the senses, H. Stanley Allen is careful to emphasise, at "an instant of time at a point in space" (*E&W* 59n.): the world of semblance, the world of Newton and of Marx which moves from action into reaction and back again until it reaches equilibrium. (The second law of thermodynamics asserts it will reach inertia, entropy.) "All systems will their own closure," remarks Hugh Kenner (*Counterfeiters,* 167), for all systems seek the sure, the safe, the secure, the explicable: They seek clarity, for they seek to predict. Their aim, then, is to avert crisis, to avoid risk.

So, Marx.

Marx, in the pages from which Zukofsky draws, speaks of *value.* It is "a jelly of undifferentiated human labour" (*Capital* 35). Henry Adams tells us that for some 300 years, from 1000 to 1270, the French spent ten million dollars a year (at the 1840 worth) building cathedrals and churches. In 100 years, from 1170 to 1270, they built 80 cathedrals and nearly 500 churches; such "intensity of conviction" has never been reached, he says, "by any passion . . . except in war" (*MSM* 94–5). Such intensity of conviction, for 300 years, "prostrated France. The efforts of the bourgeoisie and the peasantry to recover their property, so far as it was recoverable, have lasted to the present day" (*MSM* 99). Marx would call that effort, those things, those buildings, "congealed labour time" (*Capital* 8), and such definition, more abstract even than Adams's millions of dollars, becomes a mere *datum,* redolent of neither passion nor trouble, but simply *there.* To Cavalcanti, as to those French, his contemporaries, it would be a statement of No Value. "How much does it cost," William Carlos Williams asks at the beginning of *Paterson* Book 3, "to love the locust tree / in bloom?"[34]

The *Oxford English Dictionary* does not include, among its definitions of "value," one that incorporates "labour" in its terms. It lists neither Marx nor Engels among its sources. Marx, like the dictionary, was engaged in the Promethean task of bringing order to the world; balance, stability, prediction, and above all clarity. A clarity of *sense,* that is, of what is accessible through the senses: The feelings have been left behind, along with all the passions save the social or political, rolled out of the language.

> Value: *sb.* . . . That amount of some commodity . . . which is considered to be an equivalent for something else; . . . The material or monetary worth of a thing. . . . The relative status of a thing (*OED*).

Henry Adams reports that in Cavalcanti's time "a good miracle was in its day worth much money – so much that the rival shrines stole each other's miracles without decency" (*MSM* 280). The shrine, Adams says, "turned itself into a market" (106): an impulse to action? a piece of the action.

Value? In mathematics, "the precise number or amount represented by a figure, quantity, etc."; in music, "the relative length or duration of a tone signified by a note." A *measure,* then, for counting, for counting time perhaps – or, in physics, temperature, or the strength of an impulse. H. Stanley Allen, discussing the emission of electrons from hot wires, talks of "the value of the saturation current from a metal [which] increases very rapidly as the temperature of the filament is raised" (*E&W* 32). Henry Adams, in a passage I have already quoted, talks about the primacy of colour in twelfth-century stained-glass windows. The French, he says, never "cared whether a green camel or a pink lion looked like a dog or a donkey provided they got their harmony or value" (*MSM* 138). The dictionary puts it somewhat differently:

> Painting: Due or proper effect or importance; relative tone of colour in each different section of a picture; a patch characterised by a particular tone (*OED*).

And for Henry Adams, dear to Zukofsky? Value = harmony.[35] "Things related as equated values," says line 2 of the poem. Harmony is to be felt; definition, to be perceived. The poem, through the interplay of actions, of semblances, of values, generates feelings.

One might well ask, then, what Marx is doing in this poem? Why does he fill so many (twenty-two) pages of this text? Yet one should not have to ask, any more than need to ask about the Cavalcanti. The question that needs to be asked is how so many readers can see *First Half of "A" – 9* as a Marxist poem. Jacques Roubaud, for example, says that it is "Marx in verse."[36] Which it is. But it is also physics in verse, and whatever else the dictionary might bear. (One effect of the formulaic *r* and *n* is to make abstract the language of the poem.) Roubaud says that the Marx in verse of the *First Half,* which talks of "value," is answered by the second half, which talks of "love." (It is just as accurate to say that the second half poses the vocabulary of Spinoza against that of Marx – the vocabulary of the Spinoza who tried to prove the existence of God, a task by the way which, Henry Adams tells us, both Saint Bernard and Blaise Pascal thought impossible [*MSM* 129].) Eric Mottram, in a kind of street-corner or soap-box rhetoric, dismisses *First Half of "A" – 9* as "strained versifying" which "operates as as trite statement of art taking its place as labour in 1938–40," as a "virtuoso rhetoric which, although it refuses the cruder excesses of 'proletarian poetry,' verges on . . . extravagant games."[37] That the poem is, in other words, a *failed* Marxist work. But writing about *"A" 1–12* in 1957 to William Carlos Williams, who was then contemplating his preface to the whole work, Zukofsky cautioned that "those who do not read the poem carefully may call me 'Communist'" (Booth 248).

The vocabulary drawn from Marx misleads the unwary reader, for readers (and indeed some writers!) of poetry in this century have been in the habit of supposing that a poem addresses itself to one frame of reference only, and that if there is any ambiguity in a poem, then that ambiguity serves to intensify and render more complicated a "central theme" of the poem, or to reveal a covert theme or "point" of the poem which must then be reconciled to the overt statement/s the poem makes. Talking of the "resolution" of tensions and ambiguities in the poem, such readers have often identified that resolution with what they also call the poem's (and the poet's!) "integrity." It is easy to assume that the finished composition, the poem, when we finish reading the last line, is "composed" (i.e., at rest), and that such composure is a means of putting the poem to bed, like a dictionary definition set in printer's type. The anticipation of "coherence" that many readers thus bring to their reading is a result in part, in Henry Adams's words, of "taking for granted that there is an object to be reached at the end of [humanity's] journey" (*MSM* 344); in part from the assumption, fostered by the schools, that "the mind of man is not satisfied with a conception of the physical universe which requires a number of different elements for its formulation" (the words are H. Stanley Allen's, *E&W* 47); and in part from the notion that, since language is used to "formulate" a conception of the universe, then the language of the poem is a *vehicle* for the content of the poem, such content being, of course, the poet's "beliefs" or "ideas," which can be verified. Such language, used to transport content rather than readers, is the language of Bishop Sprat, where words are linked directly to things. People speak, and people write, to record their observations and to communicate them, in a cautious, rational language.

Yet any poet, surely, and certainly Zukofsky, knows that such a view of language is absurd, and what coherence the poem might have is to be found elsewhere than in the poem's "themes" and "statements." For when words *are* things-in-themselves, immediate to the senses, then they have no more "content" than has a chair, or a vacuum tube. In 1936, Zukofsky emphasized that it's nobody's business what Charlie Chaplin himself thinks or believes (*Prep.* 57): It's not the content of the scene in *Modern Times* that is so important, but the "relation . . . that has the amplitude of insight impelled by the physical, to be found in actual events themselves" (*Prep.* 61). I take the matter of "relation" here to be a matter of "form," and it is irrelevant whether Zukofsky is here a Marxist or a Buddhist. It does not matter at all. "The truth of a poem," Robert Duncan has written, is "the truth of what was felt in the course of the poem, not the truth of a proposition in whatever political or religious persuasion outside the poem."[38] The Marxism, like Cavalcanti, like the physics, is the pretext of the poem: the pre-text. The poem itself, the text, is not concerned with the content, which came before: "Thinking's the lowest rung," says the close of "A" – 12, "No one'll believe I feel this" (*"A"* 260). The text is a movement of languages, of *a number of* frames of reference, held in the language of the poem simultaneously, *at once.* And it is a *felt* world, which is not, therefore, to be interpreted; one's feelings are not subject to exegesis. As Robert Creeley has remarked, *First Half of "A" – 9* is "the *experience* of valuation" (*AQG* 141). Zukofsky does not weigh Allen or Marx against Spinoza or Cavalcanti, and find them wanting: *Things,* in the poem, do the weighing. Henry Adams, describing mediaeval art, says that

> anyone willing to try it could feel it like the child, reading new thought without end into the art he has studied a hundred times; but what is still more convincing, he could, at will, in an instant, shatter the whole art by calling into it a single motive of his own (*MSM* 178).

The poem is an attempt to voice, call it "the world out there," by following Marx's notion: "If commodities could speak, they would say: 'Our use-value may interest human beings; but it is not an attribute of ours, as things. What is our attribute, as things, is our value. Our own interrelations as commodities proves it' " (*Capital* 58). "A" – 12 expresses it "Actions things; themselves; doing" (*"A"* 156).

And like Henry Adams's cathedral, "if any stone in any part, from apex to foundation, weathers or gives way, the whole must yield" (*MSM* 109–10). Isolate out from the text one element, one thread, one vocabulary only, treat the poem as "Marx in verse" say, and it does indeed as Eric Mottram says look like an extravagant game. One sees one stone very thoroughly indeed, and the verbal cathedral has vanished from the mind, from the ear, and from the eye. For the language of "A" – 9 is remarkably abstract, derived as each word is from three separate contexts at once, working – as Zukofsky is – with at least three things at once. Given the intentions Bunting reported for the poem, it is not surprising that at times we feel, reading *First Half of "A" – 9,* that just as there may have been "an intuition of the poem without any words in it, a silent structural eloquence" (which I take to be also, then, a tune struggling for words), so too there is abstraction struggling for particularity. The particularity is found in the *collage* of contexts that accretes to the words "value" and "impulse" and "action" and so forth, and the tune, shaped as it is from Cavalcanti's form, reinforced as it is by the formulaic *r* and *n,* itself arises from impulse – melody, forced by writing. The tune, in its complex musicality, makes of those contexts, those vocabularies, disparate as they seem to be, a family. Value = harmony. The tune, the text, the poem, become a family of words, all singing together. A family. It is worth recalling that from the second half of "A" – 9 on, from that part of "A" – 9 written ten years later, drawing on Spinoza and posing "love" against "value," the attention of *"A"* as a whole will shift away from Marx and to the family: Louis, Celia, Paul. Henry Adams, describing his beloved Chartres Cathedral, continually stresses – with some wonder – that it is a church of the Holy *Family,* of Mother and Son. A human place, where the best human value erected great stained-glass windows, the finest, he says, that the world has ever seen. Seen in different lights, seen as the light changes through the day and through the seasons, such stained glass itself changes, the values of the colours change. The light itself becomes the source and centre of attention, light becomes something *seen,* a thing itself, rather than instrument. So too with this poem, its words: "the *experience* of value" as the poem "fluoresces" in "the light of seven centuries of interrelated thought."

Exegesis should not be necessary.

# 5

# "Actual Word Stuff, Not Thoughts for Thoughts"

## Williams and Zukofsky[1]

Before considering what Williams and Zukofsky might have learned from each other I want to point briefly at the nature of their literary–biographical relationship, and to indicate the sheer extent (much of it hidden) of their joint literary venture. I can do this best by pointing to a collaborative poem, "Tree – See" in *I's (pronounced eyes),*[2] not the product of a collaboration between Williams and Zukofsky, but between Lorine Niedecker and Zukofsky. The poem opens "I see / by / your tree." In a note scribbled on a letter Zukofsky sent to Niedecker on 16 October 1959 about some poems she had sent him, Niedecker comments that "I answered, repeating his 'I see by your tree you draw' to show him the singularity of it, and asked 'What do you see?' " On 29 October, the day he completed the poem, Zukofsky wrote back to Niedecker saying she had given him the second (and final) stanza, "What / do you / see?"; the second stanza, he told her, is *yours,* but now, like Shakespeare's Plutarch, in the common domain.[3] "A" – 12 incorporates bits of their correspondence, and in a 1951 fragment (TxU) he chortles over the thought of scholars and pedants spending years trying to sort out who wrote what, which of them filched the other's work first, and failing wretchedly.[4] A surprising amount of Zukofsky's work consists of quotation,[5] and his relationship with Williams, almost inextricably entwined, must rank among the most fruitful of literary relationships in this century.

We do, of course, know something of it. There are the more-or-less obvious and well-known things: their essays on each other;[6] Zukofsky's poems on Williams;[7] their shared work on The Objectivist Press; Williams's dedication of *The Wedge* to Zukofsky, and Zukofsky's extensive hand in editing the contents and putting it together;[8] Williams's note on Zukofsky in the first edition of *"A" 1–12;*[9] their continuous exchange of ideas, manuscripts, and books, which only came to an end with Williams's death in 1963.[10] There is also the record, perhaps less familiar to us, of Williams finding jobs for Zukofsky – even small ones, like using Zukofsky as a literary agent around 1930 or so[11] – and giving him books (and decent meals!); and there is Zukofsky carrying *Spring and All* around with him. Zukofsky sent Williams, piecemeal, the drafts of "A" – 8 as he wrote it; he sent the typescripts of *A Test of Poetry;* and he discussed them with him. He told Williams on 26 February 1937 how helpful Williams's comments were in clarifying his intentions for the poem. When Zukofsky completed "Mantis" on 27 October 1934, he showed it to Williams, and over the next eight days wrote "Mantis: An Interpretation," a poem which, he told Williams seven years later, would never have been written but for Williams's intervention.[12]

The traffic was not all one way, however. The young poet whom Ezra Pound introduced to Williams early in 1928 was soon offering his putative mentor invaluable advice, editing, and help. By 1929 Zukofsky was putting together a *Collected Poems of William Carlos Williams,* and at the same time the two of them were collaborating on Williams's essay "The Work of Gertrude Stein," just as eighteen months or so later, in February, 1931, Zukofsky would cut, amend, rewrite, and offer suggestions for Williams's critical sketch of Ezra Pound, excerpts of which were then in the hands of *The Symposium* and later reprinted in Williams's *Selected Essays.*[13] So, too, Zukofsky worked closely with Williams on the many drafts of *The First President,* including writing a synopsis of Act 3 for Tibor Serly's use, as well as some of the text.[14] Similarly, they discussed critical theory, poetics, and science together. It may well be that Williams's interest in Einstein was fuelled in part by a Zukofsky whose translation of Anton Reiser's biography of Einstein was published in 1930, just as it may be that the use of Apollinaire in *Paterson* owes something to a Zukofsky who in 1932 wrote a book on Guillaume Apollinaire for Rene Taupin.[15]

When Williams sent Zukofsky a carbon typescript of his "Note on Poetry" (which appeared in the *Oxford Anthology of American Literature,* 1938), he inscribed it to "Louis Zukofsky, with whom much of this has been developed" (WCW to LZ 13 March 1937; TxU). And Zukofsky reworked many of Williams's manuscripts – how many we shall probably never know, but including "Primavera" (1930), "Old Doc Rivers" (1930), "The Colored Girls of Passenack – Old and New" (1932), "St. Francis Einstein of the Daffodils" (written 1921, revised 1934), "Mounted as an Amazon" (1957 as "Swivel Hipped Amazon"), and the still unpublished "A Democratic Party Poem" (1930–1). One can guess at others[16] – like, for example, "Perpetuum Mobile: The City" and even "Choral: The Pink Church" (which Celia Zukofsky set to music). The story of their relationship will remain fragmentary, of course, until we get a careful edition of their correspondence, including a careful scrutiny of the surviving manuscripts of both writers. It will probably always be fragmentary. What needs an accounting, perhaps, is *why* they should have been so close, these two: Williams, the expansive, whose motto might be "write carelessly so that nothing that is not green will survive" (*Pat* 129); and Zukofsky, the inclusive, astringent, careful writer who could literally spend months worrying at a single phrase.[17]

What are the qualities in Zukofsky's work and life that would draw Williams to him, and perhaps point to what Zukofsky found in Williams? Let me list them, and then discuss them. They are interrelated, and I hope I can show how they come together. My list is by no means exhaustive:

1. line breaks and lines;
2. English is a second language for each of them, and hence
3. Zukofsky's language, like Williams's and unlike say Eliot's, avoids symbolism, moves towards opacity; hence it is full of what I can only call the essential duplicity of words;
4. they both prefer Spinoza to Descartes, Apollinaire to Valéry, and hence write predominantly paratactic verse.

I

I can best get at line breaks and lines by looking at the familiar and the obvious: Williams's "The Red Wheelbarrow."[18] I choose this because Williams wrote it six years before he met Zukofsky, when Zukofsky was fifteen or sixteen years old.

so much depends
upon

a red wheel
barrow

glazed with rain
water

beside the white
chickens

I choose this poem because it is in *Spring and All,* which Zukofsky first read in 1928, after Williams gave him a copy. Zukofsky called it "my favorite of all your books," and carried it about with him in his pocket.[19] The whole dynamic of this poem rests on the line breaks, which on the one hand establish the form by playing into the syllable count, and on the other move the meaning around in play: The reader is continually kept off balance waiting for completion, for a coming to rest, which is continually promised and then withheld, always suspended. There is not even a period at the end of the poem. Insofar as the line breaks make for play of meaning, they make for play of *mind*.

The poem is put together as a series of pairs, the movement of each echoing or invoking the movement of the first. There is a curious little suspension at the end of the first line – that word "depends," with its kinship with other words which *pend,* hang, leaves us waiting, up in the air, until it comes down to rest, giving us relief, a nice little satisfaction, in the single word of the second line: "upon." But the semantics and syntax of that second line do not let us rest, for the small completion brought by that word "upon" also insists on a continuation: "So much depends upon *what?*" And the second pair of lines begins to tell us, and opens the lyric catalogue with "a red wheel," which *syntactically* completes the utterance. But "wheel" leads to the fourth line's "barrow" and we see that the completeness was only apparent. From this little surprise, where in one word the act of continuation plays against the sense of completion, the poem modulates down through the repetitions of the third and fourth pairs to a sense, not exactly of completeness, but of satisfaction brought about by the emphatically adjectival "white." The poem proceeds through a whole series of apparent stops and starts, working by the syllable, throwing you off balance while at the same time precisely formed by its steady syllabic count: 4 2; 3 2; 3 2; 4 2. It is quite like Apollinaire.

This sort of movement, where the line breaks into a single word, a movement that enacts Gertrude Stein's *period,* where stopping "has something to do with going on,"[20] occurs at all stages of Williams's career. In "Landscape with the Fall of Icarus" (1960; *CP2* 386) it doubles back on itself, re-verses, as the poem revolves around the word "near":

> the whole pageantry
>
> of the year was
> awake tingling
> near
>
> the edge of the sea
> concerned
> with itself

This device, where the end word of a line (in this case "near") ends one statement but unpunctuated also starts the next, acting as the pivot on which the next line turns, is utterly characteristic of Williams's poems. It is a grammatical / syntactic play known to students of classical Greek as *apo koinou*[21] – and in Williams's hands it is, as syntactic play, as play of meaning, the play of the mind, a form of *logopoeia*.

Zukofsky does the same thing, and often condenses it. It is a frequent device in his poetry, especially in *"A"*; an especially clear example is his poem "And Without" (*CSP* 131; MS at TxU), written on All Fool's Day, 1950. It is an extremely difficult poem, and I am not sure I understand it at all. Two stanzas long, the poem is strongly like a musical canon, the second stanza identical to the first but for the omission of two words (*here, lonely*) and the move of the opening line (*And without*) to the end, so that the poem closes "A spring. And without" instead of simply "The spring." The line breaks, assisted by the lack of internal punctuation in the poem's three sentences, are the principal sources of the poem's difficulty: Ambiguating the meaning, they permit many feelings to flood in at once.

Such close repetition of the first stanza in the second, combined with the line breaks, is a technique remarkably close to that in such poems as the first of Williams's "Calypsos," playing variations on "Well God is love so love me" (*CP2* 426).[22] It is a technique that derives, perhaps, from something like Williams's "To a Poor Old Woman" (1934; *CP1* 383):

> They taste good to her
> They taste good
> to her. They taste
> good to her

(where, one might note, the line break in the first and last lines serves as a period). But there is a key difference between the two poets: I cannot find a paraphraseable content in the Zukofsky – yet it is a fine poem. "And without," the poem begins:

> And without
> Spring it is spring why
> Is it death here grass somewhere

Does it say "Outside it is spring; why?"; "Lacking spring, it is nevertheless spring; why?"; "Outside the season of spring it is still the season of spring; why?" That "why" is *apo koinou,* for the question continues. Do we understand the question to ask "Why is it spring?" or "Why is spring death?" or "why is death *here?*" And that *here,* midline, is *apo koinou* also.[23] I might note that the second stanza is much clearer, for the first line is an affirmation: "Spring, it is spring."

This technique, whether in Williams's or in Zukofsky's hands, demands concentration – both in the sense of intense thinking or mental alertness and in the sense of density: Both poets write distilled poems of great intellectual concentration, and they force the reader into alertness by continually throwing one off balance. I think Zukofsky learned this technique from Williams, and uses it for a somewhat different end: The line break in Williams serves to intensify what the poem says – he is playing around with meaning; but Zukofsky plays around with meaning *for the sake of the sound.* "And Without" is the sort of poem that Zukofsky on another occasion called a "Song of Degrees" (*CSP* 145) – its movement is essentially musical, and as we attempt to voice the poem we discover how meaning determines tones and tones determine quantity. So it's a little tune.

Another technique closely related to this has to do rather with lines than with line breaks; it is easy to see in Williams's "Portrait of a Lady" (as it appeared in *The Dial* 69 [August 1920]: 162), and in the opening of Zukofsky's "A" – 13 (*"A"* 262; 1960). Here is the Williams:

Portrait of a Lady

Your thighs are appletrees
whose blossoms touch the sky.
Which sky? The sky
where Watteau hung a lady's
slipper. Your knees
are a southern breeze – or
a gust of snow. Agh! what
sort of man was Fragonard?
– as if that answered
anything. Ah, yes – below
the knees, since the tune
drops that way, it is
one of those white summer days,
the tall grass of your ankles
flickers upon the shore –
Which shore? –
the sand clings to my lips –
Which shore?
Agh, petals maybe. How
should I know?
Which shore? Which shore?
– the petals from some hidden
apple tree. Which shore?
I said petals from an apple tree.

This is a poem written in lines, rather than in line breaks; its comedy depends almost entirely upon the way each line undercuts, mocks, renders ridiculous the posturing of its predecessor, the whole in an impatience of utterance that, urgent, continually throws the reader as well as the poem off balance, and we observe again how concentrated, how condensed, the poem is – for each line does the work a whole stanza might be asked to do by another poet – and how much of it is movement of the mind. One observes, too, an abhorrence of the decorative as well as of the conclusive. The language perpetually challenged as soon as uttered, lest it freeze into a settled complacency of the definite, the poem ends up where it began: "apple trees," the flat words pointing to the ridiculousness of the literary posture, parodying it and avoiding the sentimental: the play of the intelligence through the words, to get at / release the feeling. The shape of the poem is determined by the drive of the intention – this is a self-mocking yet erotic poem – and by the refusal of the voice to settle into something as clear as explanation, as definition.

Zukofsky, too, can write in lines, each of which offers a statement, each of which is a coherent and identifiable syntactic unit, where the line breaks herald another statement, another phrase, which often in its sheer unpredictability and disconnectedness undercuts the last, throws the balance. But there is a difference, for while both write poems that resist conclusiveness, Williams's poems nevertheless have a current of intent, of meaning – a direction, if you will – to carry us along: The relationship between one line and the next, between one thought and the next, is accessible to us even if not immediately apparent. In his more discontinuous poems, like say "Perpetuum Mobile: The City" (*CP1* 430) or "The Rose" (in *Spring and All, CP1* 195), the title, or the opening line, usually declares a subject, a theme, which the poem will explore: "the rose is obsolete." With Zukofsky, more often than not the connection between one line and the next is obscure. The difference is rather like that between say Impressionism and Cubism – or rather, between Stuart Davis's drawing at the beginning of *Kora in Hell* and the collage Zukofsky describes in "A" – 12 (*"A"* 239–40). Davis's landscape is recognizable, and recognizably coherent, identifiably a picture of *something,* though there are blurs and distortions, disruptions of perspective, so that virtually the whole picture is foreground. Zukofsky's collage is made up of recognizable objects: an engraving of Duncan Phyfe's house, workshop, and store; a postcard of a painting by Chardin; and a scrap of doodling. But the objects are in no immediately recognizable or coherent order: colour, contrast, and opaqueness predominate. The whole is an arrangement.

"A" – 13 is a partita, a suite of five variations. I cannot explicate the opening lines of Part 1 (I wish I could) for they are (characteristically) virtually immune to such activity:

> What do you want to know
> What do you want to do,
> In a trice me the gist us;

Don't believe things turn untrue
A sea becomes teacher;
When the son takes his wife

There's an astonishing interplay here between the sense we derive from each line, the sense we derive from each stanza, and the sense we derive from each sentence. This strikes me as writing by procedure rather than writing according to plan, and we end up with a complex interweaving of puns, advice, self-deprecation, self-satisfaction, mockery, and affection. And it is *speech:* presumably Louis, aged fifty-six, to Paul, aged sixteen[24] – for Celia is mentioned in the pun at line five – and Louis is the father, almost elegiacally reminiscing over his own son, over himself as son (thus echoing "A" – 12), and giving, in a series of aphoristic, almost gnomic, lines, platitudinous and sometimes baffling advice. Yet claiming to wisdom: "in a trice me, the gist us": the individual in the family, the family in the individual – and wise, like Hermes Trismegistus. And sounding like Polonius, pompous and foolish, or like the stereotypical Jewish father of cliché. "When the son takes his wife," ended the second stanza:

Follows his genius,
Found in search
Come out of mysteries.

The husband who fights –
Doctors don't heal;
Watch out

The tone of knowingness – knowing the rules to get along in the world – and of male self-centredness, is reinforced by the line breaks, indeed depends upon them:

Marriage is fast, wit
Less than fate
Look to love.

She'll have a son
And he honor, her heart desires
You let

She'll have a son (this is stanza six); and he, being her son, will have honour, which is what her heart desires. Or is it that he, the husband and father, will be *on her,* which is what her heart desires? The tone, and the line break, permit the slightly crude pun, and we begin to suspect that "A" – 13 is perhaps a tone poem. That pun is condescending to women, for this is man-to-man talk, derogatory of the female. Or is it?

For "you let" runs into the next stanza, and there's another reading, *at the same time.* "You let"

> Her correct you,
> No one will hurt if
> You can't count zeros.

In fairly complex *apo koinou,* "she'll have a son, and he will have honour; his heart desires that she correct you" – that *she* be the teacher (schoolteacher). There is affection there. And then? "No one will hurt if / You can't count zeros" means what? That school doesn't matter? that grades don't count? In math, a zero doesn't count anyway. It was not Polonius but another father in Shakespeare who told his offspring that "nothing will come of nothing."[25]

The point I'd like to make here runs like this: that until stanza seven we've been habituated to *apo koinou* operating through the line breaks, for it is precisely through those breaks that the poem acquires its density, its puns, its air of many-things-at-once, simultaneity. But the final two lines of stanza seven can only be run on: The break is of a different sort. And we are thrown off balance. It is as though, over the space of eighteen lines, Zukofsky has taught us how to read, and then as soon as we've learned, he changes the rules. The whole of "A" – 13 works like that: As soon as we settle down, we are thrown off balance, and the text becomes well-nigh impenetrable until we learn the new rules, and then it shifts again. No wonder he called it a partita: It's a suite, or set of variations, which keeps changing gear. And we cannot see how one line – or one section – leads to or arises from another, as in line four to line five in stanza two, or the last two lines of stanza three. And the point that arises from this reflection is twofold. First, that for Zukofsky the poem must have *no point:* A poem isn't trying to "prove" anything; and hence, second, the poem is deliberately baffling: Zukofsky withholds the poem from the reader, leaves it opaque, in order that its opacity may engage us.

## II

The third line of "A" – 13 reads: "In a trice me, the gist us." The dictionary tells us that "in a trice" means "in a single quick motion." Movement, then. And this phrase occurs in the third line of a poem written almost entirely in *threes,* tercets (there are 124 tercets and 2 pairs in its 376 lines); occurs in the third line of a poem which is about three: Louis, Celia, and Paul, the family of three. The pun is inescapable, and the language bears it without trouble; yet there is no legitimacy to it so far as the dictionary is concerned. There is, then, no etymological or historical ground for the pun. It is the kind of pun we might expect of a speaker or writer who did not grow up in an English tradition, with English as his native tongue. It is the kind of pun made possible, not by etymological knowledge, but by an orthographic sense of the kinship of words; we might say it is the kind of pun that relies on the *suppression* of history, of historical knowledge, of etymology, and that relies on the immediacy of the language. It is very much to the point that, like Gertrude Stein, *both Williams and Zukofsky learned English as their second language,* and so are free to use English without the clutter of its history.[26]

Let me add to this one other circumstance. Both Zukofsky and Williams want poetry that is allied to speech, "that which is heard from the lips of those to whom we are talking in our day's affairs" (*KIH* 59). "A" – 13 is speech, but it is speech recorded. In the canonical situation of utterance, face-to-face, the circumstances giving rise to speech, the immediate and simultaneous causes of the utterance, are indissolubly wedded to the words as they are being uttered – and they cannot be replicated once that moment is past. In the special situation of utterance, page-to-face, the precise circumstances of those words, of that utterance, are lost, the cause becomes irrelevant, and we are left with written words, words bereft of their immediate history, bereft of their occasion. So we find, in both Williams and Zukofsky, that one possible source of confusion in reading their work is our inability to sort out the parts of speech in a given utterance. They both, assuredly, play around with the parts of speech in their verse, so that (unsettlingly) what we thought was a noun is suddenly seen to be an adjective (as in "lavender" in the second line of "Nantucket," *CP1* 372) or a verb (as in the first word of the same poem):

> Flowers through the window
> lavender and yellow

Neither Williams or Zukofsky play around with or rely on the connotations of words, so that there is a difference indeed between Eliot's "multifoliate rose" in "The Hollow Men" and Williams's "rose." Eliot, however, is close to the English tradition, playing for the connotations, moving towards the symbolic. Williams and Zukofsky are (like Gertrude Stein) struggling to establish the American. As he told Cid Corman on 27 December 1959, Zukofsky saw himself as very much of this age, his elders ending off something European.[27] The density of Williams's and Zukofsky's language arises from the immediate context in which the words appear, not from their evocation of a tradition; it takes part in what Williams, in his critical sketch of Ezra Pound, called "the principal move in imaginative writing today – that away from the word as symbol and toward the word as reality" (*SE* 107). Zukofsky's progress through

*"A"*, indeed, seems to be toward rendering more and more narrow the immediacy of context, until in "A" – 22 it is almost simply words one-at-a-time, on the page.

Almost from the very beginning (*Poems* 1909) Williams wanted a flat factual matter-of-fact language, and hated symbolism; his words on it, in the Prologue to *Kora in Hell* and in *Spring and All,* are too well known to need quoting here. Zukofsky, however, seems not to have been so sure. There is a curious little exchange with Lincoln Kirstein and *The Hound and Horn* in 1930 about the word "newspapers" in Zukofsky's poem "Aubade (1925)" (*CSP* 30–1). Kirstein suggested Zukofsky drop the word because "at the time you wrote it, newspapers were a perfectly simple and evident symbol, but I think that they have become a kind of dusty irony" (Kirstein to Zukofsky, 17 July 1930; CtY). Zukofsky agreed, but when the poem was in proof stage, changed his mind, changing *papers* back again to newspapers on the simple grounds, as he told Allan Stroock, 12 December 1930, that no symbolism was intended, they just happen to be newspapers (CtY).[28] Like Williams, and perhaps encouraged by him, Zukofsky was suspicious of symbolism because it is a language of disguise where, talking about one thing, you are "really" talking about something else – and avoiding the thing, the object. So, just as Williams insists, one way or another throughout his life, that

> The province of the poem is the world.
> When the sun rises, it rises in the poem
> and when it sets darkness comes down
> and the poem is dark
>
> (*Pat* 99)

so too Zukofsky insists that his language is transparent. In 1959 he assured Cid Corman that he was nothing if not direct, echoing what he'd said to Niedecker in 1941, that if you read carefully the clarity of the poem is inescapable. The clarity of the writing is always paramount in Zukofsky's mind – which is why, perhaps, he instructed Niedecker always to think of the obvious meaning of the words. But then, he added, not always: It's a *general* rule.[29] Zukofsky recognised that his poetry is not always clear, of course, especially not if we expect the poem to be *saying* something.

It is instead dense, even opaque. It is language visible. Words are, in this poetry, deprived of their history and their spoken context; they are dense, visible. One reason for this is that Zukofsky often withholds from the poem its pretext or occasion, though the title sometimes affords a clue. Another is that, pushing for multiplicity of meaning, our attention is focussed on the word itself, and its possible locutions within the written context in which it appears before us. Another reason is Zukofsky's resistance, which he shares with Williams, to *explanation* as a mode of writing, and this is why he continually throws the reader off balance. Blockage of some sort is imperative to the dynamic of Zukofsky's poetry, essential to it, to ensure that the poem – and the reader! – will not move into the settledness of the expository, the descriptive, the certain, into what Williams called "copy" (*CP2* 274), the realm where "minds [are] like beds, always made up" (*Pat* 109). Thus, too, in "A" – 18 Zukofsky (quoting Samuel Johnson) tells us "I set limits / to my work which would in time be ended / tho not completed" (*"A"* 396). Which is to say, the poem is *man thinking,* not a man's *thoughts.* Or, as Zukofsky put it in 1930–1, "Writing occurs which is the detail, not mirage, of seeing, of thinking with things as they exist" (*Prep* 12). Verb.

Such a remark aligns Zukofsky with a Spinozan rather than a Cartesian view of things, with Apollinaire rather than Valéry: thinking (activity) is preferable to thought (statis – or, as George Bowering puts it, Saint As Is).[30] Both Williams and Zukofsky demonstrate this over and over again. Zukofsky told Lorine Niedecker that you exist first and then think, not the other way round, that thinking is no proof of existing, but existing includes it (fragment, 1950; TxU); in a 1941 lecture to the YMHA he defined the poem as the action of writing words to be set to music.[31] Williams, in both "To Daphne and Virginia" and "The Mind's Games" sees the mind as villainous insofar as it insists on abstracting and conceptualising and being dogmatic, making itself up like a bed. "The mind is the cause of our distresses," says Williams (*CP2* 247) – but it is so because we do not know how to use it. So too Zukofsky in a notable passage in "A" – 8 (*"A"* 94) calls Paul Valéry a "mule" and then quotes from his essay "The Future of Literature: Will It Be a Sport?"[32] In that essay Valéry talks of language as a "creator of illusions," and of poetry as a hobby. Valéry counts, as one of his masters, Spinoza's adversary Descartes;[33] which is to say, *thought,* not thinking. In "A" – 12 Zukofsky says "Thinking's the lowest rung" (*"A"* 260); he once wrote an essay, now lost, called "The Superstition of Intelligence." Intelligence, in Cartesian–Valérian terms, comes to conclusions, proposes a finality, moves towards closure, something we can think of as "knowing." In *Paterson* Williams draws much from Apollinaire, and quotes him in translation,[34] while in the early 1930s Zukofsky wrote, for René Taupin who translated it into French, an extended essay on Apollinaire. Such was the revelation that Apollinaire afforded that the publication of *The Writing of Guillaume Apollinaire,* Zukofsky exuberantly told Carl Rakosi on 7 December 1932, should push Valéry and the rest into the back seat.[35]

Zukofsky's poetry is peculiarly without anxiety precisely because on one hand it does not deny the activity of the mind, and on the other because "thinking's the lowest rung"; which is to say that the poetry does not seek to persuade the reader to adopt a particular set of ideas or conclusions, so neither Zukofsky nor the reader has a vested interest in what the poem *says,* in getting the "message" *right.* The attention is on what the poem *does;* the mind acts on particulars, the particulars of language, of the poem, because *then* it is *man thinking.* A piece of writing as dense as "A-Bomb and H-" in *Bottom: On Shakespeare* is as dense as it is, is as active as it is, precisely *because* it is a direct descendant of *Kora in Hell,* where Williams discovered how to set thought free, into thinking.[36] It is little wonder that Williams, when Zukofsky sent him "Poem Beginning 'The'," should say in enthusiasm that this is "actual word stuff, not thought for thoughts" (*SL* 94). On another occasion Zukofsky asks for thought that is without "predatory intent" and is thus self-sufficient (*Prep* 16).

The corollaries are as follows: First, that Williams and Zukofsky both write paratactic verse – in their syntax there is no subordination; there is rather a stringing out of beads on a string, as Aristotle complained, where everything is of equal importance.[37] And hence, paradoxically, the thought does not move in a line, but holds bits in suspension as it were until, all at once, they make a field. Williams called it, in 1948, a field of action (*SE* 280–95). Second, that the poem is an object. What is interesting here is the language in which Williams greeted "Poem Beginning 'The'" in his 1928 letter to Zukofsky: "It escapes me in its analysis (thank God) and strikes against me a thing (thank God). There are not so many things in the world as we commonly imagine. Plenty of debris, plenty of smudges" (*SL* 94). A thing. In her 1909 essay on Picasso, Gertrude Stein distinguished between things, things seen, and things known,[38] a distinction that reminds us of the ineluctable and intransigent quality of things: unknown, probably unknowable. The poem as a thing is resistant, and must baffle us, leave us shall we say at a loss? Hardly, but it cannot at any rate be "accounted for." Which is exactly why Williams liked Zukofsky: "it escapes me in its analysis" – and rightly he added the words "thank God." A sigh of relief. Elsewhere, and earlier (1918), in the Prologue to *Kora in Hell,* Williams remarked that "it is chuckleheaded to desire a way through every difficulty" (*KIH* 17). The named world is, at some point, the known world, and hence tucked away, safe, and dead. In 1913 Williams told Harriet Monroe that "life is above all things else at any moment subversive of life as it was the moment before – always new, irregular" (*SL* 23–4). In her lecture on "Poetry and Grammar" Gertrude Stein voiced her dislike of nouns, names.[39]

I close with a quotation, from an essay written jointly by Williams and Zukofsky, on "The Work of Gertrude Stein":

Movement . . . must always be considered aimless, without progress. This is the essence of all knowledge. . . . The whole of writing . . . is an alertness not to let go of a possibility of movement in our fearful bedazzlement with some concrete and fixed present. The goal is to keep a beleaguered line of *understanding which has movement* from breaking down and becoming a hole into which we sink decoratively to rest.

(*SE* 117–18. Emphasis added.)

# 6

# "Only Is Order Othered. Nought Is Nulled"

## Finnegans Wake *and Middle and Late Zukofsky*

> *"Well, be it so," said Belle; "for this evening you shall command." "To command is* hramahyel,*" said I. "Ram her ill, indeed," said Belle; "I do not wish to begin with that." "No," said I; ". . .* hramahyel *is a verb of the second conjugation."*
>
> George Borrow, *The Romany Rye*[1]

From 1932 to 1935, with his friend Jerry Reisman, Louis Zukofsky completed an as-yet-unpublished film script of Joyce's *Ulysses* using Max Ernst inserts for their emotive value, evoking as they do through their surreal and occasionally nightmare qualities, imaginary states of feeling. Joyce seems to have liked it, suggesting that George Arliss play Bloom and John Ford direct it.[2] Zukofsky had already completed the first seven movements of *"A"* by 1930, and he would not start work on the eighth movement until the film script was complete, finishing it in 1937. *Ulysses* left its traces on that movement. That five-year interval was echoed by two other fairly large gaps in *"A"*'s composition; the first, from 1940 to 1948 (between the composition of "A" – 10 and of the second half of "A" – 9), and the second, from 1951 (the completion of "A" – 12) to 1960 ("A" – 13). During that last interval, Zukofsky worked on two thoroughly Wakean texts: *Bottom: On Shakespeare,* which took thirteen years to complete (from 1947 to 1960), and (with the collaboration of Celia Zukofsky) a translation and transliteration of the whole of Catullus, which they started in 1958 and completed eight years later, in 1966. It is these books, in which Zukofsky explored and amplified Joycean techniques, incorporating them into his own work, that constitute Zukofsky's deliberate preparation for the last great movements of *"A"*, that released him into the power and polyvalency of his final and great works, *"A" 22 & 23* (written 1970–4) and *80 Flowers* (written 1974–8).[3] *"A" 22 & 23,* indeed, were written after a two-year hiatus in the writing of *"A"*.

These late poems constitute a radical and major shift in Zukofsky's work, and are of seminal importance in the course of poetry written in English in this century.

"A" – 22 opens with three thoroughly Joycean lines which act out a Viconian reading of history through etymology whilst preserving and insisting on the word as object. These three lines, first published by the Unicorn Press of Santa Barbara on a postcard in May 1970, were written on Valentine's Day, 1970:

AN ERA
ANY TIME
OF YEAR

It is followed in *"A"* by a 100-line lyric, later published as *Initial,*[4] which begins:

Others letters a sum owed
ages account years each year (*"A"* 508)

Deceptively simple, easy to say, perhaps because each line opens with a vowel and all but one of the consonants come from the front of the mouth. Quite fast; a neat little song for a Valentine. An appropriate opening for a pair of poems which tells, in the course of 2,000 lines, without naming names, the geological and then the political history of the world – 6,000 years of historical record without dates or names, and takes in a great deal else besides. Zukofsky's remark on the blurb to the one-volume edition of *"A"* that "the story must exist in each word or it cannot go on" has close affinities to Joyce, since it expresses the desire to say everything in one word. James Atherton has remarked that "in *Finnegans Wake* words are constructed so as to contain within themselves sufficient data to allow the structure of the entire work to be deduced from any typical word."[5] If the *whole* story can be in each word, then not only can a whole era be in an instant (a century in a moment, any time of year) but, given the topics these poems deal with, so too can universal history. Both writers seem to share Vico's etymological view of history.

Six words, three justified lines, two words per line. Eight syllables, distributed 3, 3, and 2; nine consonants, nine vowels. Eighteen letters, distributed among the lines 5, 7, 6. Three vowel sounds per line. And the right-hand half of the poem is three nouns, about time: ERA, TIME, YEAR. The left hand gives us one preposition, OF, an indefinite article, AN, and an adjective ANY. Those justified lines, the poem a rectangular block on the page, invite the eye to read the poem like a sum, set up in columns: on the left hand, AAO; on the right, AER. And if this is what the EYE hears, what does the EAR see? rhymes, and puns: AN Era/

ANY time; yEAR/ ERa. Quite Joycean in its possibilities: an earer, for instance, is one who ears; an error, on the other hand, is a mistake (Joyce would say, and does a great deal of the time in the *Wake,* that an error is a name of Ireland). "Look in your own ear and read," says Zukofsky in "Peri Poetikes" (*CSP* 213); "What can't be coded can be decorded," says the *Wake,* "if an ear aye seize what no eye ere grieved for" (482. 33–5). The notebook page on which AN ERA first appears includes what are almost the last words of *Initial* ("happy new year / any time of year" [*"A"* 511]), presumably giving Zukofsky a terminus to write toward, and providing him, no doubt, with the problem of how to get there. Most of the page records an investigation of AN ERA's etymology, giving us a Zukofskian lesson in how to read.

Zukofsky customarily worked out of four sources: a Funk and Wagnalls "desk" dictionary, a ten-volume *Century* dictionary, Lewis and Short's *A Latin Dictionary,* and Liddell and Scott's *A Greek–English Lexicon.* The *Century* is instructive about ERA: *there* we discover that era, which can mean "a series of years having some distinctive historical character" or "Loosely, . . . a point of time noted for some event or occurrence," comes from the Latin root *aera,* an item of an account, "a sing. formed from *aera,* pl., the items of an account, counters, pl. of *aes,* ore, brass, money."[6] The entry goes on to say that "Some refer the LL. word to Goth. *jer* = E. *year.*" An era is, then, a fixed point in time, *and* a series. It has to do with money, and with counting. It is, too, phonetically related to the right-hand column of the poem, AER, its anagram (another of its anagrams, EAR, also has its relevance to the poem).[7] *Aer,* says the *Century,* is "ordinary air of the atmosphere," and (under the entry for *air*) "air, breath, wind"; Zukofsky's notebook explores era's Latin and (selected) Greek antecedents, and cross-refers *aera* and *aes* to Lewis and Short. *There* we find *aes alienum, "the money of another; hence, in reference to him who has it, the sum owed, a debt."*[8] *Aes* can be wages, or pay; it can also be a reward. And, once again, in its plural *aera,* "the items of a computed sum." There is even *aer summus,* the highest point.

> Others letters a sum owed
> ages account years each year

The opening lines of *Initial* begin to make sense. In its permutations and transmutations of several dictionary meanings of *aera* and *aes,* and its puns, it is a condensed exegesis and explication of AN ERA.

Yet it is far more complex than this. Zukofsky later noted that the left-hand pair of the poem's seven columns selectively added up to ANNO, another etymological gold mine. Michele Leggott has written a detailed account of the permutations and combinations Zukofsky found in this poem of six words, demonstrating how Zukofsky generated all

100 lines of *Initial* from it: Her account fills eighteen closely packed pages.[9] Such dense etymological and linguistic play is Joycean; and so is one other element in this short poem: arithmetic. Zukofsky shares with Joyce a delight in numbers, computation, and the counting of words. Zukofsky added the number of letters in AN ERA: 18 = 1 + 8 = 9 (nine vowels, nine consonants). Nine is the number of Muses, of planets, of orders of angels, of rivers of hell, of Worthies, and goodness knows what else besides. It is also of course the square of three, another magic number; three is important to Zukofsky among other reasons because it is the number of his family – Louis, Celia, and Paul – and the family is, in the middle and late sections of the poem, the centre and source of all value, the spring of the poem's being. The sum of the poem's letters (18), reversed, is 81, which is 9 squared. When the poem was printed as a postcard, Zukofsky was most anxious that the poem be set in upper case, and that its letters form a square (it doesn't, of course, for typographical reasons). The schematic for the whole of "A" – 22 has similar numerological features, for the poem is to be 1,000 lines long, divided into three sections: the first will be 103 lines, the second, 800, and the third 97. Adding these integers, Zukofsky noted, gives figures of 4, 8, and 16 respectively. Adding the last two of these, Zukofsky got 24 (the number of movements in *"A"*), while adding all three makes 28. 2 + 8 = 10, which (adding again) gives a total of 1, the same as the sum of the integers for the whole poem, 1,000. The Pythagorean relationship of 4 and 1 had long fascinated Zukofsky, who in "A" – 19 had noted (following Pythagoras) that not only is the "Pythagoreans Four / justice the / first perfect / square product / of equals" but that the sum of the first four integers is Ten ("holy tetraktys," said "A" – 15 [368]), which, its integers added, makes 1: "Four really / ten a / central fire." Hence, "divine number begins" with 1 (419). Pythagoras will turn up again in "A" – 22, when Zukofsky, reflecting on the Pythagorean lifespan recorded in Diogenes Laertius's *Lives of Eminent Philosophers,*[10] notes that

> Pith or gore has 4
> seasons, 20 yet boy, 40
> young, 60 ripe, 80 aged. (517)

What all this means I leave open, but observe first that it reinforces our sense of those opening three lines as integral to the whole of "A" – 22, to which they stand, emblematic, as a kind of initial. Music, harmony, indeed all things, in Pythagorean thought, originate from and resolve into number. Second, that *looking* at the line of the poem which immediately follows AN ERA, we see "letters a sum," and *listening* to it we hear "letters a sum ode" (o-d-e). Eye, then, and ear. Joycean indeed!

It was the Joyce of *Finnegans Wake* that made this writing possible.

Zukofsky once told Cid Corman (in 1960) that he virtually grew up reading Joyce; I believe that from his earliest reading of Joyce he saw that what Joyce was doing was of great importance for an *American* writer (a point I shall return to later) and with full deliberation *chose* Joyce as a source for his own writing. I think, however, that he also saw his own work as an extension of Joyce's. Despite differences in age, nationality, and the genres they customarily worked in, the similarities between Zukofsky and Joyce are startling and close. He wrote to Cid Corman on 12 July 1963 that he felt close to Joyce, not as a writer to imitate, but because, like Stein and Apollinaire, he worked with syllables, utterly without pedantry, pedagogy, and dogmatism – the words *tell*.[11] A sight of their manuscripts[12] suggests that they both want everything – the whole of the work – visible at once, crowded in on one page, visible (but not to be comprehended) at a glance, and suggests something of their affinity: They are both inclusive writers, seeking not simply to contain the whole world in their work, but also – as Zukofsky said of his own writing – to contain the whole of the work in each *word*. Stephen Dedalus, observed Zukofsky, "works in all he knows" (*Bottom* 23) and Zukofsky's insistence that "the story must exist in each word" leads him to formulate a writing that relies heavily on syntactic distortion and pun to achieve simultaneity of effects and multiplicity of meaning – a polysemousness akin to Joyce's. Though Joyce is polyglot and Zukofsky is not (at best he is trilingual), he grew up in a polyglot environment and sought to find a means in his work to convey a simultaneity of tongues and significations, eventually – in the late work – adopting strategies closely akin to those of the *Wake* – indeed learning them from Joyce.

Both Zukofsky and Joyce wind in as many meanings as possible; both consequently cultivate an opacity of text – for if the text is to contain the world, then it must, like the world, in its quiddity stubbornly resist the hermeneutic act; Adeline Glasheen's description of *Finnegans Wake* as "a model of a mysterious universe, made mysterious by Joyce for the purpose of striking with polished irony at the hot vanity of divine and human wishes"[13] is not inappropriate to Zukofsky's late works. For each writer, a work that is (in Joyce's phrase) "about an idea"[14] is anathema, and hence they write books that undermine the validity of belief structures in an age of sheer self-serving systems and ideologies. *Bottom: On Shakespeare* (written over the thirteen years 1947–60) is, Zukofsky told both Lorine Niedecker and Cid Corman in September 1959, a book of philosophy which – as his blurb to the book puts it – "takes exception to all philosophies."[15] It commits, then, as he told Cid Corman, the very sin it attacks. In being sinful yet redemptive it thus acquires an essential contrariety characteristic not simply of Zukofskian but also of Joycean work and play, and there recur through the whole of Zukofsky's work sequences of writing that practise what they preach against. Hence a fine passage in "A" – 12 in which Zukofsky balances Veblen's notions of history against Vico's ends with Zukofsky's sardonic utterance, "Why bother more." And he continues: "Give some thoughts to a performance / of your *Pericles,* Celia" (*"A"* 257). *Performance.*

"Thinking's the lowest rung," he says a few pages later: "No one'll believe I feel this" (*"A"* 260). Like Joyce, Zukofsky is a trickster, sowing clues which sometimes are misleading, sometimes not: The entry for "eyes" in the index to *Bottom: On Shakespeare* refers the reader to the whole book; the entry for "Culture, a graph," refers you to pages 33–443, which is virtually the same thing. Zukofsky, like Joyce, exhibits virtually an obsession not only with eyes and ears but with history and its processes.[16] And he is, again like Joyce, neither a philosopher of history nor a convert to theories. *Finnegans Wake* is (so most readers seem to agree) among other things what Vico would call "history as made by humans."[17] *"A" 22 & 23* is, among other things, a geological and political history of the world, but one without names ("History's best emptied of name's / impertinence" says "A" – 22 [511]).

The extent to which Joyce himself subscribed to a Viconian notion of history is a matter of some debate, for, although Joyce commented that the Viconian cycle was simply a "trellis" for the *Wake,* thus justifying its presence on simply structural grounds, he was characteristically equivocal when, referring to Vico and Bruno, he said that he "would not pay overmuch attention to these theories, beyond using them for all they are worth,"[18] a remark whose essential ambiguity leaves the matter nicely unresolved. The importance we give to Vico and the role we see him playing is a theological question, intimately connected with how we view both any literary text and the world – is, indeed, a matter of how we read and what we think reading is. But there is one passage in the *Wake* that, I think, can serve to characterise at least something of Joyce's notions of history in the *Wake.* This is the passage from Edgar Quinet's commentary on Vico (281.4–13), which though parodied elsewhere in *Finnegans Wake* is nevertheless one of the few almost verbatim quotations in the book. I quote McHugh's translation:

> Today, as in the time of Pliny and Columella, the hyacinth disports in Wales, the periwinkle in Illyria, the daisy on the ruins of Numantia; & while around them the cities have changed masters and names, while some have ceased to exist, while the civilisations have collided with one another & smashed, their peaceful generations have passed through the ages & have come up to us, fresh & laughing as on the days of battles.[19]

The notion of the perdurable and perdurably lovely world of nature existing alongside and unaffected by what Pound in "Hugh Selwyn Mauberley" called "the march of events,"[20] of the perpetual recurrence of floral disport around and through the grim eternal tragic cycle of human existence, of permanence within change, finds echoes in a passage from Zukofsky's "A"–12, written in 1951 (*"A"* 130–1). It is a striking evocation of Vico:

> If each time a man writing a word
> Thought it most completely distils him
> Or did not write it –

a notion of distillation echoing, surely, the blurb on the dustjacket of *"A":* "The story must exist in each word, or it cannot go on."

> All of his legend five minutes old moving thru the sixth
> The strata under six – eons and eons –
> He might type *camions* or *cars*
> Instead of scribe as in the fourth minute
> *Chariots and horse.*

The thematic rhyming of eras with minutes – surely the sort of distillation and condensation that this "man writing a word" most seeks – offers a series of archaeological strata in which *type* is seen as an echo of *scribe.* "The words written down must live" (this too is from the dustjacket blurb) "and not seem merely to glance at a watch":

> The study of history –
> The tree, the knee, the tea,
> Societally and cyclically –
> Sees through a glass darkly:
> Walsinghame;
> Waltzing it an era,
> Dusty unseen harps,

As is often the case, the words generate the course of Zukofsky's writing and thus of the thought: "Walsinghame" breeds "Waltzing it," for instance (and do those "dusty unseen harps" of the next line play "Waltzing Matilda?"). It also generates out of sonic necessity not the echo of *cars* with *horses* (we might well expect *cars* to find their historical equivalent in *chariots*) but (as the rhythm tells us) the echo of *camions* with *chariots.* That word *camions,* of course, has embedded in it (like a stratum?) the previous line's *eons.* Such echoing generates the comic rhyming in the lines that follow: "The study of *his*tory"/"tree"; "knee"/"tea"; "So*cie*tal*ly* and *cy*clical*ly*":

> So rich in determined loss
> The loss flames and reacts,
> Radiates in words,

> The inert less than an eyelet, a flower ray,
> The sixth layer is Troy.

Those archeological strata, eons under eons, are layered in *felt time* rather than in the *seen ground* (earth, the soil), and the condensation of an era into a minute means that in the very act of writing one word the writer reenacts the whole of human history. In the drafts Zukofsky fiddled with the close of the second line, wondering whether the record distils the writer or his *time,* and in the fourth whether the "legend" moving through layers of time was his own or all Man's, before cottoning on to the actual word he was writing: "history" is "his story," after all. And it is "determined," which I take to mean "beyond our control" but at the same time calling for that sort of stamina and persistence we call "determination." History is seen as cyclic, and this at first sight perfectly straightforward passage of expository writing acquires, through those seemingly innocuous conjunctions ("horses" and "cars", say) which I have called rhymes, something of the flavor of a palimpsest – a not unusual effect in either Zukofsky or Joyce. In so doing, and in demanding in its concentration the concentrated attention of the reader, it not only enacts those cycles but makes us see that, indeed, each *word* (as the poet demanded in line one) carries human history, "all of his legend." Quinet's lovely and perdurable flowers are here not only in that "eyelet," that "flower ray," but also in the sheer recurrence through time of the simple acts of every day, "particulars — historic and contemporary" (*Prepositions* 16), historic and present.

There is more to be said, however, for those Viconian cycles (if they are indeed Viconian) are concurrent. It is the nature of the palimpsest to keep the past visible and present, archaeological strata on the (written) page, archaeological strata in the language. When Vico, Joyce, and Zukofsky see, each in his own terms perhaps, that the whole of history is concurrent, simultaneous, and a *repeat,* then (in the words of Donald Phillip Verene) "as gods, heroes and men began at the same time . . . so these three languages [of the three ages] began at the same time,"[21] and the three kinds of speech (that is to say, of language) are simultaneous and concurrent. They represent the directions taken *immediately* and thenceforth simultaneously by consciousness from the original existence of Jove. "AN ERA / ANY TIME / OF YEAR."

Not only is all history simultaneous, then – or contemporaneous – but language is in its onomatopoeic aspect essentially polyglot: a simultaneity of languages; a reflection of as much relevance to Zukofsky as to Joyce. For both writers, history is embedded in language, and punning, whether etymological or cross-linguistic, is one way of discerning it, releasing it, making it present. In *The First Half of "A" – 9* (1940) Zukofsky translated Cavalcanti's canzone *Donna mi pregha* into English, in language taken exclusively from a physics textbook by H. Stanley Allen[22] and from the Everyman edition of Karl Marx's *Capital,* thus incorporating into the language of Cavalcanti's Englished poem both the language of economic philosophy and the language of physical science – an early means, for him, of getting at the history embedded in language. So, later, he incorporated into the language of "A" – 11 the vocabulary of Henry James, Paracelsus, and Spinoza, so that a poem that records the history of his own family evokes as part of that history the worlds of these previous writers: a sort of intertextuality in which Zukofsky puns James puns Paracelsus puns Spinoza, and the alert reader realizes for her- or himself the history that is present in the language. The punning in *Finnegans Wake,* intertextual though it may be, does not work in the same way, for Joyce permits himself what Zukofsky does not, recourse to a lexicon not confined to the English dictionary.

## II

It was after completing "A" – 12 in 1951 that Zukofsky, working on his huge prose work *Bottom: On Shakespeare,* a book which as it progressed became increasingly multiplex, "a graph of culture" as well as a book on prosody as well as a poet's autobiography as well as "a long poem built on a theme for the variety of its recurrences" as well as an attack on "all philosophies" (*Prep.* 166), found an urgent necessity to extend the resources of language.[23] In the course of writing *Bottom: On Shakespeare* (1947–60) and then *Catullus* (1958–66) Zukofsky extended his repertoire, exploring in considerable detail the possibilities of syntax and of cross-linguistic pun as means to achieve simultaneity, while at the same time cultivating – toward the same end – habits of extreme compression. They are his *Wake.* The density of Zukofsky's writing in *Bottom* is exemplified in the section "A-Bomb and H-" (97–9), a curious breed of discursive prose that, apparently ample and expansive, is highly concentrated and impossible to paraphrase. It is not discursive in the sense that it offers a logical argument; the prose is so dense, the syntax so difficult, that we must read it as carefully as we would a poem. If we are tempted at the beginning of the piece to treat the prose as metaphorical, the ambiguity (perhaps "punning" is a better term) of the terms gives us pause. What on earth can a "residual perceptive stand" be, especially in "the *rout* of an original formation of flesh-and-blood life"? Is it a grid through which we see? The difficulty is in part that these terms (and they are pretty large terms) stand virtually *contextless* – the effect is of a series of terms habitually used in one discourse being suddenly transferred into another and completely unrelated one;[24] the net effect of the passage is that it makes the reader DO what the passage is talking about: intellectual rarefaction.

In *What Is Called Thinking?* Martin Heidegger commented that "multiplicity of meanings is the element in which thought must move in order to be strict thought."[25] The suppression of context we find in passages like this one from *Bottom* expands meanings, multiplies them, so that it is only by dint of hard and concentrated thought that we can come to grips with this nonlinear, unhierarchic writing, this generative incoherence.[26] The play on "stand", "rout," "explosion," and the like doesn't help. By the time you get halfway through the fourth sentence – the one mentioning "intellectual rarefaction" – the syntactic oddity of "the actual rarefactions of bombs . . . in particular times and places they explode" draws you up short, since they seem to be exploding the times and places themselves, rather than exploding *in* them; by the time you've mulled that one over and figured out that yes, indeed, the kinds of bombs he's talking about *DO* explode particular times and places, your eye has reached the next three words and you realise that "the intellectual rarefaction" he's talking about is what *you're* experiencing, and that YOU are the "particular time and place" in which this particular and "actual" rarefaction has exploded. And then you see that "actual," containing as it does the word "act," is a pun, and that the whole passage you're reading is *itself* a bomb, "A- or H-", and the writing enacts its content. This is a performative discourse in which the context of those large terms gets established as you read. Whatever else Zukofsky does he refuses to *explain*. The same could just as properly be said of some of the processes of *Finnegans Wake*.

Not all of those processes, of course. One place where Zukofsky and Joyce part company is in the matter of syntax. A single stanza from a poem written in December 1950 (while Zukofsky was still writing "A" – 12 and was in the early stages of *Bottom,* then) is representative of his habitual practice: the third stanza of a poem called "Air":

> For all their metal we are not alone –
> Hedge and human
> As it were sun winds met on Sunday
> High up and in a street of stone. (CSP 132)

The syntactic ambiguity in the third line, its *apo koinou,* is a Zukofskyism, but not I think characteristically or frequently a Joyceism. Does the line say that "hedge and human met, as if (like) sun and wind"? or, "hedge and human met (as it were – i.e., so to speak); the sun met the winds on Sunday"? (I ignore the chimes/ rhymes/ and hence latent punning in "metal" and "met on," "sun winds" and "Sunday," and so on.) Later in the same poem we read "But, under a bridge a river, to harbor / With a thought / . . ."; is that word "harbor" a verb? harboring a thought? or a noun, a destination? Both, of course.

This sort of syntactic foolery is perhaps easier to do in poetry than it is in prose, since prose lacks the help line breaks give. For whatever reason, though, there is little of this sort of play in *Finnegans Wake*. Zukofsky, in his syntax, characteristically plays with parts of speech, leaving the role of words essentially ambiguous. He foregrounds semantic play through fooling with syntax; Joyce, foregrounding through puns, tends to leave his syntax pretty straightforward. Roland McHugh overstates the case, I think, when he claims that "nearly every *Finnegans Wake* sentence observes the formalities of English syntax,"[27] for although there is (often) an implied – or an evoked – syntactically conventional undertow to the text, the puns have crucial syntactic reverberations. Some examples, from the *Wake:*

> – Now from Gunner Shotland to Guinness Scenography. Come to the ballay at the Tailors' Hall. We mean to be mellay on the Mailers' Mall. And ***leap, rink and make follay*** till the Gaelers' Gall. Awake! Come, a wake! Every old skin in the leather world, ***infect*** the whole stock company of the old house of the Leaking Barrel, ***was*** thomistically ***drunk,*** two by two, lairking o' tootlers with tombours a'beggars, the blog and turfs and the brandywine bankrompers, trou Normend fashion, I have been told, down to the bank lean clorks***?***
>
> (510.13–21. My emphases.)

The only syntactic irregularity in this passage – if we ignore the final question mark – clings to that word ***infect,*** which we might read as an imperative verb. We are not likely to, of course, once we meet the main verb of this sentence, ***was . . . drunk,*** and quite possibly we don't read it as a verb at all, for by the time we meet this word (even if all we've read is the words I quote) we have already noticed the strategy of substitutions Joyce is working here, and ***leap, rink and make follay*** is so obvious a set of substitutions that we are likely to read ***infect*** EITHER as "except" in which case we can identify the phrase it introduces as adverbial, OR as "in fact" in which case the phrase is in apposition. Joyce's strategy in passages like this is one in which we are so used to the act of substitution, reading thereby the ambiguities of the subtext (except? in fact?) that the syntactic disruption the pun makes is minimised. The horizon of our syntactic expectations undergoes modest but constant modification.

So, to a second sentence:

> – And this pattern pootsch ***punnermine*** of concoon and proprey went on, ***hog and minne,*** a whole whake, your night after larry's

night, [up to here the sentence is pretty straightforward – all those phrases are adverbial, with the possible exception of ***hog and minne,*** which ***could*** be adjectival if it refers to ***punnermine*** – and then the sequence gets rather complicated:] ***spittinspite*** on Dora O'Huggins, ***ormonde caught butler,*** the ***artillery of the O'Hefferns*** answering the cavalry of the MacClouds, . . .

(519.3–7. My emphases.)

***Spittinspite*** is imponderable. It surely looks like a verb, since we tend to break it down into its three components and turn it into an indicative *or* an imperative; but the subtext turns it to either "spitting spite on Dora" (a participial phrase) or "in spite of," which I *think* makes it an adverbial phrase. It functions in this sentence, that is to say, in a manner comparable to the ***infect*** of the last example, though it is more complex. The real difficulty in this passage is with ***ormonde caught butler,*** which is an independent clause. The syntactic irregularity here is simply a comma splice, and we can and presumably do read ***the artillery of the O'Hefferns*** . . . as an absolute construction. There seem to be a lot of comma splices in the *Wake* – as a strategy they strike me as related to Zukofsky's, when he abandons punctuation altogether, leaving the reader with a series of multiple choices over how to link words, phrases, and clauses together. It is significant, however, that Joyce relies heavily on cross-linguistic puns, metonymies, permutations from one word to another, anagrams, and a whole host of other (often polyglot) devices to effect the syntactic distortion, or on what Fritz Senn calls "dislocutions"[28] – what amounts to a recontextualizing of the word – as he does in the sentences immediately before the one just quoted:

But ***twill*** cling ***hellish like engels opened to noneuropeans,*** if you've sensed, ***whole the sum.*** So be vigil!

(519.1–2. My emphases.)

Here I read a comma splice after ***sensed,*** in which case ***whole the sum*** is either a fragment (another common strategy in *Finnegans Wake*) or we read ***whole*** as a verb, presumably imperative. The first part of the sentence is problematic in a different way: readers of standard formal English are so used (from their reading of Shakespeare if of nothing else) to ***twill*** as an abbreviation of "it will" that it is tempting indeed to ignore the fact that, if we take ***twill*** as a noun (singular) then the verb is in the wrong number, and the clause is ungrammatical; ***hellish like engels*** is, if we read ***twill*** as a noun, a simple adjectival phrase; if we read ***twill*** as a verb, then ***hellish*** presumably is adverbial, and we should add ***ly,*** and change the whole diagramming of the sentence. This immediately suggests that Joyce is working in doubled (or more) syntactic readings.

***Opened to noneuropeans*** is a straightforward participial phrase. A sequence like this one is comparatively unusual in the *Wake* in that, though heavily punning, it uses no neologisms whatsoever: All the words, if we take ***engels*** to be a name, are ordinary English words. Writing that follows this sort of strategy in the *Wake* is especially effective in undermining the authority of the standard English sentence. And it is not, after all, in its intensifying of language, so very different from Zukofsky's generative incoherence.

And it is to that I wish to return, for in writing *Catullus* in collaboration with his wife[29] Zukofsky learned certain Wakean tricks, or at least learned how to apply them on a grand scale. In his prefatory note to the book, Zukofsky says that "This translation of Catullus follows the sound, rhythm, and syntax of his Latin – tries, as is said, to breathe the 'literal' meaning with him." That word "literal" is in quotes. In a draft of the preface, printed on the dustjacket, Zukofsky writes "I might be said to have tried reading his lips that is while pronouncing." Like *Finnegans Wake,* there is no work like it in the language, and reading it is almost totally bewildering, for we have nothing to hold on to, to hold our balance. The early readers of the *Wake* must have felt the same way: The turbulence is astonishing; the sound is amazing; as in *Finnegans Wake,* the writing creates the situation to which it refers. Here is *Catullus 112.* First, Catullus's Latin:

> *Multus homo es, Naso neque tecum multus homost qui*
> *descendit: Naso, multus es et pathicus.*

Zukofsky used Cornish's edition in the Loeb Classical Library, which translates the poem:

> You are many men's man, Naso, but many men go down town
> with you: Naso, you are many men's man and minion.[30]

This hints at Naso's promiscuity but in favouring Naso's obsequiousness hardly gets at the sexual currents running through the poem, and certainly underplays the scorn. Celia's pony, carefully inscribed above the Latin, translates *multus* as *much,* and, other than offering two possibilities (*pathic* and *lascivious*) for *pathicus,* sticks strictly to the word order of the Latin and quite closely to Cornish's English diction. In Zukofsky's hands it becomes quite astonishing, the at first sight impenetrable first line,

> Mool 'tis homos' Naso, 'n' queer take 'im mool 'tis ho most *he*

(syntax and vocabulary both highly fluid), followed by an equally recalcitrant final line:

descended: Naso, mool 'tis – is it pathic, cuss.[31]

There's a possible compassion in those last four words.

*Mool,* the *Century* tells us, is a dialectal variant of "mold"; the *OED* says that as a noun it means "fine soft earth, friable soil; the earth, the ground; a clod of dirt; soil for a grave; material, the matter of which anything is formed"; as a verb it means "to cover with mold; to grow musty, cold; to cause to contract mold, as 'damp, moldy cheese;' to crumble something to powder," and, in Scots dialect, "to associate intimately with" as in "lads and lasses mooling together." What has this to do with the Latin? Consulting the *Century,* we find that English *homo* derives from Latin *homo:* "a man, . . . usually connected with L. *humus,* earth, the ground," and cross-refers us to *humus, human, humble,* etc., pointing along the way to the Greek *chthon,* the ground. *Homo* in Greek, of course, means "the same," and in modern slang usually means homosexuals: "queer," as Zukofsky's version puts it. The other two words that might be slightly puzzling are *pathic* and *cuss.* The *Century* tells us that *pathic,* from Latin *pathicus* ("remaining passive"), as an adjective means "of or pertaining to disease"; as a noun it means "a male that submits to the crime against nature; a catamite," which last term means "a boy kept for unnatural purposes." *Cuss* is a "low" American word, which as a noun means a curse, either "as imprecation" or as a "symbol of worthlessness"; and "a fellow, a perverse or refractory person." As a verb it means to curse or swear at. But there is another entry for *cuss:* Referring us to Chaucer the *Century* tells us that it is "an obsolete variant of *kiss.*"

Catullus's Latin poem is notable for its *double entendre,* and its meaning is indeed indeterminate in several respects, since the text itself is, as Neudling remarks, "much disputed."[32] No one seems to be sure what *multus* means, though a man of many friends, a man generally known or known in many places, a large man (as in "there's a great deal of him"), and even a busybody, a talkative person, have all been suggested. Robinson Ellis says that "it is possible that the word *multus* had popular meanings which have not reached us for that very reason: at any rate, none of the commentators quite establish the sense they give it," and Kenneth Quinn suggests that the *whole poem* is "apparently a pun on two (or more) meanings of *multus.*"[33] What is clear, however, is first, that the position of *tecum* is "designedly ambiguous" (Ellis 391); second, that in the final clause *multus* is defined by *pathicus:* and third, that *descendit* is an overt pun that has survived into this century. Lewis and Short list one of the meanings of *descendo* as "to go down from the dwelling houses . . . to the Forum – ie going downtown" – and another as "to sink down, penetrate into anything . . . in an obscene sense" ("Descendo" I, B, 1 & 5). It looks as though Catullus packed a great deal into his fifteen Latin words, and that Zukofsky, unpacking it carefully, stowed it all away again in twenty-one very unusual sounding English words, in the process utterly dislocating a vocabulary. Zukofsky's poem cannot be paraphrased, nor summarised. Reading the poem is a demanding and difficult process if you assume, as Marjorie Perloff suggests conventional readers do, that a literary text "limits its mobility by following a fixed set of rules, guaranteed to produce 'clever' effects";[34] or that the act of reading is a matter of attaching a single or dominant meaning to words, establishing hierarchies of significance; or that the act of reading is the act of looking through the words at something that you assume lies behind them, thus withholding primacy from the text; or assuming that hypotaxis is a virtue and parataxis a vice.

Zukofsky's writing, like Joyce's, makes such assumptions irrelevant and impossible, for it forces movement. Tracking the gaps, figuring out how one word leads to the next – or back to the last[35] – the reader discovers a text that (as Perloff says of the work of Gertrude Stein) allows for free play, "constructing a way of happening rather than an account of what has happened, a way of looking rather than a description of how things look" (37). With the book before one, Catullus's Latin text on the left-hand page and Zukofsky's on the right, the eye, as Burton Hatlen remarks, travels back and forth from one to the other, recursive, noting similarities and differences, perhaps puzzling out from the Latin what the poem "should" mean, but, surely, alert to what the poem is doing. A salient feature of *Finnegans Wake* is that the very punnish nature of the book invites us to translate while ensuring that translation is impossible; a similar punishment lies in store for the reader of *Catullus*. This strategy, of withholding intelligibility while seemingly offering it, is absolutely essential to both books (and, I might add, has its ironic counterpart in their authors, two great modern writers who withhold their work from their readers whilst wanting it to be on every drugstore book rack). It is not, of course, that neither book is intelligible, but that they profoundly disturb our notions of intelligibility: Like the world, the text must stubbornly resist the straitjacket of determined meaning and the singularity of intellectual order. The writing does not offer a vocabulary as a lexicon of terms but as a repertoire of activities (the distinction is Meredith Yearsley's),[36] and the question, reading both Joyce and Zukofsky, is not a question of meaning but of procedure: Not, what does it mean? but, how do we read it?

The most remarkable feature of the *Catullus*, to my mind, is what it does to our sense of English as a language. At every point of his translation Zukofsky seems to have given priority to two things: keeping track of the sound, and picking the *un*obvious English word. This has two principal effects, and it is in these that we find, perhaps, that Zukofsky comes closest to Joyce. When in his preface Zukofsky said that he wanted to "breathe the 'literal' " in the Catullus he put *literal* in quotes, as Hatlen observes (347), to point at the *littera*, the letters, out of which Catullus's words are made: They are visual and aural, sensory objects. Zukofsky wants us to apprehend the words as sensory objects, and – as he says – track the Catullus syllable by syllable rather than word by word. Very often the translation makes no "sense" apart from Catullus's Latin, which must be seen alongside, and the act of reading is largely the act of apprehending the relationship between Zukofsky's and Catullus's language as we *sound* the words. As Burton Hatlen puts it, this translation refuses "to pander to our fear of language, our hunger to escape from words into 'meanings'" because Zukofsky's "first goal as translator is to establish the physical reality of his own English words, thereby forcing us to come to terms with the physical reality of Catullus's . . . Latin words" (347). Zukofsky took pleasure, as Joyce must have done, in the reflection that in Hebrew the word for *word* and the word for *thing* are the same.

Picking the *un*obvious English word helps the reader, of course, to focus on the sound of it, and to experience the word as a physical reality, rather than to view it simply in terms of a message to be interpreted, straightforwardly paraphraseable. In thus rendering unfamiliar English words in a pattern determined acoustically by Latin sounds – and this is the second effect – we view the English through the perspective of the Latin, we hear it as a non-English speaker might. Indeed it seems like a foreign language. As early as 1958, when he had only translated six of the Catullus poems, he affirmed to Cid Corman in a (perhaps deliberate) echo of William Carlos Williams's demand for an American idiom that this transliteration of Catullus into English was simply a further stage in his attempts to make an *American* English, and an American music. It may be hard to see the language of *Catullus* as an AMERICAN language, but no harder, surely, than to see the language of the *Wake* as a brand of Irish.

Zukofsky's deliberate alienation of the reader from the language, using the Latin so he can *see* the English, is exactly the counterpart of Joyce's activities in *Finnegans Wake*. Their emphasis on the materiality, the *wordness*, of language is a confrontation with and successful undermining of a canonical and indeed patriarchal authority, a retrieval of language from its domination by a single, imposed standard of correctness for speaking, writing, thinking, knowing, or meaning; what Charles Bernstein has called "a unitary cultural canon."[37] Imperial. "How different are the words *home, Christ, ale, master,* on his lips and on mine!" reflects Stephen Dedalus in *A Portrait of the Artist as a Young Man,* faced with the Dean of Studies. "I cannot write or speak these words without unrest of spirit. His language, so familiar and so foreign, will always be for me an acquired speech. I have not made or accepted its words."[38] And to establish a language that they can accept, Joyce and Zukofsky drew on similar means: Joyce, by an act of exile removing himself from that language, dwelling in Zurich, Trieste, and Paris, making Italian the language of daily affairs; Zukofsky, who as a child learned English as a second language, by entering the realm of a language *he did not know,* Latin, and through it and through the dictionary, removing it and making it foreign again. I think that Zukofsky decided to limit his vocabulary in the *Catullus* to the dictionary because for many speakers and readers of American English (and not only those who learned English as their second language) *only those words authenticated by the dictionary have a place in the language,* are "real." Hence, in *Catullus* it is *written* rather than spoken language that generates the work (which is probably one reason why his work has been so attractive to the language writers); it is worth remembering again that in the mid-1930s Zukofsky wrote a fiction called "Thanks to the Dictionary."[39] Not knowing Latin enabled him to objectify its sounds.

Joyce and Zukofsky each grew up in a culture which perforce expressed itself in a colonial language; and each writer, in his major work, successfully threw off that imperial English language and discourse. Both writers thus exposed the canonical language as (in Charles Bernstein's words) "an artifice denying its artificiality" (86), and both, by thus inhibiting a natural or unconscious acceptance of the relation of words to things, undermined also the sway of the imperious intellect which, assigning single meanings and unity to the world and asserting that it is thereby intelligible, concocts formulae for the control and mastery of the world. Gertrude Stein, a writer Zukofsky much admired, believed that the United States was the first country to enter the twentieth century, a century where, as she wrote in her book on Picasso, "nothing is in agreement, neither the round with the cube, neither the landscape with the houses, neither the large quantity with the small quantity."[40] A century where, then, categorizing and naming will not do. Working on the *Wake* Joyce said that he was writing "*au bout de l'anglais*"; even in *Ulysses* he said he needed "a language which is above all languages."[41] To be at the end of language is to be at the point at which not only must all finalities be disturbed but the definitive must be made transitive, the point at which we recognise the sheer inadequacy of ordinary language and of the presuppositions of conventional syntax. The world is indeterminate, plural, and heteroglot, of nonlinear time, acausal events, and nonrationality. If Zukofsky is trying to bring what he sees as a dead American language to life, there is indeed astringent irony in his use of Latin (once the language of Authority and a language long dead save in Joyce's Roman Catholic Church) as a means of revival, as a means of achieving simultaneity. It is an act of Joycean (and Viconian) translation.

# 7

# "To Make Glad the Heart of Man"

## *Bunting, Pound, and Whitman*

*The only tokens of history continually available to our senses are the desirable things made by men.*

George Kubler[1]

A poem is a desirable thing. And made by man. I cannot see, else, how it might last, like say Sappho even in fragments, or even as William Carlos Williams, without Greek, translates:[2]

> That man is peer of the gods who
> face to face sits listening
> to your sweet speech and lovely
>     laughter.
>
> It is this that rouses a tumult
> in my breast. At mere sight of you
> my voice falters, my tongue
>     is broken.
>
> Straightway, a delicate fire runs in
> my limbs; my eyes
> are blinded and my ears
>     thunder.
>
> Sweat pours out: a trembling hunts
> me down. I grow
> paler than grass and lack little
> of dying.

I too lack Greek, so cannot say how distant this is from the original.

But that original is only putative – like, say, the world "out there." I do not *think* Sappho can be translated. Or Catullus. Or, who can know,

Propertius. The text that history has transmitted is uncertain – a fragment, or a muddled pastiche – but our relation with the past is tenuous at best, and only an antiquarian might want the "real thing." Some learn Greek so that they might read Homer "in the original," but who knows *what* it is they read. We need not, of course, step so far afield: We guess the text of *Pericles, Prince of Tyre* even as we guess its author. We argue over the texts of Whitman, preferring one to another. William Carlos Williams was so careless of his manuscripts that even *he* seems not to have "known" what his text was – but he, unlike Bunting and Zukofsky, resisted the definitive. We have no clear text of Pound's *Homage to Sextus Propertius,* though at least one scholar claims to have established it. There is much we *never* knew.

We have forgotten much, by choice, by necessity, by accident. And there is, still, what we *know:* the poem.

> Under molde he leggeth colde
> And faleweth so doth medewe gras.

(That is Thomas Hales, who was a Franciscan, writing before 1240.) A desirable thing. How else would it survive these 700 and more years – or this, say, for the next how many:

> AN ERA
> ANY TIME
> OF YEAR

To be printed as a two-inch square, said Zukofsky. Nine vowels. Nine consonants. An E; Any; Y. Ambiguous Y. Playful repeats and variations. So simple as to be cheeky and daring – like the astonishing opening line (Bunting's),

> A thrush in the syringa sings.

An extraordinary lyrical grace and beauty. It is an opening line anyone might covet, yet few would dare to think or write, so fine is the path it treads.

If it cannot be translated (and what poem can?), assuredly it cannot be explicated – nor need it be. "Understanding" is only one kind of perception, and "explanation" is not one at all. One can only point – and the deaf, who cannot hear the music of the poem, nevertheless have to be sung to, while the moving finger points. And in pointing, I would distinguish (though George Kubler does not) between the desirable object and the useful object; indeed I would oppose them. The desirable object is self-sufficient in a way in which the useful one is not, for the useful always gestures towards its purpose, points away from itself. Occasionally we find tools whose function we no longer know, and it is then that we are struck by their beauty. The tool is anthropocentric, for it serves human-kind. But the poem does not. "A drunken soldier singing 'Eskimo Nell,'" Basil Bunting once said to me, "is serving God, while a parson preaching temperance and thrift is serving only man." Or words to that effect. Children hop, skip, dance, on their way to school; a thrush in the syringa sings. "O gay thrush!"

For much of his career Ezra Pound struggled with the notion that poetry should be useful. He seems to say with Yeats that its purpose is to ennoble, and with Eliot that its purpose is to purify the dialect of the tribe. His incursions into Confucius propose in part at least that the poem is therapeutic for the State if not for the poet, for it will put the language in order, and the heart, and the house. Such need for poets to justify themselves, to defend their craft and art, should surprise no reader of *Hugh Selwyn Mauberley,* say, or of Margaret Anderson's and Harriet Monroe's autobiographies. The title *My Thirty Years War* sounds more accurate a note than does *A Poet's Life,* and that note is not, one might add, at all peculiar to the opening decades of this century, and to North America. Matthew Arnold's *Culture and Anarchy* of 1869 elaborates in specifically aesthetic and literary terms what Dickens had fifteen years earlier said in *Hard Times,* and asserts a function for art. When Basil Bunting sailed from Italy to the Canaries in autumn 1933, penniless though he was, he was treated royally by the officers and crew (moved to a better cabin, even) because he was "*poeta!*"; when he was in Persia (and perhaps still, for all I know) Firdosi's epic *Shah Nameh* was recited serially on national radio every morning. At such times and in such places, the poet needs no defence, and need not pretend to be of use. But in a culture that places man at the centre, whose "humanism," demands the greatest happiness for the greatest number, and which sees "that which ministers to the material needs of man" as good (the words are Benjamin Franklin's, I think), then everything is thought of in terms of that end, in terms of "use"; use is thought of as the only good; and all is subservient to some "human" end. (Our notion of "human" is as fuzzy as our notion of what we call, or used to call, "God.") Good, and virtue, become quantifiable, and the word *measure* as an arithmetical rather than a musical term begins to creep into discussions of poetry.

*Hard Times* is a plea for the imagination, but Dickens's great insight (following Swift, I suspect) is into *fact,* which reduces the world to the verifiable. Verification rests on the appearance of things, and on the rather curious assumption of constancy or stasis in the universe, that events can repeat themselves, that conditions or circumstances can be – let us say – replicated. Words thus become counters which are used to record the appearance of things in propositions which must be verifiable. If the real can be described, then it can be verified, and the test of reality comes to lie in how far it can be reduced to discourse in the language of the senses. Reality is not, then, a matter of experience and feeling, but of observation and record. The known and indeed the knowable becomes what can be verbalised. And words, *then,* point to and somehow correlate to observable reality and can – in the case of someone like Bitzer – be wholly mistaken for it. What is a horse?

> "Quadruped. Graminivorous. Forty teeth, namely twenty-four grinders, four eye-teeth, and twelve incisive. Sheds coat in the spring; in marshy countries, sheds hoofs, too. Hoofs hard, but requiring to be shod with iron. Age known by marks in mouth."
> Thus (and much more) Bitzer.[3]

– and *now,* Gradgrind tells the unfortunate horse rider's daughter, "You know what a horse is." The real is experienced or perceived, "understood" let us say, only through words used as counters, in the language of definition. We demand our language be precise, as though there could be an absolute correspondence between the words we use and the things we refer to – yet the only precise languages are of mathematics and logic, both of which, *outside their own systems,* are sterile.

Hence Eliot, not at all unlike Arnold, can talk of seeking to lift the language *out of* the realm of the verifiable – the world we call "mere" – but does so by talking of the *use* of poetry and the *use* of criticism. Bunting is a dissenter (he is a Quaker), and to my knowledge, he never has. In a much-quoted remark he has said that there is no use for literary criticism. (William Carlos Williams, taking a somewhat different tack, talked of lifting things to the imagination.) Poetry does not make language more precise, though Eliot fondly hoped that it did, and "use" is a sign of man's rapacity. Zukofsky called it "predatory." Pound resisted poetry as useful, among other ways by relieving *The Waste Land* of much that was more or less directly (Pope-ishly) satiric, and it is quite clear that the early drafts of that poem are the product of a writer who has something he wants to say: as though the poem had a *use,* as though he had a use for the poem. It is not wholly an accident, surely, that through such rigorous editing as Pound gave it *The Waste Land* acquired a more or less clear musical structure (Bunting once commented to me that if you remove Section 4 it sounds like a sonata). And with the exception of *The Pisan Cantos* and perhaps such early work as *A Lume Spento,* the least "useful" of all Pound's poems is also one of his best, *Homage to Sextus Propertius,* which Bunting in a 1932 essay called "the most important poem of our time, superseding alike 'Mauberley' and 'The Waste Land.'"[4]

If the point of translation is to make available in one culture a work produced in another, undoubtedly *Homage* fails: It is not, that is to say, very useful for the purposes of "cultural transmission" (whatever *that* might be). If the point of translation is to provide in one language a work that is in some sense equivalent to one originally written in another, then *Homage* fails, if only on the grounds that Propertius, as Pound's critics and commentators never tire of saying, was neither as mocking nor as satiric as Pound's work implies. Even the poem's staunchest admirers, such as Sullivan or Richardson, point to what they consider weaknesses – though I must say right now that these only look like weaknesses if you expect the poem to be *doing something*. *Homage* is not, indeed, a useful translation. Richardson thinks it is addressed to the reader who, knowing Latin, reads the text with Propertius at his side, or *en face,* so that he can appreciate "the value of possibilities that appear in the Latin itself as it strikes the eye, imagination and wit"[5] of the translator who, writing *Homage,* gives us a poem which records the processes of translation. Sullivan complains of inaccuracies left in for the sake of the sound, and of interpolations – especially in Section 4 – that "have no connection at all" with the poem, but are there for the sake of "*mere* word-play and phrase-mongering."[6] Sullivan assumes, however, that "as living poetry the classics *can* only exist in translation" (22), which not only immediately ascribes a purpose to *Homage* but also, in its notion of "classic," suffers from the archaeological fallacy that the experience the original audience had of the poem can somehow be replicated (after, of course, it has been somehow discerned). In so doing, he completely misses the skill and beauty of Section 4 of *Homage,* which he finds "very obscure" (56), and indeed he misses the poem altogether, since he demands that it have a "point," be *about* something. And if *Homage* is satire, as many readers have claimed, then certainly it can hardly be successful (useful) if critics and readers are still arguing (as they are) over who or what exactly is being satirised. The value of the poem – what makes it a desirable object – lies elsewhere. It is a *tour de force* of voice, of tones of voice: "weary with historical data," says the opening section of the poem, "they will turn to my / dance tune." There is a deflation in that "dance tune," and what follows is, as many readers have noted, a series of verses of great skill and diversity, of freedom and range of tone; a collection of more and less complex tunes. Eliot called it "a most interesting study in versification."[7]

In "Prince of Poets," his obituary notice of Ezra Pound,[8] Basil Bunting wrote that Pound

> said in the Thirties that Eliot had got stuck because he could not understand Propertius, and all the rest had got stuck a few books earlier still. I think he excepted Louis Zukofsky and myself.

T. S. Eliot excluded *Homage* but not *Mauberley* from the *Selected Poems*. *Mauberley,* like *The Waste Land,* has been taken as a poem of some use because it is, identifiably, saying something, and perhaps saying something that matters. *Homage,* I suspect, has been spared the classroom because, though skilled and painstaking, it looks naive and facile. It also looks more bookish than it is. Bunting tells the story that when Zukofsky was staying with him in Rapallo in August 1933 (which is when Eliot, that is to say, was seeing *The Use of Poetry and the Use of Criticism* through the press), the conversation turned to the *sound* of poetry, and to *Homage* which they got Ezra to read. They were surprised at his orotund declamation, and so remonstrated, whereupon Pound got Zukofsky to read first, then Bunting. Instead of reading *Homage,* Bunting read Whitman's "Out of the Cradle Endlessly Rocking" – and to his astonishment heard Pound reciting it along with him. Eliot, I recall, called Whitman a writer of prose, and a writer of bad prose at that.

That Bunting should have turned to Whitman and to "Out of the Cradle" in such a context is not perhaps too surprising. "Out of the Cradle" is indeed one of Whitman's more obviously "musical" pieces, almost a set piece in fact, not only rhythmically (as in the repeat, almost onomatopoeic, of anapaest–iamb in "Out of the cradle, endlessly rocking," patterned with such things as the spondees of "out of the ninth-month midnight," where the tone almost completely suppresses the accentual nature of the verse, pushing it towards quantitative measures so that "midnight" is *in duration* a spondee); not only rhythmically, then, but also in the activity of the vowels and consonants and the patterns they make, and in its movement from line to line. "It's a matter of making the rhythms," Bunting told Jonathan Williams and Tom Meyer, "develop and shift around themselves."[9] When he was fifteen years old Bunting was sought out by Whitman's old friend Edward Carpenter, on the strength of a prize essay he had written on Whitman, "a more or less national prize – a national prize for Quaker schools."[10]

Bunting is a dissenter. He is also a progressivist: He demands of his verse that it do something no one else *quite* did before. Hence Ode 36 of his *First Book of Odes,* "See! Their verses are laid," is an extension of Yeats. And a progression can be discerned from Whitman through Pound to Bunting. This is a conscious working, I believe, but it is *not* to say that Bunting draws on ("uses"!) all of Pound (what poet could? "There are the Alps, fools!"). Nor is it to say that he is wholly derivative (or, even, at all). It is to point to a progression. It is to say that there are clear similarities between "Out of the Cradle," *Homage,* and *Briggflatts* (if not indeed *all* of Bunting, for of the three, Bunting is the most insistently and consistently "musical"). Comparing them we see a movement progressively further and further away from the movement of blank verse (and, incidentally, from the long blank-verse poem and *its* organisation), progressively further from the stressed language of accentual verse, and especially the iambic. Whitman's rhythms only *seem* largely accentual, and Bunting's, one is tempted to say, are not at all. Much has been written about Whitman's "prosody" in terms of stress patterns; so too of Pound, and of *Homage* in particular, as "rhythm." In the next few pages I examine various patterns other than the crudely rhythmic ("stress") that occur in three short passages, fragments indeed, from these three writers. Naturally it would be helpful if the reader kept the larger context of each passage in mind (I discuss only a part, for example, of a sentence by Whitman). What I have to say will certainly be clearer if the passages I discuss – and the discussion itself – were *read aloud,* voiced.

Whitman, Pound, and Bunting. I believe, though I shall not attempt to show it here, that these patterns are of a kind that do not occur in English writers before Whitman (or if they do, they occur only rarely, as in Campion, say, or the sadly neglected William Barnes of Dorset), and that they are not to be found in writers like say Eliot, who I think got somehow stuck in the iambic. Whitman brought something new into English verse (and it has to do with the cadences of English prose – or, better, speech), and Pound and Bunting picked it up, refined it. What Whitman brought is a new kind of noise, a new kind of song if you will. It has to do, that newness, with the organisation of the verse – and that, obviously, cannot be entirely divorced from what the verse says. The quantity of vowels, for example, has to do with the *tones* of words, and tone is related to syntax and diction. Fuzzy thought gives a fuzzy voice.

That should be obvious. Here are the passages:[11]

*I.* *Walt Whitman.* "Out of the Cradle." 1891 "Deathbed edition," lines 1–4:

> Out of the cradle endlessly rocking,
> Out of the mocking-bird's throat, the musical shuttle,
> Out of the Ninth-month midnight,
> Over the sterile sands and the fields beyond, where the
> child leaving his bed wander'd alone, bareheaded,
> barefoot,

*II.* *Ezra Pound. Homage to Sextus Propertius,* 6. 1926 *Personae* text, lines 1–6:

> When, when and whenever death closes
> our eyelids,
>
> Moving naked over Acheron
> Upon the one raft, victor and conquered together,
> Marius and Jugurtha together,
> one tangle of shadows.

*III.* *Basil Bunting. Briggflatts,* Canto 4. Oxford University Press edition of *Collected Poems,* 1978, lines 1–7:

> Grass caught in willow tells the flood's height that has
> subsided;
> overfalls sketch a ledge to be bared tomorrow.
> No angler homes with empty creel though mist dims day.
> I hear Aneurin number the dead, his nipped voice.
> Slight moon limps after the sun. A closing door
> stirs smoke's flow above the grate. Jangle
> to skald, battle, journey; to priest Latin is bland.

I shall also, at times, point to lines following these. What I hope to get at is the way in which each line indeed *grows* out of its predecessor, so that the two make a kind of figure of their own, and each is linked to each in a kind of perpetually altering pattern, occasionally stabilised by a recurrence – of rhythm perhaps, or of image, but *usually of a sound* of some sort, so that the stability, the framework if you will (such verse as this, however, always threatens to overbalance), establishes itself through variation and repetition. Establishes *itself.* Recurrencies. It all has to do with what the voice can carry and what the *ear* remembers – more or less arbitrarily I'd say the ear remembers up to some seven or eight lines. Each passage preserves the word order of speech.

If we look at sentence length, there is at first sight little similarity at all between the three passages. Whitman's opening sentence is 208 words (22 lines) long; Pound's is 28 words (6 lines); and Bunting's, 19 words (2 lines). In 7 lines Bunting gets 5 sentences of roughly 12 words each, but two of those sentences are compound or compound-complex, making them look, syntactically, like 7 sentences. Bunting's sixth sentence, however, beginning on line 8, is 38 words – 4 lines – long. Yet there are indeed close similarities, for all three passages proceed in a cumulative way, piling phrase upon phrase or (in Bunting's case) sentence upon sentence paratactically, a lyric catalogue. There is hardly any subordination at all: In his whole opening sentence Whitman has three subordinations (in lines 4, 6, and 10); in his first 11 lines, Bunting has three (in lines 1, 3, and 10); in his opening sentence, Pound has none. Pound is interesting because the opening "When" (with its repeats) leads us to expect a subordinate adverbial clause, and what we get is a fragmentary sentence – though we do not recognise it as fragmentary until the last line of the sentence. The effect of piling these phrases, one upon the other, within an apparently subordinate clause, is to resolve the whole pile in "*one* tangle of shadows," and this comes about through the curious suspense or suspension of the breath at or just before that "one," as the eye runs ahead of the voice to the period at the line's end. The suspense involved – and resolved – is not unlike that in Whitman's larger and indeed looser strategy, where the cumulative delay through prepositional phrase after prepositional phrase comes to a head and is nicely resolved, compacted, in that "I" at the beginning of line 20, which invites us, sandwiched as it is between two commas, to expend a good part of a whole breath on it.

The Bunting moves somewhat differently, for the element of suspense has been (comparatively) suppressed and, where Whitman and Pound both move in what might be called a periodic sentence (the predication held till the very end), Bunting moves through a series of comparatively straightforward, rather short, more-or-less expository sentences. The connecting thread between them is not at all obvious (this is the source of the suspense, where Whitman and Pound use syntax), and they move to a generalisation towards which they did not seem to point, for they did not seem to point anywhere:

> Today's posts are piles to drive into the quaggy past
> on which impermanent palaces balance.

The generalisation itself, however, rounds out the progression and balancing (the stabilising of the pattern) of "I hear Aneurin," and at the same time signals a shift and the start of a new progression, announced in the next line's "I see Aneurin's. . . . " That series of sentences, moreover, comparatively straightforward though they may be, is nevertheless noticeably interrupted by the syntactic variation and surprise (we have been led to expect something else) of line 7:

> to skald, battle, journey; to priest Latin is bland.

An apparently simple syntactical repeat or progression (to skald, to priest) gives us pause as we wonder whether "priest" is a verb or a noun, while the "is" comes as a surprise since the first half of the sentence (before the semicolon) has no verb at all, though we may feel one is implied. The effect is not unlike that in Pound. All three passages move somewhat paratactically: The reader is given few signposts whereby to organise the data.

Within this rather general and crudely sketched overall pattern there are a number of elements common to all three passages, which serve to tie the lines together, and presumably to generate them, to generate repetition. Let me simply list them:

*1. Repetition of phrases and words.* This is obvious indeed in Whitman and Pound, subtler in Bunting. "Out of the . . . ," and "when, when, and whenever"; Whitman, with his greater expansiveness, plays the variations of "Down from," "Up from," and so on as well. Bunting: "I hear

Aneurin number the dead," "I hear Aneurin number the dead" and "I see Aneurin's. . . . " And, Whitman to Bunting very clearly, the variation on this: "Out of the cradle," Out of the mocking-bird's," and so on, and "number the dead, his nipped voice," "number the dead and rejoice"; "I see Aneurin's pectoral muscle swell" – and one hears the "S . . . LL" of "muSCLe" and "SweLL," which is another kind of repeat and variation. Pound, I might add, repeats "together," rhymes (if that is the word) "closes" and "shadows," and half-rhymes "Jugurtha" and "together" – a device to which I shall return (in Number 3).

2. *Repetition of vowel–vowel, vowel–consonant, and consonant–consonant sequences* (and variation). Bunting is so dense in this that it is hard to know where to start. I have already mentioned "muscle/swell." There is also the more-or-less continual chime of the A of "grASS . . . thAt hAS . . . bAred . . . Angler" and the variants (of which "bAred" is one) which push toward the E of "lEdge," the length of "dEAd," and so on. Variation of vowels (i.e., lengthening) leads to a transformation into another vowel. There is also such a sequence as "MIST DIMS DAY," which is a lovely interweaving utterly characteristic of a writer like Whitman ("SHOwer'D HALO" "pLAY of SHADOWS" – which also, incidentally, involves an inversion) and this too points toward Number 3. It is precisely this kind of interplay which largely holds Pound together, both tonally and rhythmically: the sequence "vowel–R–vowel," for example: "OUR EYe . . . OVER AChERON . . . victOR And . . . togethER,/One." It is worth noting that the W of "one" is in turn a repeat (and variation) of the opening "when," and that the slight juncture between "one" and "raft" echoes this pattern, as does the minuscule pause between "tangle" and "of." Pound, like Whitman, is astonishing in his use of vowels.

There are interlockings, too: Whitman's "NiNTH-MONTH MidNight" (and the pacing here is important), Pound's "moviNG NAKed Over ACHerON" – which also patterns "movINg nakED OVER AcHERon" (one might also notice Pound's use of N in these six lines), Bunting's "MIST DiMS Day." The difficulty with all three passages is that as soon as you start noticing such patterns, repetitions, variations, at all, you tend to be overwhelmed by them. There is a subtle shift, for example, in the DL of "craDLe" and "enDLess" in Whitman (who rhymes "rocking" and "mocking" to draw your attention to the sound patterns – note the play of "the" and "throat"). One can endlessly point, when all one need do is hear.

3. *Shift from unvoiced to voiced* (or the reverse). Again, prominent in Bunting, but present in all three. "THE ninTH-monTH midnight" also shifts D and T – with interweaving. "MisT Dims Day" (again!) also weaves

S and Z; and "vicTor conquereD TogeTHer . . . JugurTHa TogeTHer" also weaves K and G, while the V is a voicing of the F of "raft." In Bunting there is the astonishing and lovely "skeTCH a leDGE" – and, in a clause hard to understand, "janGLe / to sKaLd." I note simply that unvoiced-to-voiced shift is T to D, S to Z, F to V, K to G, among others. The shift from P to B is only *apparently* rare in all three since they occur elsewhere than in the three samples: in *Song of Myself* Whitman "Bends an arm on an imPalPaBle certain rest" (which is unusually fine); I have already quoted Bunting's "imPermanent Palaces Balance." And I notice, too, that in Pound the K occurs only in the first four lines, and G (overlapping a shade) in the last three.

4. *Consonant clusters and juncture (pause).* All the devices I list (and others) affect the pace and rhythm of the verse; not only do the consonant clusters have the most clearly audible effect upon pace and rhythm, however, they have a profound effect upon stress, and push the verse towards quantity. All three passages are rich, here, and Bunting once again most. The only sensible way I can see to show this is simply to copy out, once again, each passage, using small capitals to show the consonant clusters that force a pause, and indicating the pause with a slant (/).

*Whitman:*

Out of the cradle endlessly rocking,
Out of the mockiNG- /BiRD'S /THROaT, /THe musical
shuttle,
Out of the NiNTH/MONTH MiDNight,
Over the steriLE SaNDS /ANd the fieLDS /BeyoND, /WHere
the chiLD /LeaviNG His beD /wander'd aloNE,
/BareheadeD, /Barefoot.

*Pound:*

WheN, /WHen aND /WHenever deaTH /CLoses
our eyeliDS,
/MoviNG /Naked over Acheron
Upon the ONE /RaFT, /victor aND /conqueRED /Together,
Marius aND /Jugurtha together,
ONE /Tangle of shadows.

*Bunting:*

Grass /caught IN /willow teLLS /THe flooD'S /HeiGHT /THaT
/HaS /subsided;
overfaLLS /SKetch a leDGE /To be bareD /Tomorrow.

No angleR /HOmes /with empty creeL /THough misT /DiMS /Day.
I hear AneuriN /Number the deaD, /HIS /Nipped /VOiCE.
/SLiGHT /MOON /LiMPS/After the sun. A closiNG /DOOR
/STiRS /SMOKE'S /FLOW abovE /THE graTE. /JanGLE
/TO skaLD, /BattLE, /Journey; to prieST /Latin is /Bland.

It is, perhaps, worth remarking that the pause resulting from consonant cluster is occasionally emphasised by punctuation (usually a comma) or a line break. It is also worth noting that a similar kind of quantitative pause occurs when a slur from consonant to vowel might lead to confusion ("closes/ our," for example). If we read "priest" in line 7 of Bunting as a verb, the quantity and tone are changed, because the stress is changed. Bunting uses a great deal of aspirate H. His verse tends to be more turbulent than Whitman's and Pound's.

5. *Shift from front to back vowels, or the reverse.* I am not at all sure about this. Each poet exhibits a movement towards back (open) vowels, which we associate with the noise of *song*.[12] The problem here is that the English language seems to exhibit a tendency to *middle* its vowels – we drift, that is to say, towards *schwa*. It is easy, at any rate, to confuse the two movements. But there are, nevertheless, interesting variations and interlacings. I point to two, both Bunting, both vowel transforms: "slIght mOOn lImps after the sUn." Here the diphthong of *slight* (front lower A to front upper I) becomes the I of *limp* (a sort of clarification, I suppose) whilst the back upper *moon* becomes middle *sun* (though the value of the U will shift if you pronounce it Northumbrian, which shifts down and is perhaps more voiced). But there is an interweaving, I think. A similar shift seems to occur – this is all very tentative – in "A closIng dOOr stIrs smoke's flow," which is more clearly a move towards roundness and the full-voiced open-throated noise of song. A similar shift, perhaps, occurs in from "when" to "one" in Pound, and even in "OUt Of thE crAdlE EndlEsslY rockIng" (quite complex).

This is very impressionistic, but I think all this means that as you move from Whitman through Pound to Bunting your mouth has to work a great deal more, moving around all those vowels, voicing all those consonants. Bunting seems to be fighting against the centering tendency of the language (he uses back/front/back moves a great deal). All three writers, however, seem consciously to be forcing certain kinds of articulation: As the voice moves towards middle, towards *schwa,* it moves towards *slur;* words begin to blend together, and the noise of speech begins to get fuzzy and vague.

Which is to say what? NOT that Bunting, Pound, and Whitman see poetry as a way to keep the speech muscular. But that they push for the *variety* of sounds that makes our speech and makes for subtle effect, and seek weavings and patternings that make for what we think of as song. It would be interesting indeed to examine the work of Eliot in this way, for I suspect (and indeed hear, though I have not worked it out) that his intent on the *use* of poetry has locked him into iambics, and into a comparatively limited range of sound indeed; so, too, one might look at/listen to Zukofsky, for *he* I suspect (and indeed hear) is pushing for the full range of the voice, upper limit music, lower limit speech. The four of them, Whitman, Pound, Bunting, Zukofsky, provide I think a resource for the poet in a way in which, say, Eliot (my convenient whipping post in this note) does not. It may indeed be that *Homage* outlined a door; Bunting, I believe, tells us where it might lead. Words as song.

# 8

# *Six Plaints and a Lament for Basil Bunting*

*"When I stop liking tea and cigarettes I'll send for the undertaker."*
Basil Bunting[1]

Who was this man whose death at eighty-five is so saddening? Looking back: images, words –

1. *Late 1941. Alloa, Fife:* Bunting, B., Leading Aircraftsman, Serial number 1119305, learning how to drive an army lorry, at the front of a large convoy, spots up ahead an archway, on the left side of the road, on which, as he gets nearer, he can read "George Younger's Brewery." So he leads the whole convoy into the yard. "We all got a free drink," he said. *April 1971. Ontario:* "A sign in Prescott caught my eye ST PAUL ST BILLIARDS. Popular saint, that last." *November 1984. Hexham:* Waiting in a shop to get his watch fixed. "There's a watch that has an eye in it where it shouldn't have." Facing us, a placard promoting ACCURIST. Our slow wits took some time to read "accurst."

Basil Bunting: an attentive and opportunist eye (and ear) with little or no respect for authority, save that which he chose to recognise for himself. "You cannot be useful and retain possession of your mind," he told Zukofsky in 1947[2] – this, when he was in Teheran, being very useful indeed to the British Foreign Office.

2. *September 1972. Wylam, Northumberland:* "Did I tell you about the cats? The snake-and-lizard man came to see me, hunting a lizard said to have been seen in Northumberland, where it had no business to be. I mentioned casually the wild cats (Felis Sylvestris) now plentiful in the border forests. He got enormously excited, got on his motor-bicycle and rushed off to the forest, where he found three wild cats in a single evening.

Apparently none of the farmers or forestry people had ever thought of mentioning wild cats to the naturalists, so it was news to *Nature,* which ran an article, and to the BBC's natural history section. They asked Simms *who* was an expert on wildcats, and the damn man said I was; so for a week the BBC was ringing me everyday, trying to get me to admit that I knew all about wild cats. Now I had never even seen one loose, only heard about them in the pubs near the forests. They wouldn't believe me. At last I choked them off (their photographers got a good picture of one eating a pheasant), and went out for a ride, which took me into the forest. Coming down a very narrow remote lane I stopped to examine a hedgehog, deciding not to take it home to our garden because the dog and two cats would have gone mad trying to bite it, and just as I was about to get in to the car again I saw a wild cat, stalking a couple of young rabbits. It was unmistakeably the wild creature, heavier on the haunch than the domestic cat, and with a head smaller in proportion to the body. So that was that." *The late 1950s. Throckley and then Wylam:* Working 5 P.M. to 2 A.M. for *The Newcastle Daily Journal,* cycling back and forth from home to Newcastle, getting to bed perhaps by 3:30, sometimes not till 4 or later, obliged (to keep his job) to "remain an 'expert' on foreign affairs" by reading "very fully" the foreign despatches in the *Times* and the *Telegraph* and other papers for two or three hours after he got up and before he went to work, long, long days, cycling in the "tolerable" autumn night and in the winter, often, struggling against a gale, stupid with fatigue, "tired of fools," hating it.[3] But at Corn Close, nearly thirty years later, he told Jonathan Williams (and a BBC crew): "That was worth doing. In the middle of the night you saw all sorts of creatures on that road that you never see in the daytime. Every kind of owl I got familiar with, and foxes carrying chickens in their mouths, and things of that sort. It was very nice in some ways, of course you were terribly tired, a tiring business being up all night working on a newspaper and then trying to sleep when everyone else is up and about in the day."[4]

A love of animals and wildlife; a hatred of pomposity; a mischievous eye.

*3. September 1973. Connemara:* "I had a conversation with three donkeys. They were wandering along a road, where I was taking a morning stroll. I patted the first that reached me, whereupon it instantly laid its head in my bosom, while its mates joined it. One donkey isnt too hard to manage, but three, all trying to eat your jacket at the same time, are a handful. A tourist car arrived and couldnt get past. The man honked awhile, then stuck his head out of the window and bawled: "Take your bloody asses out of my way!"; so I let on to be a bit stupider than I am, and held him up quite a while." *April 1973. Wylam:* "Columbia Broadcasting did a film of me in December. . . . I rashly took them to Blanchland for lunch, and they'd never seen anything like that before, so I was kept reading poetry and walking about in icy winds on the fells near the top of Bolt Law for three days. . . . There was some fun. When I was feeling fed up I warned them that the place swarmed with vipers, and enjoyed watching them step delicately around, examining every tuft of heather before gingerly putting their feet down."

A ready glee, often, at the back of those alert and curious eyes, forever alive with mischief and with sheer delight at human oddity. Telling a story, reading a poem, the brown eyes glance back and forth among his listeners; smiling and chuckling to himself, stroking his beard, smoothing the hair behind his ears, dragging on his cigarette.

*4. June 1949. Teheran:* "A friend of mine – another Ezra – was returning from my house to the city in a small open car, when he was hailed by an Arab crying 'Stop'. He didnt stop, whereupon the Arab began to abuse him thoroughly in his own language. As it happens, Ezra is bilingual in Arabic and Persian, so he stopped the car, beckoned the Arab over, and hit him on the head with the handle of the jack. A police car which was passing took both of them to the police station and before the magistrate. The magistrate asked: 'Why did you hit this man on the head with the handle of a jack?'

Ezra said: 'Because he abused me.'

The magistrate asked: 'What did he say?'

Ezra told him. The magistrate turned to the Arab and asked: 'If someone said this to you in Baghdad what would you do?'

The Arab said: 'I would rip up his belly'

The magistrate gave sentence:

'I cannot let you off. You were seen to hit this man over the head with the handle of a jack, so I fine you the minimum, five tumans. If you care to pay twenty tumans you may hit him over the head with the jack itself.' "[5] *September 1972. Wylam:* "One day I stopped at the Farmer's Arms in Muker, in Swaledale, for a sandwich. I ordered two, one beef, one cheese. I'd forgotten I was in Yorkshire, where people really eat, and the sandwiches were enormous by English standards (You wouldnt gasp at them in North America). The girl brought them in and set them down and went off to the kitchen again. Within a minute a man came in, went to the bar and ordered two sandwiches, one beef, one cheese. The barman hollered out to the kitchen: 'Another beef and another cheese, quick', and there came back the most astonished voice I have ever heard saying: 'What! Has he eaten them *already!*' "

Human absurdity. He hated the city, all his life. In 1938 he talked of "the foulness of town life,"[6] and thirty years later complained in an interview that cities "cut you off from trees, wild life – all the things you ultimately rely on."[7] Yet he liked Los Angeles, and Isfahan; when he lived in London in the 1920s and 1930s, sporadic as that domicile may have been, he found great interest and even delight in the indigenous working-class population, in what he called "the common people";[8] he knew a great deal about music halls and popular entertainment, and wrote at least one fine essay on "Folk-Song in London." What he despised was "suburban cleanliness" and "cultured minds," preferring "peasant comfort" to "middleclass convenience."[9] He went for life and vigour in a place, not its respectability. When in 1957 he moved from Throckley to Wylam he was pleased by the closeness of animal life, and his great delight in the company of children was a delight in their unabashed and vigorous curiosity. On 8 August 1972 he reported, on his return from an appallingly wretched year in Victoria, that "little children in the next houses have taken to ringing the bell: 'Please can Mr Bunting come and play with us?' " In London in 1928 he noticed that "the chief singers are the children,"[10] and when in 1977 he moved to Washington, Tyne and Wear, his great tolerance of and patience with children extended to, embraced, and delighted in children of three shouting "fuck off!" or "kick the dog in the balls!" In Washington he lived in a bare and ugly row house in a cramped jungle of concrete-block and brick boxes in dead-end curving streets where by car it is a mile or even two to a neighbour's house less than fifty yards along the footpath; impossible to police; crammed with unemployed (like many another "new town"); hundreds of snotty-nosed kids running round with nothing to do and nowhere to play except scruffy minute patches of grass, or the dead-end street.

5. *August 1977. Washington, Tyne and Wear:* "Children alone make the place endurable. Four or five boys last night who had made their bicycles horses to drag home-made chariots racing round our nearest spot of green at a great pace, in defiance, apparently, of the police, who do not notice that if they prohibit such an entirely harmless infringement of the laws there'd be nothing left for the boys to do but break street lamps, telephone kiosks and people's cars. They got on fine with me, made me Emperor to start the races. Or two little boys and a little girl so loquacious that she kept me sitting ¾ of an hour on my doorstep without ever closing her lips for ten consecutive seconds, telling me about a deceased goldfish."[11]

Patience and common sense; delight in spontaneity and contempt of hypocrisy. Practical. A kind of astonished amazement at stupidity; a ready dismissal of fools; thorough impatience with the smug. If he hated cities, he hated petty officials of all sorts, but civil servants ("desk and pen vermin")[12] even more – and pedants. Proofreading a university journal in a printer's shop in the early 1950s "enormously increased my regard for soldiers and politicians, not usually thought of as very intelligent or scrupulous classes, but less dishonest and less fatuous than academics."[13] He called himself (with Edgell Rickword) the last of the Victorians; he preferred the small and delicate to the large scale and grandiose: the delicacy of Persian to the colossal aggressiveness of Roman and Egyptian architecture, the clarity of Dowland and Byrd to the weight of Wagner or of Beethoven's symphonies, the music of Wyat to the bombast of Shakespeare; he held the autonomous family as a unit before the village before the town before the city before the state and said that the bigger the autonomous unit gets the worse it is for everybody. The only hope for our children, he thought, was to destroy uniformity, centralisation, big factories, big states, and big cities. "I like the common eye," he told Pound in 1954, "cleared maybe, and very sharp, much better than the inward one or the lens-aided dissecting eye."[14] He said our morals need enlarging, and did not believe that man's highest aim is his physical comfort or even his physical sufficiency. *August 1948. Teheran*: "The most upright, religious, even saintly, man I ever met after regaling me [in India] with utterly uneatable dishes of mixed peppers decided to entertain me the remainder of the night by taking me to a series of brothels. To revisit Pompei AFTER seeing something of India throws a light on the ancient world that one isn't given at school. . . . All this is shocking and therefore must not be mentioned or seen. But unless we stop being shocked and receive these things as part of human nature, and by no means an ignoble or uncivilised part, where the hell are we going to get to? Only to new, self-erected blank walls."[15] He saw principles, beliefs, theories, abstractions, as so much mumbojumbo designed to keep men content with the shoddy, the third- or even twelfth-rate; to keep them subject to an authority not their own. "Prohibition," he told *Contempo* magazine in 1932, "is the most effective red-herring yet invented. It beats even religion for keeping people from thinking about more fundamental structural defects in their society. It beats even baseball."[16] A practical intelligence, forever alert to detail: In 1934 he wondered why slum dwellers (such as those in the Tyne Dock) didn't shoot a few policemen now and then, so their plight might be noticed and attended to,[17] and called the idea that abstract nouns have other than a grammatical significance a "lunatic notion."[18] He kept insisting to Pound that he look at the practical implications of his ideas, told him that "if you start thinking about economics in terms of eats and drinks and sleeps it's liable to be less misleading,"[19] and broke with him in 1938 because Pound (as he had said three years earlier), helplessly monotheistic in his intellectual habits, had never considered "the implications of polytheism in action"[20] and was probably incapable of doing so. Uncompromising, then; a Northerner. Solid.

6. *March 1934. Tenerife:* "I knew several miner's leaders at one time and another, from checkweighmen to old William Straker (the chap who had found out in the course of fifty years or so of mining politics that billiards was worse than booze.) I even talked once or twice to old Charley Fenwick, before he died, a man who had been a Northumberland miner's official since the middle of last century and went down the pit to work at the age of nine. Damn it, I was brought up in all that, Joseph Skipsey is said to have dandled me when I was a baby, and he'd been down the pit before the first factory acts touched them. I was on the spot when the View Pit was flooded and forty-five men drowned, I heard what the men had to say about it and the whole cursed system when there wasnt any question of politics, mining or otherwise, but just sheer human commonsense. My grandfather, whom I knew pretty well when I was a kid, was a miner, son of a miner. I know the solidity of those people, and I watched it break up in 26, when I was all the time in a mining village, took the chair at one of Cook's meetings, stuck a knife in the tyres of a government strikebreaking lorry and tried unsuccessfully nearly every paper in the country to get the scandalous faked benches of magistrates who condemned the strikers to years of hard labour shown up. Not even the independant labour party's rag would publish the facts."[21] *November 1984. Whitley Chapel:* "One girl, 16, wearing her mothers wedding dress because there was nothing else in the house for her to put on except her factory working clothes. The Bishop of Durham is quite right about the extreme poverty of these people, though no one in the southern newspapers does anything but mock." *1968. Wylam:* "I like to go to museums and look at things people have made: brocades, pots, furniture, durable things. Poems should be durable too. Potters work in space, and poets in time, but the results are much the same. They make something beautiful and lasting."[22]

An insistence on the tangible world, a scrupulous attention to detail. Hence, his edition of Skipsey's poems in 1976: "one small lifelong commitment discharged at last";[23] a passionate love of the North, and a detailed knowledge of its history. An empiricist, he insisted on the primacy of the sensible world; he was an anarchist "who believes nothing because he can't, not because there are no pleasing or even useful beliefs to choose from";[24] he rejected all belief that went against the available evidence. Despising journalism for its continual compromise with the truth, loathing it, he was nevertheless (in the words of a *Times* editorial) "scrupulously fair and objective"[25] and one of the great *Times* Correspondents. Attention to detail: Whatever else his poetry is, it is flesh and blood: "I like a new landfall," he told Dorothy Pound in 1948; "certain graces of men and trees and hills, the greased leathern hides of Zulu girls, the lack of cupidity in remote places and places grown out-of-date, Portuguese sailor's shirts. I like the monkeys to be in the trees, not on chains; bougainvillea; the banyan; the snake-guarded wild bananas in bush you must cut as you go, a life more physical, less logical, less covetous, less distilled out of the past, than the chained life we lead. That's . . . why I hate earning a living."[26] An anarchist (and a Quaker) he did not believe in causes, disliked Bunyan's prose ("He's alright if you want to *preach*"), did not believe in *raisons d'être,* "never felt the need of one. Do exist, anyway."[27] The details he paid attention to were always immediate, always physical and tangible. When he sent Pound his *Collected Poems* in 1968 Pound read them onto a tape, but broke down – after several false starts – at Page 122, "On the Flyleaf of Pound's Cantos", and in October, 1970, a depressed Ezra Pound wrote him in Vancouver: "If I had paid your attention to detail, I might have done something decent."[28] A keen eye, a clear sense of priorities, an insistence on clarity of knowledge and of thought. The eye of a poet, the eye of intelligence. A sense of the concrete that serves men well in times of war: "de-briefing," he told Dorothy Pound, "is taking a pilots report and crossexamining him to compare what he actually did on a sortie with what he was instructed to do. In a Fighter Squadron, the Operations Officer and the Intelligence Officer are one and the same man. He receives a rather general order from H.Q. and works out all the implications down to the exact minute of every detail, using not only all the official information he has on file, but also his personal knowledge of his pilots, their capacity & temperament. He then 'briefs' everybody concerned – passes on the now exact orders together with every scrap of useful information he can get – where the flak is, what the route looks like, what sort of bloke commands any enemy squadron likely to intercept them, & so on. He checks the planes as they go off, investigates crashes at take-off & reports to H.Q. When the sortie is over, he interviews each pilot separately and compiles an exact narrative of all that took place or was seen. That is the 'de-briefing,' which has to be done like lightning and still remain perfectly accurate. It is good mental training: you can almost feel yourself getting shrewder in your estimate of men. I am glad I had a year of it (even though, in action, as we mostly were, you get hardly any sleep or food, being always at work), & I think it probably helped me in surpassing other political intelligence officers and minor diplomats who had not had any similarly strenuous training."[29] The clarity of prose is remarkable, and derives from Hume, Halifax, Swift, and Darwin. His favourite novelist was Dickens.

7. *December 1971. Vancouver, British Columbia:* "The war did me a lot of good: it gave me confidence, assurance in myself as a man of action; it gave me power of decision under great responsibility. It gave me authority: I learned my Wing-Commander-act." *March and April 1951. Lucca:* "War: . . . an activity which has pleasures of its own, an exercise of certain faculties which need exercise: in which death is neither a bugbear nor a consummation but just happens."[30] "Freedom from war, like freedom from poverty, can be pursued at the expense of things better worth preserving than peace and plenty, of which, I should say, the most important and the most threatened, is personal autonomy."[31] *October 1971. Victoria, British Columbia:* "I can say with complete immorality that I enjoyed the war very much. I managed throughout to keep things lively for myself."[32]

A thorough man; whatever he did, he did completely. A varied war: basic training at Royal Air Force Padgate, then June, 1940, barrage-balloons, escorting North Sea convoys to Murmansk as Mate on the converted yacht the *Golden Hind* (and getting nearly blown out of the water by a too-near depth charge). 1942, as interpreter to Persia (via Sierra Leone, Kenya, Natal, India), where he lost some teeth to scurvy. 1943, four weeks in a convoy of eighty lorries, from Baghdad across Arabia Petraea to Tripoli and the battle of Wadi Akarat; the last weeks of the Siege of Malta; an intimate view of the Sicilian campaign from Eisenhower's war room (which he helped set up), and then from his fighter squadron in Catania (where in the famine he set up a peasants' market and a missing persons' bureau). 1944, Naples (where he was nearly blown up), then by sea to England in time for his squadron to cover the invasion of Normandy. Late 1944 or early 1945, back to Persia, as Squadron Leader, Vice-Consul in Isfahan and then in 1946 to Baghdad as Chief of Combined Intelligence for an area that included the whole of Saudi Arabia, Iraq, and Persia, and more. He found work "a habit-forming vice, like opium"[33] and action "a lust that is hard to abandon."[34] He stayed in Persia until the middle of 1946 and went back in February 1947: "I'm afraid I shall want to be moving and at grips with people and outwitting them until I die,"[35] he said, and managed, off and on, to stay in Persia – either with British Intelligence and/or as *Times* Correspondent – until 1950 when he lost his job with the *Times.* So the Foreign Office sent him to Italy to stop a Russian takeover but some fool from the embassy met him at the plane and blew his cover: He was shot at a few times (just as, when he went back to Persia for the *Times* in late 1951, Baqai and his thugs would start riots and throw stones at him), but he did what he could, and he made a start on *The Spoils.* A thorough man: Under his care the Tribal Map of Persia, the first of its kind outside India, was completed (and is still unpublished, buried in the Foreign

Office archives), and detailed histories of oil concessions, of the Qajar dynasty, and of much else besides, were done. He spent, in Persia, all of his Foreign Office allowance, and all of his war-time savings (what little they were) to get the job done – and what was his reward? Mossadeq threw him out of Persia in 1952 (the thugs had done their work), and when he reached England, after driving from Teheran with his pregnant wife and two-year-old daughter (the journey took a month), he could not pay the enormous Duty on what few possessions he had been able to rescue from Mossadeq; the *Times* could not or would not give him a job, and when he got to his mother's house in Throckley he was virtually penniless. "My very considerable services to the state," he told Zukofsky in March 1953, "havent entitled me to anything whatever."[36] Because he had spent the last few years living outside the country, he did not qualify for unemployment insurance; that same month he told Ezra Pound that "none of us is entitled to any of the benefits of the welfare state except free medical attention."[37] Whenever a potential employer asked him what he'd been doing for the last umpteen years his claims sounded extravagant; if he wanted to write something, what could he write? the Official Secrets Act stopped that. *July 1953. Throckley:* "I cant get a job at seven quid a week (no experience) let alone get listened to. What they mean by experience Lord knows. Last board that interviewed me simply refused to believe my record. Wouldnt even take the trouble to check up and find it true. 'You mean to say a former GSO2 and Counsellor is applying for a piddling little job like this? Make your claims more modest next time.' "[38] *June 1953. Throckley:* "The government is applying a last turn of the screw, demanding duty and purchase tax on the car the Times abandoned to me. I cant pay, I'm not even allowed to sell the car which is running up debts in a garage. But if now they fix a government debt on me I'll end in gaol for having refused to falsify news to the disadvantage of our government. Such is democratic gratitude. . . . my children must starve and I be denied any chance to show sagacity elsewhere. This week we cannot pay the butcher. And little worms who hardly know enough Persian to construe a few pages of the Chahar Maqaleh have lectureships, because they listened to professors nearly as ignorant as themselves, but I who know their literature – and the ways of their tribesmen – I cannot be the slightest use, or at any rate, cannot be paid for it."[39] *September 1953. Throckley:* "the Air Force expects me to keep my uniform handy for the next war 'to serve in the same position you occupied before demobilisation,' ie, chief of intelligence for a very big region. I wonder, by the way, how many General Staff Officers, Grade Two, are now drawing public assistance?"[40]

Human absurdity, blindness, stupidity. His own damn pride no doubt got in the way, that Victorian or is it Edwardian rectitude, that code of gentlemanly conduct, of not making a fuss, of not airing your linen (clean or dirty) in public. But if he was at all bitter in his later years he had every right to be. Because he had lived so much abroad, he did not qualify for a full old-age pension, which at 65 was pitifully small. So at the Queen's pleasure he was awarded a Civil List pension to make up the difference – but, indexed at a lower rate and taxed at a higher one, it barely paid for his cigarettes. In the middle 1950s Basil Bunting and his family, valued servants of the state, were supported with food parcels sent by Ezra Pound, inmate of St. Elizabeths Hospital for the Criminally Insane. The British treatment of Basil Bunting is a national disgrace. So in his late sixties and early seventies he underwent a series of voluntary exiles: Santa Barbara, Vancouver, Binghamton, Victoria. *July 1971. Wylam:* "Can you imagine me teaching poor devils to read Bellow, Styron (who's he?), Cary, to say nothing of Lawrence, Brecht, Beckett, Fitzgerald; or in another course Stevens, Hart Crane, Berryman, Lowell, somebody called O'Hara, Cummings, Duncan? The prospect appals me. If I hadn't dependants I'd never pretend to do it. It makes me quite sick to anticipate it, and the only comfort is that . . . I should save enough to live a year or more without working, if the work doesn't kill me first. This syllabus will prevent me being the only real use I can be to the university, which would be to let them know of the existence of David Jones, Zukofsky, MacDiarmid and so on. Even by A-level standards their syllabus is fifteen years or more out of date. By what I'd reckon of university standards, thirty years." His treatment has been shameful.

And the critics, the professors, and even his publishers – all the people supposed to *know* – have treated him no better. They took too much at face value his too-often-quoted estimate of himself as "minor poet, not conspicuously dishonest," as though self-advertisement was characteristic of all writers. But self-promotion was not part of his stock in trade, and he did not elaborate on the meaning of "minor," nor its context. His own stubborn pride, perhaps, forbad any such thing. But in private he would relax, and talk a little. *December 1970. Vancouver:* After reading MacDiarmid aloud, over some beer, in the evening, a list of major writers ("to aim at less is to aim lower") and a list of "secondaries" (Catullus, Chaucer, Sidney, the troubadours, Eliot). The majors? Homer, Ferdosi, Manuchehri, Dante, Wyat, Spenser, Wordsworth, Whitman, Pound, Yeats, Zukofsky, Jones, MacDiarmid. *August 1953. Throckley:* "I've been thinking . . . about how and where I got whatever I know and feel about poetry, and the more I think the bigger Malherbe's part in it seems. Wordsworth, when I was a small kid, showed me what it was; Rossetti's translations from the Dolce Stil people, in my teens, and Whitman at the same time, enlarged the scope. Horace gave the first inkling of how it was done (odes). Malherbe produced all I afterwards found in Ez's writing except what I'd already got from Horace. Ez and Spenser, great galleries of technical accomplishment. Lucretius. Dante. And after that, Hafez for what I got from Horace (and Ez from Chinese) only more, taken further: Manuchehri, greater and more splendid gallery than Ez and Spenser: Wyat: the Mo' Allaqat: and for sheer pleasure, when I am not out to learn or have my mind fixed, for diversion, for sheer living, Homer and Ferdosi."[41] *November 1970. Vancouver:* " 'How Duke Valentine Contrived' is not worth keeping; it's got a few good lines but it's an exercise. Its main if not its only virtue is the accuracy of the landscape, of the directions – and that virtue is Macchiavelli's. I'm sure when Shelley drowned he thought 'If only I could get my hands on the works. So I could destroy them. They're no good.' "

As a poet Basil Bunting was a progressivist (though he did not believe in progress): Each poem he wrote must do something different, that had not been done before. What minor poet of this century – or for that matter, what self-proclaimed or widely anthologised "major" one – would reject as "better lost" such a poem as "Per Che No Spero"[42] which, capturing so nicely as it does the sound of a dinghy (or, more accurately, a cutter) being slapped by the waves, originally formed the opening lines of a longer and untitled poem, itself destroyed. An old man's casting up of accounts, that poem ended with a bit of Hadrian's hymn, "anima, blandula, vagula":

> Poor soul! Softly, whisperer,
> hanger-on, pesterer, sponge!
> Where are you off to now?
> Pale and stiff and bare-bummed,
> It's not much fun in the end.

What *minor* poet, looking through *The Spoils,* would worry: "Is the falcon stuff too commonplace?"[43]

> Have you seen a falcon stoop
> accurate, unforseen
> and absolute, between
> wind-ripples over harvest? Dread
> of what's to be, is and has been –
> Were we not better dead?
> His wings churn air
> to flight.
> Feathers alight
> with sun, he rises where
> dazzle rebuts our stare,
> wonder our fright.

He himself preferred the fowler passage, just before these lines: Their use of rhyme and of consonant pattern is not so obvious.[44] A minor poet? What other poet in this century, besides perhaps Zukofsky in the opening of "The Translation," would RISK that astonishing line: "A thrush in the syringa sings?" A minor poet? "I'd rather have somebody who is thinking of Horace call my poems bloody bad," he told Zukofsky in 1949, "than hear them praised by somebody who is thinking of – who? oh – Dylan Thomas."[45] If the very few translations he did (not all of them collected) are anything to go by, he is – or could have been – the best translator of Horace we have had. What makes his death so extraordinarily sad is not simply the neglect he suffered, though God knows he suffered that, but the sheer *loss of work* that neglect caused. And the misery he had, feeling that loss. "Minor poet, not conspicuously dishonest"? *September 1964. Wylam:* "I owe poems to . . . Cooper Stephenson, who was killed in the great battle of March 1918, the closest of all friends I've had; and to Peggy Greenbank and her whole ambience, the Rawthey valley, the fells of Lunedale, the viking inheritance all spent save the faint smell of it, the ancient Quaker life accepted without thought and without suspicion that it might seem eccentric: and what happens when one deliberately thrusts love aside, as I then did – it has its revenge. That must be a longish poem."[46] He wrote *Briggflatts,* and the poem for and on Cooper Stephenson gestated. It, too, would be a Northern poem, and would include the Cliffords and the Percys and the Rising of 1569. *May 1972. Wylam:* "There is a conspiracy to pretend [teenage girls] dont exist until they reach 18, and the P&O is in it. For a few days [on the *Canberra,* coming home from that hellish year in Victoria] I was a general grandfather–confessor to them and thought I'd extend my knowledge of these pleasing creatures, but then the youngest of them all suddenly annexed me, led me about the deck etc, and all the others sheered off. This is in fact a fortunate event. I'd been looking at the new moon, the April new moon that takes the attitude of Wordsworth's "little boat" in *Peter Bell,* Ezra's barge of Ra-Set, I think the most convincing new moon I ever saw: and the next night an occultation of Jupiter who vanished of a sudden behind the old moon's corpse and then reappeared as a drop of molten silver slithering down the new moon's flanks; and I was fresh from this when I saw Linnaea, slim as the new moon and even blonder (and, alas! as remote as the moon), and there she was, Selanna, chick of Leda's egg immeasurably beautiful and not suspecting her beauty and the responsability it lays on her. All I've been meditating for three years and could get no sense into lay around like blocks that have found their keystone, and I started picking them up to see how perfectly they fell into their places. So this little lass had only to look out of the corner of her eye to find an obedient servant. . . . A bonus: her name, grandmother to granddaughter for six or seven generations, is a feminine form of Linnaeus, and though there's no certainty she seems to be descended of the man who named the flowers, as Adam did before him. Not Selene only, and Helen, but Persephone too. The difficulty is going to be how to translate what the myths imply into a mythless modern tongue." The drafts of *A New Moon* that he destroyed were good enough for most poets of his time, indeed better. A minor poet?

> Such syllables flicker out of grass:
> 'What beckons goes': and no glide lasts
> nor wings are ever in even beat long.
> A male season with paeonies, birds bright under thorn.
> Light pelts hard now my sun's low,
> it carves my stone as hail mud
> till day's net drapes the haugh,
> glaze crackled by flung drops.
> What use? Elegant hope, fever of tune,
> new now, next, in the fall, to be dust.[47]

Sound. Consonants. Quantity. The attentive ear. But a progressivist: Destroy it. "A poet's business is to get a language that won't have to rely on anything so slipshod as algebra,"[48] he once said. Every word must be *new*. *November 1950. Lucca:* "You and I, [Louis,] have more than the whole ruck of others who have done well out of poetry. And I'm not even noticeably eccentric on the page! Why? What has dogged us?"[49] The price an attentive eye (ear) pays is its subjection to the immediate; it is attentive to it and vulnerable to it. *November 1932. Rapallo:* "One absorbs a fragment of somebody else's technique and in the process of absorbing it, something gets written, but whether that something is a poem or a technical exercise one cant tell – at least I cant – for some time."[50] *April 1967. Goleta, California:* "while I am reading Pound Yeats and Eliot for one class and Williams, Zukofsky or David Jones for the other, I find I cant write a line which does not turn out to belong by right of rhythm or structure to one of these poets rather than to me, so that I've not had as much use for leisure as might be expected." The price of forced exile, teaching, is our loss. It is the very spareness and turbulent concreteness of his language; it is the astringency of his eye; it is his integrity and his refusal to compromise and his knowledge ("Nobody, it seems, has ever thought of setting Yeats' 'John Kinsella's Lament for Mrs Mary Moore' alongside of Juan Ruiz (archpriest of Hito)'s lament for Trotaconventos. They never cease to astonish me, these learned men, for they know so little"); it is what he reminds us we have lost; above all, it is his utter refusal to compromise that makes his death so sad. He distrusted splendour, the colossal (and therefore brutal), the magnificent:

"Life includes splendour but is not sustainedly splendid,"[51] he said, and he denied, thereby, all euphemism. His favourite prose writers were Hume, Swift, Butler, Dickens; and his own prose, in hundreds of letters, in essays, in lectures, is amazingly clear. The bane of our age, he said, is our not "having to face what a man has made with deliberation and all his skill. . . . Every syllable you publish [of letters, biography, of casual utterance] will divert attention from the WORK."[52] Living is a difficult business, demands a tenacious eye.

He was one of the four great Northern poets. The other three are the Gawain poet, Edmund Spenser, and William Wordsworth.

# 9

# *Exploring the Mere*

## *A Note on Charles Reznikoff's Shorter Poems*

*When Edschmid says, "But there were young people in every period," it was, whether intended or not, Lord, O Lord, give me strength, a banality. . . . Yet I am aware that not all . . . statements are banalities. The reader has to decide for himself. For "There is an essential something in us that can explode greenly" (Th. Däubler). Whether "Lord, O Lord, give me strength" is banal, I don't dare decide considering the quantity of explosiveness being appealed to, maybe it's Expressionist. Lord, O Lord give me your storm! After all, it is a direct order uttered by a man who feels powerless. . . .*

Kurt Schwitters (1923)[1]

Charles Reznikoff's shorter poems pose problems for me, and I must confess I'm not wholly at ease with them. They seem, much of the time, to be *near*-poems, narrow misses. So many of them don't quite make it. Yet so serious and constant, so persistent has Reznikoff's career as a writer been, that his disclaimer at the end of his life – "the oak has many acorns / that a single oak might live"[2] – strikes me as disingenuous. Rather, the short poems challenge my notions of what a poem is. I don't think I'm going to solve the problem in this note; I hope, though, that I can narrow it down somewhat.

It has to do with lucidity, and it may have to do with subject matter – or to put it another way (and to reverse the order), with the thing, and with the treatment of the thing. A major orthodoxy of our times, current perhaps since Whitman but observed more with the lip than with the deed, has insisted that the poem can be about *any*thing, made with anything. Even shopping lists can be poems, Williams told Mike Wallace: "anything is good material for poetry. Anything. I've said it time and time again."[3] Yet like Yeats Williams distinguished poetry from rhetoric and quarrelled with Robert Duncan for trying to build poems out of it. Similarly, we live in an age so steadfastly given to the pursuit of the mannerist and the baroque that we have (to our cost) almost completely ignored those major voices of our time, each in his or her own way notable for lucidity: Bunting, MacDiarmid, Niedecker, and of course Reznikoff.

Lucidity. "Transparency of thought or expression"; what is "easily intelligible" (*OED*). If we do not belong to a tradition that believes poems should be difficult (for that is the road to Arnold's "high seriousness"), then we are almost perforce conjoined to those whose words have, as Pound noted of Williams in 1917, "opacity."[4] The trouble with lucidity in poems is that it seems cryptic, because we don't quite believe our eyes anymore – or our ears. The poem can't be quite *that* simple: We want it to be *more,* and we neglect to ask, "more *what?*" Here is a poem:

> A dozen pigeons on a roof
> idling away the day.
> But above them, part of the weathervane,
> working away in the sun and wind,
> head lifted,
> the gilt rooster. (*CP* 2: 209)

This is fairly simple and straightforward; certainly it proposes an easily intelligible contrast between the lazy animate and the industrious inanimate, the creature of nature and the "creature" of man, and the irony is neatly punched home, the point held back to the throwaway last line. It seems deliberately slight, yet is skillful indeed.

Two fragmentary sentences long, the poem operates through metrical and syntactic play. The first line (iambic tetrameter) is exactly twice as long as the last (which is dimeter); the second is twice as long as the penultimate. And in between, the filling to this sandwich, is a pair of iambic pentameters. "Working away in the sun and wind," alliterating the w of "weathervane," picking up the "away" of line 2, acquires its tenth syllable in the pause between "and" and "wind," necessary if we are not to hear "dwind" (inescapably suggestive of "dwindle"); and these long lines serve as prelude to (dwindle into) the metrically irregular "head lifted," a *phrase* containing the only finite verb of the poem, a finite verb serving as adjective – with the result on the one hand that "the gilt rooster" comes as slightly anticlimactic, and on the other that it is only the inanimate rooster who *does* something: head *lifted.* The syntactic irony neatly reinforces the ironic juxtapositions and reversals of roles that are the poem's theme; and the compression of the scene is neatly encapsulated in the terminal words: "roof, day, weathervane, wind, lifted, rooster." Yet the voice in the poem refuses to judge, and we can draw our own conclusions: It is morally neutral, favouring neither the inanimate nor the animate, whilst at the same time it invites the reader to come to a judgment. "Idling away the day" is, after all – like "gilt"! – a cliché of moral discourses which treat, and usually correlate, beauty and idleness. This poem inverts the traditional correlation, yet the reader may well be puzzled to determine whether nature is here to be seen as dependent on (and thus perhaps "inferior to") the mechanical/artificial, or as liberated by it. This is really quite a remarkable little poem, with unobtrusive yet skillful visual and aural patterns and contrasts, and much compression. Yet so unobtrusive are its implications that it is indeed easy to dismiss it, to shrug the poem off as "a rather pretty picture" or "an imagist-sort-of-poem." Reznikoff is a moralist; he is a didactic poet in an age suspicious of the didactic: The poem unavoidably drives toward a point – it *says* something – and yet, and yet.

The compression, and the neutrality of voice, drive the poem toward the cryptic, and Reznikoff himself seems to have been so uncertain of his reader (or of his craft?) that he gave the poem a title: *Machine Age*. The net effect of this seems to me twofold. First it declares that this is a poem *about* something, that it is more than simply a picture, and in so doing points to what should be obvious (which is, I think, one reason why so many of the titles of Reznikoff's short poems are so unsatisfactory). Second, it opens up the implications of the contrasts in the poem, the ironic juxtapositions, wider than they *might* otherwise be, thus rendering judgment more difficult while at the same intensifying the invitation to judge: By providing a sort of editorial gloss it announces, that is to say, that the poem moves toward a conclusion or conclusions, while at the same time it renders those conclusions less possible. I think, too, that it implies that Reznikoff wanted the poem to be *more*. I shall come back to this, for it raises a central question, but first I want to look quickly at two other poems. The first is an early one, this time untitled.

> The girls outshout the machines
> and she strains for their words, blushing.
>
> Soon she, too, will speak
> their speech glibly. (*CP* 1: 29)

This is a swift thumbnail sketch: the observer, detached, knowing the ways of the world as "she" does not yet; the factory or mill scene implied by "machines"; her naivete and innocence embedded in "strains" and "blushing"; and in the third line that interstitial "too" carrying with it the implication that the girls themselves were once like her. Again, then, a picture of great compression. But here the inevitability of her shift into knowledge (or into acceptance by the others, or into the habitual world of the ordinary or even "vulgar," take your pick) is amplified and reinforced by verbal and metrical patterns which serve to throw the whole weight of the poem onto the last word, "glibly." It is really quite brilliantly done, and is a narrative drawing on unobtrusive lyrical elements: the alternating stress and unstress of line endings, which accentuates the dying fall of the last line – a fall that is also reflected in the length of the lines themselves (two long, followed by two short). The grammatically different *kinds* of enjambement in line 1 and line 3; the speech pattern of line 3, with its "too" at midpoint, completely overriding the metrics of the first two lines and flattening out its *own* metrical organisation, so that we find, when we reach the last word of the poem, that it is glibness which has shut down the metre, that "ordinary" language has closed down the possible song. To say nothing of repetition and alliteration, of small patterns of contrast in "shout" and "speak," "strains" and "glibly" – so that our sense of inevitability comes from an overall pattern which pivots on the fulcrum of "soon" and rests its weight on that "glibly." I think of this poem as Reznikoff's Theodore Dreiser/*Sister Carrie* poem (though he wrote more than one), for when he wrote it, some time before 1920, it was somewhat different.

The version we have is condensed from that in *Poems* (1920), where it reads

> Blocking hats with a boy helper
> he tells of the sluts he visits.
>
> Girls outshout the machines
> And she strains for their words, blushing.
>
> Soon she, too, will speak
> Their speech glibly. (*CP* 1: 196)

Not only is this less interesting prosodically, but it is more explicit. The theme is more-or-less overtly sexual, the implications are narrower in range than in the revised version, and on the whole the poem is *more* lucid, not less, for the opening lines declare not only that this narrative has a point, but what the point is. It is much more overtly a poem of social commentary, and Reznikoff is much more obviously the didactic public moralist.

Which brings me to my third poem, for this is Reznikoff's characteristic position, and of the three poems I am looking at, this one is at once both the most and the least lucid of the three I have chosen. It is from "A Short History of Israel; Notes and Glosses," published in *Going To and Fro and Walking Up and Down* in 1941. It has, then, a declared subject matter.

> A dead gull in the road,
> the body flattened

and the wings spread –
but not to fly out of the dust
over the waves;
and a robin dead beside a hedge,
the little claws drawn up
against the dusty bundle:
has there been a purge of Jews
among the birds? (*CP* 2: 24)

A gull and a robin – ordinary birds. Everything in the first eight lines reinforces the sense of helplessness and vulnerability so strongly suggested by the sharply seen, and augments the contrast between live and dead. But the grim sardonic reflection of the last two lines, faintly whimsical, turns the poem round, comes as a surprise: Is this then a world in which even the ordinary and familiar persecute one another and fight among themselves? What a disturbance of nature! The picture of the gull is astonishingly vivid, and that "dusty bundle" successfully lifts the lines on the robin from the sentimentality they skirt. But the editorial gloss in the last two lines is still whimsical; it subjects the first eight lines to interpretation, and the reader likewise. The final lines impose a reading, a significance, that is not inherent (or even apparently implicit) in the scene as presented – it was no bird, after all, that flattened that gull – and in the long run the poem is unsatisfactory. It is as though Reznikoff has been going to and fro and walking up and down looking for the meaning he wants, observing and then writing with predatory intent.

Perhaps I put that too strongly, but what I am trying to get at is that the last two lines push the poem towards a lucidity that the opening lines do not have and toward which they do not point: Sharp and clear as *they* are, they are nevertheless open-ended in implication, and it is the open-endedness of that clarity which not only makes them so fine but also makes them *less* lucid, just as the straitjacket of interpretation in the final lines makes the poem *more* lucid. For lucidity is, as I said at the beginning of this note, what is "easily intelligible" (which is different from what is "easily seen"). The sharpness of the insight/picture in any lucid work (for example by Halifax, or Swift, great masters of lucidity) turns us into reading content; lucidity tends to drive us, if not into silent response, into thematic criticism and reading, and the subject matter of the poem tends to be the interpretation – what the writer thinks is the meaning – rather than what gave rise to it, *materia mundi* (and if we are not to be preached at, lucidity demands the exercise of wit). Hence the ending of the poem closes the poem down, instead of leaving it open, and it is the sort of closure that risks banality, risks being *mere,* because it declares that the poem indeed *has* a subject matter, and a meaning we can all agree on, and is hence instructive.

It is this that makes Reznikoff so very close to Williams, yet at the same time so very different from him. For although the opening lines of the third of the poems I chose, or the little thumbnail sketches, remind me of the Williams of say "The Term" or "Between Walls" or even of "The Red Wheelbarrow"[5] – which, oddly enough, without a point, starts out as though it had one: "so much depends" – they are nevertheless sharply different. Reznikoff is the poet who finds words for what others *think*, Williams, for what they *see*.

Between Walls

the back wings
of the

hospital where
nothing

will grow lie
cinders

in which shine
the broken

pieces of a green
bottle

Williams, proceeding by syllable count, shapes his poem by breaking the count in lines eight and nine and leaving the poem completely open-ended. "He does not 'conclude,' " Pound said of Williams in 1928, and Williams's deliberate pointlessness frustrated and angered many readers, who found his work cryptic, or – as Cleanth Brooks did – "quite inert."[6] Small wonder then, that Pound continued: "his work has been 'often formless,' 'incoherent,' opaque, obscure; obfuscated, confused, truncated, etc."[7] Reznikoff provokes a similar response, save that instead of "so what?" we get "is that all?": Hayden Carruth once called the language of *Testimony* "uninteresting"; William Dickey called that poem "dishonest," written from "a very simplistic kind of moral perspective indeed."[8] Trivial, then.

This is the central problem. Our whole sense of the banal depends on social or moral experience and criteria: It is not, strictly speaking, a literary matter at all. Theoretically there is no reason whatsoever why a fine poem should not be composed of commonplaces – and indeed in Samuel Johnson's "On the Death of Dr. Robert Levet" we have a clear example of one – but nevertheless we do indeed (for Romanticism has intervened between Dr. Johnson and us) often ask of the poem that it be more than it appear to be. We feel, perhaps, that a poem is not doing enough, that it is *merely* light verse, it is *mere* words, and so forth. Now, "banal" is a curious word, and so too is "mere." *Banal:* "Of or belonging to compulsory feudal service"; hence "open to the use of the community"; hence "commonplace, common"; hence "trite, trivial, petty" (*OED*). (Of *use,* note.) *Mere:* "Of wine: Not mixed with water"; "Of a people or their language: Pure, unmixed." Hence, "That is what it is in the full sense of the term: nothing short of (what is expressed by the sb.); absolute, entire, sheer, perfect, downright," and hence, "Having no greater extent, range, value, power, or importance than the designation implies; that is barely or only what it is said to be" (*OED*).

That Reznikoff was aware of the risks he ran in his poetry there can be no doubt: The difficulty for the public moralist, for the didactic poet, for the writer whose task it is to put into words what oft was or should be thought, is that of raising the banal, the mere, the *lucid,* to the level of poetry – a problem directly analogous to Williams's, of "lifting to the imagination those things which lie under the direct scrutiny of the senses, close to the nose."[9] Williams solved his problem by dropping the interpretation, dropping the pointedness; in composing *Kora in Hell* he learned to make of *the act of writing* a self-sufficient act, to make it "mere" in the old sense: nothing more than, but nothing less than, what it is. But Williams's solution cannot be Reznikoff's, for Reznikoff seeks to make *thought* self-sufficient, and attempts to solve the problem either by opening the poem up (as in "Machine Age" or the second of my three poems) or by closing it down, to a specific application, thus making it of use. Neither solution is wholly successful, for as soon as you open the poem up, you escape the mere, the language of the poem is no longer self-sufficient but is subservient to the thought, the signifier is subservient to the signified; and as soon as you close it down, you risk banality. Even in the sharpest of his short poems, where the detail is most luminous, that didactic note is still there, the intelligibility:

> This smoky winter morning –
> do not despise the green jewel among the twigs
> because it is a traffic light. (*CP* 1: 116)

He is an old-fashioned poet, and as August Kleinzahler says, "the plainness is so extreme it jars."[10]

# 10

# *Robert Creeley What Counts*

*We lose truth in names and phrases, as children lose themselves in a wood, for want of geographical knowledge.*

– John Taylor of Caroline.[1]

Here is a poem by Robert Creeley, from *For Love:*[2]

The Lover

What should the young
man say, because he is buying
Modess? Should he

blush or not. Or
turn coyly, his head, to
one side, as if in

the exactitude of his emotion he
were not offended? Were
proud? Of what? To buy

a thing like that.

There are not many names in *For Love,* and what nouns there are seem mostly to be abstractions: exactitude, emotion, proud, thing. It is an abstract landscape, yet it is oddly precise. What concrete nouns there are are curiously general: lover, man, head. Yet the poem is *exact:* faintly cruel, sardonic. The title. The delicious wit, wry. The embarrassed rhythm, registering possibility as *choice* and choice as permission, where what starts as question turns into flat statement. "Should he / blush or not." As if. The young man recognizes where he is and what he is (as we, as readers, do), and thereby chooses: the lover. The personal, the intimate, venturing into the world, the social "should" bewraying admission of love; the consciousness of should, forced into consciousness of self, distancing the lover from the world while bringing him into it, coy, coyly proud. And what is not mentioned is the relief, the release to the young man's spirit that one must buy Modess, the one *name* in the poem and itself familiar and *un*specific (save as its function: a *specific*). We know she is not pregnant.

The poem suggests, then, a singular occasion, a complex immediacy, of the world, and of the young man, in it, coming to it. To be precariously situate is an old New England problem. As William Carlos Williams put it, "It is an immorality that IS America. . . . There was no ground to build on, with a ground blossoming all about them – under their noses. Their thesis is a possession of the incomplete."[3] The world rendered open to judgment. A choosing, where "should" becomes "does," the waverings of choice forcing recognition, re-cognition, and the sequence of words comes to rest on the demonstrative pronoun, "that." "That," which along with Bertrand Russell's "this" might be the only *genuine* name.[4] The poem points a finger. It is a naming.

Choice is recognition (as Duncan told Creeley)[5] and Wittgenstein tells us in *Philosophical Investigations* that "one has already to know (or be able to do) something in order to be capable of asking a thing's name" (15): We can only name what we have a use for (and Wittgenstein, later in his book, tells us that meaning is use). Naming is recognition. Which is to say, with Williams (who is writing about Poe),

> Invent that which is new, even if it be made of pine from your own yard, and there's none to know what you have done. It is because there's no *name*. (*IAG* 226)

It is a curious dilemma we are in. There is only the once, the one occasion for the naming – and for the name! – for each event is a singularity, a particular act, specific. It is *the* young man (and "the," like "this" and "that," is deictic), buying *that* Modess, on *this* particular occasion. "One by singular one," says the poem "The Figures" (*FL* 147). Gertrude Stein said that "poetry is essentially the discovery, the love, the passion for the name of anything," "a calling an intensive calling upon the name of anything,"[6] and she came to see the poem as an essentially *static* register of movement, while at the same time (almost, indeed, in the same breath!) she asked "why after a thing is named write about it" (*LIA* 210). "More and more one does not use nouns," she said.

It is a curious dilemma we are in. In *Autobiographie, chapitre dix*[7] (it is the only chapter), Jacques Roubaud acutely notes that the language – words, names, phrases, "les paroles" – in which we record events, experience, exists prior to the event or experience we seek to describe or record. Such recognition that the dictionary contains only quotations leads Roubaud to ready-mades, found poems, quotations, and allusiveness. It gives his work a curiously deterministic quality, and it detaches him from the language. Like other members of *Oulipo* he is an experimenter with form and is often whimsical. It leads Creeley, however, as it led Gertrude Stein and William Carlos Williams before him, to the construction of vocabulary in a world whose words are obsolete because they predate experience. "We lose truth in names and phrases," John Taylor of Caroline complained in 1814, because the terms of our discourse are the wrong terms. To be precariously situate is an old American problem. And so Creeley, in a note written in 1953 (concurrent, that is to say, with "The Lover"),[8] said that "the process of definition is the intent of the poem" (*QG* 23). And for Gertrude Stein? "Poetry is I say essentially a vocabulary just as prose is essentially not. . . . It is a vocabulary entirely based on the noun" (*LIA* 231). The noun. "A right noun," Olson told Creeley, "is worth every color in the business. Actually a noun carries all the color with it, and rightly used, gets back, all that light has done with it, yes?"[9]

Naming is recognition. One has already to know something in order to ask a name. "But what does one have to know?" Wittgenstein asked, and answered: "only someone who already knows how to do something with it can significantly ask a name" (*PI* 15). Naming is recognition. No wonder New England's first settlers, as Williams said, "saw birds with rusty breasts and called them robins. Thus from the start, an America of which they could have no inkling. . . . but something the newcomers had never in their lives before encountered" (*SE* 134). No wonder that for American poets the great problem has been the discovery of the landscape. No wonder their thesis has been a possession of the incomplete. To be precariously situate is an old problem: "our anger cannot exist usefully without its objects," wrote Creeley in that 1953 note, "but a description of them is also a perpetuation. There is that confusion – one wants the thing to act on, and yet hates it" (*QG* 23). The name is no sooner used but one has no use for it: Our names are partial.

William Carlos Williams lies back of Creeley, breaks much of his ground, establishes it. Americans, he said, will never recognize themselves "until someone invents the ORIGINAL terms" (*IAG* 226) for – as he pointed out in *Spring and All* – "life becomes actual only when it is identified with ourselves. When we name it, life exists" (*S&A* 115). Actual: from Latin *agere,* to do. Creeley's "Lover" is uncertain, in his social situation, precisely because he does not know *what* he is, nor how he should respond (nor even, perhaps, what his response *is*) in a situation where the social aspect is suddenly dominant over the domestic: He has no name. It is as if the senses need the corroboration of the mind before the world can be accepted as real, before we can be actual. Creeley's world is an uncertain world, on the edge – at times – of falling into nightmare (or, more rarely, into joy), and Creeley is a hesitant man in it, indwelling, concentrated, inwardly focussed. The American world is fearsome, for one doesn't know one's place in it. Michael McClure has talked of hunting through old dictionaries, "forgotten languages of argot," looking for the names of things: "a man names what he sees and then puts away the fear of it," he writes.[10] The name identifies and authenticates the thing and one's sense of it, one's relation to it. "The Lover" is a name, and it is irreducible, particular, specific: the poem as singular name, the singular occasion. What philosophers call a "simple." And as Louis Zukofsky tells us, echoing Wittgenstein, "the simple is so well compounded."[11] It cannot, in its complexity, be taken apart. The occasion, social and domestic, the pretext of the linguistic occasion of Creeley's poem, is complex; the poem is a compacting. And to the thoughtless eye it is complete.

I would not argue that Creeley is a "philosophical poet" – if by that we understand Creeley's concern to be with matters of, questions of, philosophy – if only because, as Wittgenstein remarks, "when one is doing philosophy one gets to the point where one would like just to emit an inarticulate sound" (*PI* 93). But in what Creeley calls "a world that's constantly coming into being"[12] he is indeed dealing with those things which Plato called "unknowable" but "perceivable."

A name may be partial, but when we get to a name we may go no further. As Wittgenstein puts it in *Tractatus Logico-Philosophicus* (3.221), "objects can only be named." How can we give an account, Theaetatus asks Socrates, of "the elements of an element?" And Socrates answers:

> the primary elements . . . have no account. Each of them itself, by itself, can only be named, and one can't go on to say anything else, neither that it is nor that it isn't . . . if one is going to express in an account that thing, itself, alone . . . it would have to be expressed apart from everything else. As things are, it's impossible that any of the primary things should be expressed in an account; because the only thing that's possible for it is to be named, because a name is the only thing it has.[13]

"No one understands," said Creeley in a 1956 note on Philip Guston, "but some know" (*QG* 343). Or, in Wittgenstein's words, "one can know something and not be able to say it" (*PI* 36). If we get to a name we may go no further, for it is in name that the event, the experience, the perceived moment, *acquires* completion – but only, after all, for the occasion of the poem, the poem's reading. Creeley is, then, an occasional poet – but he is not by that trivial, as some would have us believe, any more than he picks a moment that is "complete" and writes about it. Far from it. Our sense of the complete – as Dewey struggled to show – is the effect of discovering the *simple,* the "not composite," and giving it a name. There are no simple parts, Wittgenstein reminds us, of a chair (*PI* 29). At least, not that we experience. And our sense of completeness is a linguistic act, derived from Name. The singular act is irreducible; like a name, it tells you only about itself. How did Olson put it? "That which exists through itself is what is called meaning."[14] And in an incomplete world, what counts is attachment: Our names are partial, as we are to them. "What I come to do / is partial, partially kept," Creeley writes in "The Innocence" (*FL* 24). What *counts.*

the trees completely
or incompletely
attached to the ground

says Creeley in "The Rites" (*FL* 22).

The difficulty, of course, is that we do not live in isolated simples, and the finger that points to a singularity is inadequate for discourse. The young man buying Modess is singularly *that* young man only for a moment; then he becomes some one or some thing else, or he is doing something else: He may still be a lover, but he will not be exactly the lover so carefully registered in the poem. We live, that is to say, in series, and it becomes necessary to count. "The natural way to count" may indeed be "one and one and one and one" as Gertrude Stein says (*LIA* 227), but for Creeley "human life" is, as he writes in *Presences,* "an accumulation of persistent, small gestures and acts, intensively recurrent in their need,"[15] and the counting is cumulative. *1.2.3.4.5.6.7.8.9.0* is the title of one his books; *Numbers* that of another. Numbers, the collection of singularities; counting, the distinguishing of names. Number is the name of a pattern, it is the measure of it. So, in the first of "Three Fate Tales" Creeley speaks of "the one pattern which cannot be broken because it is general, the collection. The numbers."[16] Number: another simple. Bertrand Russell once wrote that "I must confess it seems obvious to me (as it did to Leibnitz) that what is complex must be compounded of simples."[17] And Leibnitz, Zukofsky tells us, thought of music (number) as a felt relation of counting (*Bottom* 426). And the poem? Sing another number, one might say. To Creeley,

> poems might comment on many things, and reveal many attitudes

> and qualifications. Still, it was never what they said *about* things that interested me. I wanted the poem itself to exist. . . . (*QG* 54)

The irreducible name. The word as thing.

# 11

# *"Go Contrary, Go Sing"*

## *Robert Duncan 1919–1988*

*in order to draw a limit to thinking we should have to be able to think both sides of this limit (we should therefore have to be able to think what cannot be thought).*

Ludwig Wittgenstein[1]

The visionary. Duncan is the great transgressive poet, for whom transgression is a form of obedience. In a remarkable essay on "The Typewriter" he praised Virginia Woolf who, "shut out of a human opportunity she sees before her . . . , must free herself, her conscience, from the impositions of the societal patterning that lie back of the very privilege she speaks from – the literacy of her prose."[2] His attack on Elizabeth Drew, in "Ideas of the Meaning of Form," is in its rejection of "reasonable literary terms" a rejection of the "literacy" which, claiming "good breeding" and shunning contact with the "lower orders," in Duncan's view finally trapped Woolf into denying those possibilities she affirmed, because its fastidiousness of taste would deny the "savage," the "childish," and even (again, Woolf's words) that "illiterate, underbred book," Joyce's *Ulysses*.[3] Duncan, like Joyce, will transgress those bounds, for the morality of such literacy, in the very act of defining the unthinkable thinks it; in the very act of condemning the irrational, embraces it and denies that it does so. It forces itself thereby not only to police the inner as well as the outer world lest the unsought, the uncontrolled, and the unanticipated appear, but also to be untrue to itself.

"Reasonable literary terms," "good breeding," taste, and sensibility are social virtues; if they are not acquired in the nursery then they come from the classroom. It is these that Duncan would transgress, but cannot therefore deny. Even though Sensibility seems "monstrous to me, against man's nature," Duncan wrote, it cannot be "discarded as untrue to us, for Sensibility is most true to us." It must be "co-ordinated with unmannerly need and the flash of inconvenient temper that strikes true to what we know without claiming to be right. The truth of what we feel entire . . . must be made good in it." This "old forming of a sensibility" is "through," and shows its Gorgon face,[4] thus taking its place among the old excluded orders it would itself deny. Yet, as he wrote in the *H.D. Book,* "the old excluded orders must be included,"[5] for the truth of what we feel entire demands obedience, and cannot be transgressed. What we feel. Entire. And communal.

> Were our songs of the universe and our visions of that great Love who once appeared to Dante holding his smoking heart in his hand, were our feelings and thoughts that had flowed out of whatever originality they might have had into their origins in phrasings of melody, were our dreams and our architectures to come home at last members of no more than a classroom education?[6]

The classroom. That purveyor of facts, reasons, and known forms. In thus denying possibilities it takes refuge and finds protection in an act of knowing that is itself a stoppage of thought and response precisely because it claims to know, claims to know completely. Yet to know in a factual sense, he said to me in 1966, say that Gregory of Tours lived from 538 to 594 and was a historian as well as a bishop, is to stop the mind, close it to knowledge; but not to know even who he was is a sense of knowing him, since we know he is to be sought and can seek him.[7] "It would be sickening to know the whole field of poetry," he said. "Instead of imagining your reader to be someone intensely like yourself, sitting and reading a book of poetry somewhere in a little room, you are forced to imagine him as taking a graduate course in English. This is very disturbing to your idea of why you wrote the poem and what you wrote it about."[8] Those who know the whole field can fit the poem into its proper place, "appreciate" it, sort and classify it through acts of analysis and differentiation, find its bounds, know it. With Pound, Williams, and H. D., with Zukofsky, Olson, and Creeley, with Blaser and Spicer, Duncan stands outside the exclusive tradition of polite letters, the tradition of the academy, the tradition of the rational and humane, and is yet most himself. Of all the writers of his generation he is the one who took most directly to heart Zukofsky's dictum, "No order of the universe can finally be seen order to it,"[9] and found it his need's enquiry and ground.

In February, 1971, he mock seriously proposed a reading of "kinds of Duncan," speculating that, with its Stein, its Eliot, its George Barker, and its countless others, it would last hours and hours if not days, and lead to the discovery of new kinds. Half a year earlier, in 1970, he had described a proposed seminar at Santa Cruz in "Ideas of the Meaning of Poetry":

> I hope to realize in the course of the sessions a group of shaping essays, beginning with one on music and including poetry as "speaking" (as in "It speaks to me; you speak to me; the act speaks for itself; that there work of art speaks to me); as vehicle of identity (the identity of Man, of "English" as well as of Dante's intellect or Whitman's personality [or Spicer's "Martian"]) and spirit; as a field of communion (i.e. as a language) – as a language-machine or technique; as a *door* (the visionary *trip,* the world of the poem); as a governing formation – perspective, projection, pentagram/pentagon/pentameter, plot, web, bridge, sluice, dam, power plant, wiring system.[10]

Self-imposed tasks became enormous (and frequently impossible) because self-imposed; disobedience to plan (even one's own) and disturbance of intention (especially one's own) ground his poetics; characteristically those essays (so far as I know) were not realized, any more than was his long-promised essay on Zukofsky. Duncan's text is necessarily in flux, indeterminate and variant, in part because it is composed by the tone-leading of vowels, "the least lasting sounds in our language,"[11] and in part because, demanding that the reader be brought "closer to stages in my own work on the poem" in order more fully to participate in its composition,[12] he sees the poem in its full existence as lying ahead of us, like Whitehead's God impinging "at only one place: the moment where we are right now. . . . The poem is one means of being intensely alive."[13]

The office of poet is to enhance possibilities, transforming and sublimating, not repressing or mastering the unruly world; the poem is the place of transmutation and evolution, in which the poet follows the orders of the poem. Against a form "significant in so far as it shows control" Duncan posed a form "as creation or fiction of a universe as a way of 'knowing' the real universe. Form as a mode of participation in the real."[14] And so he learned from Pound and from Zukofsky a need for accuracy that insisted on being responsible for all errors:

> This is, sometimes I would compare it to a carpenter, in other words, view the language as a wood that if you make a mistake, you cannot correct it so that you have to face your botched work. But then in language you are concerned with the meaning of what you are doing so that it never becomes a botched work. The mistake in itself becomes the ultimate of what you must work with.[15]

This means that the disturbances of our life are our potency; that the work of the poem – and the poem itself – can never be foretold; that the immediate is not prepared for nor conditioned by the past; and that "I gather what I mean as I go. And must write as if I gathered my sense as a man would gather water in a sieve."[16]

In *Bottom: On Shakespeare* Zukofsky wrote that the risk a text takes "when it sees and foresees at the same time is that at any moment creation may become like uncontrolled water."[17] But Duncan, caught up as he is in the risk of meaning, finds in that tension the source of the great energy, passion, and humour that drive the work:

> Creativity . . . means such a change in the meanings of every part in the creation of each part that every new strictness is also a charm undoing all previous strictnesses, at once an imperative and a change of imperative. Each syllable in the poem . . . is a stricture . . . that proves in the movement of the poem to be a liberation.[18]

The risk of meaning is, too, the risk of utterance, of language, "the conquest of babble by the ear,"[19] the risk of being. In late 1978, speaking of the figures of water and of trees in his early poems, he told Aaron Shurin and Steve Abbott "I was finding my sexuality through these figures. It wasn't as if I was expressing it. I was realizing it, making it real through these figures."[20]

Such sense of writing as an act of incarnation makes the work of the poem belong to one's immediate living. "I enter the poem," he wrote in *Bending the Bow,* "as I entered my own life, moving between an initiation and a terminus I cannot name";[21] about two years earlier in 1966 he told two student interviewers in Vancouver:

> The conventional artist takes a goal and labours toward it. Whenever I see a goal I avoid it. Through this things happen in the poem because I've got to break the train of thought that's going ch-ch-ch to Chicago. I'm not designing a train line. In other words I derail and lose track of myself; I delight in doing both of these.[22]

In conversation at that time he talked of himself as the paranoiac, manically seeking and seeking for whatever does NOT belong in the plot, seeking NOT to drive that train to Chicago. "I attempt the discontinuities of poetry," he wrote in 1956. "To interrupt all sure course of my inspiration":[23] to run contrary – what Charles Bernstein calls *The Resistance.* So the poem can not be foretold. "I always feel the congruity of everything," he told KQED ten years later, "and when I am baffled I believe that the congruity is there and that I am unable to tune, to find it."[24] Yet – or hence! – "especially in *Passages* I have entirely departed from the principle or concern of *integrity,* not only in that the 'poems' are not entire in themselves, but that the series is not conceived of as an entirety.

And beyond that, . . . I do not see whatever sum of works and days of mine as having any completeness, unbrokenness, entirety."[25]

From *this* side of his dying, his work and career show an astonishing coherence, and the energy holds. It comes from the sheer persistence of his vision and of his passion, his passionate need, which drove him, poet, to watch, listen to, attend the workings of the heart in language: Possessed as he is by "the troubled awareness . . . of meanings in the common language everywhere that those about him do not see or do not consider so important,"[26] his Muse is "Her-Without-Bounds." His poems do not so much demand a response as seek an affinity, strike a correspondence in the reader. Small wonder, then, that his beautiful book *Letters* should be illustrated with five wondrous drawings of an ideal reader. Small wonder, too, that the picture of the poet, penned in June, 1953, should be part of a series of imitations of Gertrude Stein. It is a shade cozy, but it still points to one essential Duncan:

> A poet who sits in the light of words like a cat in the mote-filld sunlight of a window. Where he is in the sentence is there. And he listens. His poetry pictures his listening.[27]

# 12

# *Writing as Assemblage*

## *Guy Davenport*

> *... the link between these fragments is not that of grammatical logic, but of an ideographic logic, culminating in an order of spatial disposition completely opposed to discursive disposition.*
>
> *... Clearly, it is not narrative. It is the opposite of narrative, since narration is of all literary genres the one which most demands discursive logic.*
>
> Gabriel Arbouin, June 1914.[1]

When Guy Davenport gave the Thirty-Third Distinguished Professor Lecture to his colleagues at the University of Kentucky on 8 March 1978 on "The Geography of the Imagination," there were among the audience the entire geography department, a Jungian analyst, and some physiologists working on the brain. The lecture was about Poe, O. Henry, and Grant Wood's well-known painting *American Gothic*. "An ambiguous title," he wrote me afterwards, "can do wonders."[2] The poopsheet handed out at the door has a picture of Guy Davenport seated at his desk on which sits, next to a pine cone, a specimen bottle that once belonged to Louis Agassiz. The prose accompanying the picture says that Davenport has written "twenty-one contributions to books of essays and poetry" (such as Stan Brakhage's *Film Biographies*, Ronald Johnson's *Radi Os*, and – though this is later – Roy Behrens's *Art & Camouflage*); "sixty-six articles, 207 reviews; eleven papers read before learned societies" (including the inaugural lecture at the Center for the Study of Ezra Pound at Yale University, in 1975); "and fifteen short stories" (six of which had been gathered in *Tatlin!* in 1974), in addition to his translations of Sappho and Archilochos (some of which have been set to music by Lukas Foss and by Richard Swift); his "study guides" to the *Iliad* and to the *Odyssey;* his long poem *Flowers and Leaves* (which Thomas Merton once read, all 114 pages, to his class at Gethsemane: It is a lesson in aesthetics);

and his numerous illustrations. It does not mention his numerous paintings, nor his library table, which he built to a design by Ezra Pound. In his kitchen at home there is a saucer full of sugary water for the wasps and ants, free to come and go as they please for he likes them in the house (wasps figure centrally in the story "Au Tombeau de Charles Fourier"). A family of snakes lives under his porch, and each spring he faithfully reports their stirring from winter's long dullness. "Can you imagine the deliciousness of sun to snakes, after four months of freezing?" (2 April 1979). There is no evidence that the geographers, the analyst, or the physiologists were disappointed by the lecture.

"Guy Davenport went round in a dream the day he learned the Greek alphabet," he says (8 January 1979). And he was a late starter. "I couldn't read until very late. I began the first grade aet. 7 (being thought retarded) . . . I wasn't a bookworm, and didn't begin reading with any real interest until 13, when I broke my right leg (skating) and was laid up for a wearisome while" (9 April 1979). But the reading stuck. Some four years later, in 1944, he quit high school to study art at Duke University and ended up with a B.A. in English and Classics and a Rhodes Scholarship to Merton College, Oxford. An attentive man, who as a child was "taught how to find things"[3] in a family that devoted every Sunday afternoon to hunting for Indian arrows, who remembers everything he's seen or read, and who reports what he has found, he sees for himself; his complete unconsciousness that this is unusual turns those reports into conversation. In response to a remark that structuralist criticism is a disguised utilitarianism which hates literature, he comments that all literary critics

> are shameless scavengers. They babble Freud (who is on paper the most inept critic ever to have come out of Europe: I mean, his interpretation of Da Vinci, based on a novel which he thought, poor sod, was a biography, and if this wasn't ruinous enough he psycho-analyzed Leonardo, using his one dream (in which a grackle swoops down and touches his lip with its wing) and being so unhandy with Italian that he thinks it's a buzzard sticking its tail in L Da V's mouth, and then drags in the Egyptian for buzzard, which is *mut,* which he says is the root of 'mother' (it isn't, not by forty miles), and ends up a prize ass. (9 February 1980)

His speciality as a critic is, as he says, "finding out how things break down into components" (3 July 1979). Listening to Guy Davenport break down the components of Poe's "To Helen" and of Grant Wood's *American Gothic* is unlikely to have bored the geographers, the analyst, or the physiologists of the brain.

In less than three minutes of that lecture they would have heard what we can now read in two pages: that Nice was a major shipyard in Roman times (Marc Antony built a fleet there); that classical ships never left sight of the land, and that sailors could smell orchards on shore (and that perfumed oil was a major industry in classical times; ships laden with it, too, smell better than ships laden with sheep); that the raven was the device on the flag of Alaric the Visigoth, whose torch at Eleusis marks "the beginning of the end of Pallas Athene's reign over the mind of man"; that Lenore, a mutation of Eleanor which is a French mutation for Helen, is a name that Sir Walter Scott imported from Germany for his horse; that in 1809, the year of Poe's birth, Herschel discovered and explained binary stars (the spectroscopic double Beta Lyra and the double double Epsilon Lyra); that Poe's mother played the first Ophelia on an American stage, in a city (Boston) not only where Poe was himself born but also where stands (still! really there!) a House of Usher. And they also learned that Poe's Russian translator Vladimir Pyast went stark raving mad in a St. Petersburg theatre while reciting Poe's "Ulalume" (Davenport got *this* tidbit from a poem by Osip Mandelstam). The lecture enacts a version of the Herakleitian insight that (to quote Davenport's own translation, *Her* 18) "the most beautiful order of the world is still a random gathering of things insignificant of themselves," by retrieving for our delight the forgotten or (which is nearly the same thing) holding up for our attention the familiar. For we all know – we learned it in school – about Attar of Roses, a perfumed oil; and at the very least we might guess about orchards. Which is why the schoolboy Poe could write "perfumed seas," a phrase which has been called silly. "What I do," Davenport is fond of saying, "is very simple." He is an attentive reader who trusts the writer to know what he is doing. One of his specialities is to take up the well known or the intellectually or aesthetically unfashionable, and look at it again, afresh, clearly: He is an unprejudiced reader. In *The Geography of the Imagination* he has an astonishing little piece on Joyce Kilmer's "Trees."

After hearing the lecture, it may have come as a surprise to read, in "Finding," of Davenport's "severe compartmentalization of ideas" as a child: "school was school, as church was church and houses were houses. What went on in one never overflowed into any other." And the habit persists. "To this day I paint in one part of my house, write in another; read, in fact, in two others: frivolous and delicious reading such as Simenon and Erle Stanley Gardner in one room, scholarship in another" (*Geog* 361, 363, 364). The inhabitant of this highly compartmentalised house specialises above all else in making connections: Many of his essays and pretty well all of his stories proceed the way poems or collages proceed – through apparently random and arbitrary juxtaposition. "The house That Jack Built," his 1975 Yale lecture on Pound, juggles Ruskin,

Joyce, Williams, Olson, Yeats, Tchelitchew, Zukofsky, Queen Victoria, the Wright Brothers and the history of early flight, Henry James, Brancusi, Homer, and – at last! – Ezra Pound. With characteristic disingenuousness Davenport says "my best hope was to keep lots of chaff in the air all the way through" (21 May 1979). In fact it proceeds by ideogrammic method, careful juxtaposition making comparison possible; it is analogous to the methods and shares something of the aims of the *annales* group of historians like Braudel. "Every evening I freak out on Fernand Braudel. Last night I understood, really understood, what the Baroque is. By page 800 the elements for understanding are all there. Lordy, what a book!" (14 October 1977). In the *ABC of Reading* Ezra Pound called this the "method of contemporary biologists" and cited Louis Agassiz.[4] Guy Davenport's first published book is an anthology with commentary of the writings of Louis Agassiz. It came out in 1967 and is (predictably) not only scarce but expensive.[5]

Making connections. The habit and impulse of Davenport's mind is to knock down barriers (taxonomies, ideologies) by means of verbal/visual play and startling juxtapositions through which the world as ordinarily conceptualised and organised is freshly perceived. There is, that is to say, a strongly sensory and indeed sensual element, and the questions he asks cut across the ones we are used to. They drive towards particulars: How many great works were made by someone over eighty? Which English poets had bad eyes? They are versions of the Herakleitian question (Davenport's version, *Her* 28): "Except for what things would we never have heard the word justice?", which strikes at our assumptions about the world and forces us to go and look at it closely, to go and find out. It is a teacher's question. He is alert to pun, overlap, similarity and difference, minute detail. "Have you ever noticed the words *eye* and *ear* overlapping and dissolved in the second and third words of *Hugh Selwyn Mauberley?*" (21 December 1978). And he enjoins us to be the same. *DA Vinci*'s Bicycle by Guy *DAV*enport. Rhymes.

There used to be a quiz programme on English television (perhaps there still is) in which viewers sent in artefacts which a panel would then "read" and identify: this kind of mark can only have been made with a steel chisel; feature *X* is a result of *Y* technology, hence there was *Z* knowledge. It is a skill such archaeologists as Marshack especially cultivate. Ezra Pound thought "an expert, looking at a painting . . . , should be able to determine the degree of the tolerance of usury in the society in which it was painted"[6] – an awesome feat, even to the initiated. The expertise would tax a team of experts. Looking at Guy Davenport tackle Grant Wood's *American Gothic* is awesome indeed: It is as though, if not that team of experts, then at the very least someone like Braudel were examining not a society but a cultural iconology; Pound's injunction is being taken seriously, and I would call it a *tour de force* did not that label so readily imply a one-shot performance. *The Geography of the Imagination* – the whole book, not just the lecture – made up as it is of writings for a variety of purposes and for different audiences and occasions, is a model for those who would like to know what skills are required. At the risk of sounding like an unbearable Enthusiast, let me list them, for they tell us something of Davenport's resources, just as the essays and stories tell us something of his passions and concerns, just as the form of his writings tells us something of his habits of mind and perception.

Obviously, a good *memory*. And, with it, good *lists:* Davenport characteristically works out of up to eight journal-notebooks. Otherwise, how can you discern that the temptation of St. Antony has its place not only in a discussion of Joyce but of Eudora Welty; how else can you briefly sketch literary and graphic treatments of the subject from Flaubert through Tchelitchew and beyond? Hence, and closely related to memory, a knowledge of *history*. Or rather, of histories of all sorts. Who stayed in what hotel; what was the first painting of a man wearing spectacles; what is the first English poem to mention Cro-Magnon polychromatic paintings (it is a sonnet, by Wordsworth); what was the first American factory and who built it where, with what knowledge; who made shirt buttons out of Mississippi fresh-water mussels. On Page 262 of *The Geography of the Imagination* there is a succinct history of symbols and *symbolisme* to bolster an aside that Joyce is the first writer since Dante whose symbols are transparent on the page; on Page 25, of the lute and its transformations in Cubism, in Conan Doyle, in Rilke, and in de Nerval, to illustrate a remark about Roderick Usher; and on Page 15, of the egg-and-dart design, from the Biblical Edom to the American Midwest in the 1930s. *The Geography of the Imagination,* from one end to the other, points to or traces the movement of objects, ideas, and myths across geographical and cultural boundaries (hence its title), and takes in its purview the history of everyday objects, design, art, mythology, literature. So, too, the resources include *etymology* (which is another form of history), called upon for example to explicate "solicit" in an essay on Joyce, and *natural history* ("a boar is never 'at bay'," Davenport reproves a translator of Homer: "he attacks from the beginning"). And there is the matter of rhymes.

Davenport has a keen eye for recurrences of one sort or another, usually unexpected: "funerary chaos among American men of letters," for example (*Geog* 81), or the Hotel Albert, where Albert Pinkham Ryder painted in poverty upstairs whilst (according to one of Ford Madox Ford's anecdotes) Walt Whitman downstairs begged for a dollar. "American culture," comments Davenport, "has the eerie habit of passing itself, in narrow corridors, ghostlike" (*Geog* 77). Or (and this is from his notebook, as recorded in *Vort*) that the machinegun that killed Gaudier-Brzeska at Neuville-St.-Vaast on 5 June 1915 also killed the young De Launay, "the anthropologist who had begun a brilliant study of labyrinths." Such rhymes often form the basis of his fiction, where they become rather more speculative. In "1830" (*Tat!*), for example, a story that takes at face value Poe's claim that he went to St. Petersburg to enlist with some Russians in the fight for Greek independence, "the room where the Prince of Tavris was talking with Poe, who does not identify himself because he had no identity at that time, is the room where Lenin met the first Communist Congress after the Revolution" (*Vort* 9). Here the rhyme has a thematic function, though it also serves, as such rhymes customarily do in his fiction, a structural purpose. "The Aeroplanes at Brescia" (*Tat!*), Davenport's first story since undergraduate days (written when he was forty-three: As I noted, he is a late starter), rhymes the events of a single year (1909) when Kafka published an account (*his* first story, and hence *another* rhyme, this time with Davenport – it's irrelevant that Kafka's account was factual) of the airshow at Brescia, which Wittgenstein might well have gone to, working as he then was at Glossop airstation on the torque of the propeller. "History is not linear," Davenport says (*Geog* 67), and he collects such data, and especially dates, much as others collect baseball statistics. In proposing that Kafka saw and nearly met Wittgenstein early in this century, before either of them was anybody (they had no identity at that time), Davenport is sounding a recurrent motif. "The Trees at Lystra" (*Ecl*) recounts the story (Acts 14:6–20) of Paul and Barnabas, taking part in a myth before it *was* a myth, while it was still going on and hence before either of them was anybody. The protagonists of such stories act entirely without pretension, wholly unself-consciously (a fact that tempts the careless reader to see the stories as slightly precious), and we are reminded through such fiction of the factual everyday world out of which myths arose, and in which their materials originated. Such stories (and indeed much of Davenport's fiction) work like little essays that reintroduce to us the familiar and taken-for-granted world of cultural beliefs, and make us see it new.

These stories, and the elements making them up, are given to the reader with great panache; Davenport is above all an enthusiastic enquiring man, possessed of gusto and *wit*. He can pack what his accurate eye observes into a single adjective ("the unresonating mind of Edmund Wilson"); he can acutely characterise the work of Robert Lowell into a sentence that every student of American poetry should be *made* to read: "He is a thoughtful, serious, melancholy academic poet; if he is representative of anything beyond himself, it is of a broody school of professor –poets whose quiet, meticulous verse is perhaps the lineal and long-winded descendant of the cross-stitch sampler." The paragraph before the one in which this sentence occurs on Page 133 of *The Geography of the Imagination* is devastating, as is the passionate essay from which it comes, "Do You Have a Poem Book on E.E. Cummings?" (I might add that "The Anthropology of Table Manners from Geophagy Onward" is simply hilarious). Sometimes the writing approaches aphorism in pointing to a rhyme: "Ovid studied men turning into animals; Darwin, animals into man" (*Geog* 245). Davenport is a student of metamorphosis.

To say this is to point to one of two threads that run persistently through *The Geography of the Imagination:* the historical and geographical metamorphosis of myth – myth which is a pattern rather than a script, myth which is a behaviour, where "divergent and unsuspected features . . . fit in the same contours" (*Geog* 263). The clearest statement of this theme is in the title essay, and in the essay on Eudora Welty, which George Steiner has called "one of the finest analyses available of Miss Welty's guarded but compassionate art."[7] The other thread is the theme of the archaic. "If we have had a renaissance in the twentieth century," Davenport says, "it has been a renaissance of the archaic" (*Geog* 20); "what is most modern in our time frequently turns out to be the most archaic" (*Geog* 21). He proposes that "irrevocably alienated" from the past, "we *romantically* suppose man to have lived more harmoniously and congenially with his gods and with nature," and that the best artists of our time are those who performed "the great feat of awakening an archaic *sense of* the world" (*Geog* 27, emphases added).

There is at times in Davenport's prose an impatience, crustiness, and cynicism reminiscent of the Diogenes he has translated so well. "Nothing characterizes the twentieth century more than its inability to pay attention to anything for more than a week," he says in one of four essays devoted to Ezra Pound (*Geog* 172); and in one on Osip Mandelstam he calls it "the most miserable of ages since the Barbarians poured into Rome" (*Geog* 306). In the *New York Times Book Review* (6 September 1981) Hilton Kramer, conveniently ignoring those words *romantically* and *sense* which I italicised, attacks Davenport for appearing "to share with the master [i.e., Ezra Pound] an implacable hostility to modern society and a corollary myopia in the realm of politics." He completely misses the point. Davenport's hostility is a lament for the death not simply of the city (we are "all gypsies and barbarians camping in the ruins" – *Geog* 19) but of the *idea* of city, a local place where men and women gather in sanctuary, rest after odyssey, live in families; where flower is married to stone, and where in harmony one mind may share its understanding with another; a place of sensibility and education, where one lives and is aware of an order; the home of civilisation and of culture, the centre of historic continuity. He calls it "the unit of civilisation" and reminds us that the ancients depicted their cities on their coins as a goddess crowned with battlements (*Geog* 19). Davenport's hostility arises from the perception (which was also Louis Agassiz's) that the notion of human progress is, to put it mildly, "a complex, self-deluding idea" (*Geog* 354):

> Man, it would seem, does not evolve, he accumulates. His fund of advantages over nature and over the savage within is rich indeed, but nothing of the old Adam has been lost; our savagery has perhaps increased in meanness and fury; it stands out more terribly against a modern background. (*Geog* 67)

Ours is an age that neglects its artists, and denies that there is such a thing as a life of the mind.

Hence Davenport's praise of "an archaic *sense of* the world" (which I take to be distinct from "the archaic world"): Archaic man lived in "a world totally alive, a world in which one talks to bears and reindeer, like the Laplander, or to Coyote, the sun and moon, like the plains Indian" (*Geog* 26–7). In "The Symbol of the Archaic" he points to "the bisque-coloured, black-maned prancing tarpan of Lascaux, the very definition of Archaic painting," which was painted "in the deep dark of a cave by torchlight, an uncertainty to the man or woman who painted it" (*Geog* 22).

In 1957, lecturing at the National Gallery of Art in Washington, D. C., Siegfried Giedeon equated the end of the paleolithic era with man's declaration of himself as master of the universe, and noted that a dominant sense of the vertical then replaced the "absolute freedom of direction" in archaic art: "The space conception of primeval art is perhaps the most revealing trait of the conception of the oneness of the world: a world of unbroken interrelation, where everything is in association, where the sacred is inseparable from the profane."[8] To the untutored eye, such paintings are crude, flat cartoons, misproportioned, perspectiveless, incomplete. Our sense of *completeness* demands the separation of one object from another, one experience from another, their isolation from perceived continuities of time and space; *perspective* demands a focus of attention on hierarchies of values. Together, they assume that the universe is not only knowable but *known*. Louis Zukofsky[9] attacked Shakespeare's critics for claiming to know more about Shakespeare and his intentions than did Shakespeare himself. As Davenport puts it in "Narrative Tone and Form," "perspective commits itself to one point of view" and "finishing involves a stupidity of perception" (*Geog* 312). Davenport, like Zukofsky, knows better: "no order in the universe can finally be seen order to *it*,"[10] and we must keep our options open. The logical mode for the expression of such ideas, the form, is collage, for collage resists finality, resists categories and the notion of completeness; it resists, that is to say, any theory that does not keep open the possibilities of meaning, and always keeps a firm eye on the world of perception before it heeds the erring brain.

This is a theme Davenport sounds again and again. "There are several maturations," he says in his essay on Agassiz (*Geog* 244), "not one final fructification." He is determined to resist any stasis of a systemic or more importantly a systematic articulation, for as he says "the way we live" is "an incoherent buzz of experience" (*Geog* 265). Following Wittgenstein (and Olson) he avers that the meaning of the world is outside the world (*Geog* 268). But we are in it, and it is essential that the mind remain curious. This is why so many of his stories are about people taking part in a myth before it *was* a myth, while it was still going on and thus before they were anybody.

Perspective and completeness demand a linear mindedness, and linear mindedness reduces the world to simple equations of cause and effect, value and money. Davenport's hostility to the twentieth century arises from his perception that in an industrial and technological age and culture the sciences "explain the mechanics of everything and the nature of nothing" (*Geog* 27), sundering the wholeness of the world into linear compartments. "The nineteenth century . . . put everything against the scale of time and discovered that all behaviour within time's monolinear progress was evolutionary" (*Geog* 151). As he told Catherine O'Neill in 1979, "no-one is monolinear,"[11] and it is a distortion of attention to treat them as if they were. The writers Davenport admires are like Joyce, whose "correspondences are not linear parallels; they are network" (*Geog* 290); like Pound, whose "restorations of relationships now thought to be discrete" close such gaps as those between mythology and botany (*Geog* 151); and like Olson, who saw that "a shift in attention lets the jungle in" (*Geog* 87). Civilisation is at best fragile: man's "advantages over his fellow creatures are all mechanical and therefore dependent on the education of each generation: meaning that an intervening generation of barbarians destroys all that has been carefully accumulated for centuries" (*Geog* 19). The line of distinction has been misdrawn, he says. "Redraw it to zone sensibility from barbarity" (*Geog* 238).

So the main activity of the writing is to shift the writing *back* again, to keep the jungle out. If metamorphosis and the archaic are two threads of *The Geography of the Imagination,* the prime activity of the book is retrieval: to restore what has been forgotten, to join what has been divided. To teach.

"I consider all my writing as extensions of the classroom," Davenport told *Contemporary Authors* in 1973; much of it clears the ground, shifts the focus. The essays and stories are alike acts of foraging, seeking connection: "it is the conjunction, not the elements, that creates a new light" (*Geog* 194). So Davenport proposes an idyllic world in the deep archaic past, which rests on attention, alertness, and *unselfconsciousness*. As Davenport draws him (and as we see him revived in the Adriaan van Hovendaal series of stories) archaic man was not the self-declared master of Nature, but a part of it, unreflective and unselfconscious; he owes something to the Samuel Butler of *Erewhon,* and he owes something to the notions of Charles Fourier. And above all, he is the figure of the artist.

> Art is the attention we pay to the wholeness of the world. Ancient intuition went foraging after consistency. Religion, science and art are alike rooted in the faith that the world is of a piece, that something is common to all its diversity, and that if we knew enough we could see and give a name to its harmony. (*Geog* 270)

An insistent note through the whole book is that the world is knowable if we but look, and imagination is but a way of seeing the world; metamorphic, "it makes up nothing" (*Geog* 193). It is no coincidence that Davenport's first published book was an anthology of writings by Louis Agassiz, who at the end of his life said that the ability to combine facts is a much rarer gift than to discern them, and whose knowledge was what Whitman sought for himself, encyclopaedic.

To summarise the book in this way is to do it grave injustice. *The Geography of the Imagination* is a book remarkably free of theoretical statements and of theories and systems, whether of art, writing, history, or culture. Like other Romantics of our time, Davenport seeks to change the way we see, to redeem our vision, but he does so through practice and example, not through theology. His language, marked though it may be with what George Steiner calls a "baroque, precious, crazily inventive" vocabulary, is completely free of fashionable jargon. Not only does he point to what he sees, but he does so in a way that resists generalisation, that avoids conclusions, and that parrots no critical schools or scholarly catchphrases. His essay on Olson ends approving Olson's refusal to "articulate images and events which can be left in free collision" (*Geog* 99).

Hence, the form of the writing is an enactment as well as an embodiment of vision. Packed with information, it demolishes customary boundaries between fact and fiction, between essay and story, between picture and language. "The Aeroplanes at Brescia" started out as a research essay on Kafka. The story 'Tatlin!' itself was originally . . . a kind of plan for a history-of-art book" (*Vort* 3). The first sentence of "Au Tombeau de Charles Fourier" is a drawing of Gertrude Stein at the wheel of her T-model Ford, and the last is a drawing he identified in a letter as the earliest known mask of Dionysos, from Hauran (3 July 1979) – it is the earliest known example of the actor's mask. Reviewing Alexander Marshack's *The Roots of Civilization,* Davenport observed that "when language emerges, the verb *to draw* is the same as the verb *to write*" (*Geog* 64; Davenport's emphasis); all his stories are written as though they were drawn, and hence call attention to themselves as *made* works. The drawings that accompany the stories and are to be read as part of the text are often copies of photographs and are to be understood as quotations, as pictorial allusions rather than pictorial facts, as quotations of ready-mades. So a note in *Da Vinci's Bicycle* tells us that the final paragraphs of "Au Tombeau de Charles Fourier" are by Gertrude Stein; a note in *Ecloques* that "The Daimon of Socrates" is a "kind of translation" of Plutarch, with added quotations from other sources.

These are erudite and bookish stories, then, and they have been assembled or composed as much as they have been written. "My writing unit is such that I start literally with scraps of paper and pages from notebooks," he told Barry Alpert. "Every sentence is written by itself; there are very few consecutive sentences in my work. . . . The actual writing of any of the stories in *Tatlin!* was a matter of turning back and forth in a notebook and finding what I wanted" (*Vort* 5). Even the sentences themselves, indeed, are assembled. "A Field of Snow on a Slope of the Rosenberg" (*Da V'sB*), for example, opens with one of Davenport's extravaganza sentences – those sentences meant, he told me (3 July 1979), "to be what Ives called the God Damns in his music." It is worth quoting in full:

> For a man who had seen a candle serenely burning inside a beaker filled with water, a fine spawn of bubbles streaming upward from its flame, who had been present in Zurich when Lenin with closed eyes and his thumbs hooked in the armholes of his waistcoat listened to the baritone Gusev singing on his knees Dargomyzhsky's *In Church We Were Not Wed,* who had conversed one melancholy afternoon with Manet's Olympia speaking from a cheap print I'd thumbtacked to the wall between a depraved adolescent girl by Egon Schiele and an oval mezzotint of Novalis, and who, as I had, Robert Walser of Biel in the canton of Bern, seen Professor William James talk so long with his necktie in the soup that it functioned as a wick to soak his collar red and cause a woman at the next table to press her knuckles into her cheeks and scream, a voyage in a hot-air balloon at the mercy of the winds from the lignite-rich hills of Saxony Anhalt to the desolate sands of the Baltic could precipitate no new shiver from my paraphenomenal and kithless epistemology except the vastation of brooding on the sweep of inconcinnity displayed below me like a map and perhaps acrophobia. (*Da V'sB* 149)

Davenport's speciality as a critic is in finding out how things break down into their components, in noticing how they are put together. This sentence, he told me (3 July 1979), is built thus:

image of candle burning in water: from Ernst Mach (a dream he had, opining on waking that it was a profound meditation on the unbelievable fact that water is two atoms of hydrogen and one of oxygen, gasses that love to burn)
Lenin in Zurich: from Valentinov's memoir of Lenin (who wrote a book against Mach and Avenarius, whom, as he admitted, he had not read: purest idiocy – Valentinov was a Menshevik; his study of Mach must therefore, by political argument, be anathema to Bolsheviks, and Mach is still banned in the USSR)
Manet's Olympia: from a newspaper feuilleton by Walser
Schiele and Novalis: put in as likely by GD, a guess
Wm James and the soup: made up
the balloon trip: described by Chris Middleton.
Note that bubbles in line 2 have become one big balloon bubble.

Davenport's prose is crafted as carefully as verse, as carefully as his drawings. In this long ideogrammic sentence, built like the opening of an epic with its long delay of the main clause, the details whilst we wait for the main point are so many, crowding one after another in subordinate clause after subordinate clause, that our experience reading it is very like that of reading a list – almost a lyric catalogue. It is entirely in keeping with the idiom and syntax of poetry in our time: though the subordinating (hypotactic) syntax is perfectly straightforward, leading to "the voyage could precipitate no new shiver" as the main clause, and culminating in the bathetic "acrophobia," the subordinated matter is as important as the main clause, if not more, and thus ceases to be subordinate, and the overall syntactic effect is paratactic: the syntax of juxtaposition. Playing on our expectations, the anticipated climactic "I, Robert Walser" is appositionally related to the "who" of the first line and hence subordinated to the voyage – although the preceding hundred or more words point to the speaker as centre of perception – and its climactic effect is diffused by the paratactic addition of apparently incidental details. The data in the sentence are held in the mind in an equivalence of value; the relations of cause and effect are suspended, replaced by the experience of addition, and we are thereby enjoined to contemplate the writing as surface, as writing texture, rather than as a vehicle of conceptually ordered information or as narrative. It is a form of writing closely analogous to the surface deployment of objects, images, and materials in collage (or more precisely, in *assemblage*), and occurs on the larger scale of the whole work, as well as in the sentence.

"Au Tombeau de Charles Fourier," for instance, appeared in the *Georgia Review* (Winter 1975) divided into thirty-three unnumbered sections which ranged in length from 1 paragraph (a fourteen-word sentence) to 24 or more paragraphs, all indented; each section treats or draws upon a single subject matter: wasps, the early history of flight, Dogon cosmology, Gertrude Stein in Paris, whatever. When he prepared the typescript for *Da Vinci's Bicycle,* however, Davenport reordered his materials (sometimes, especially in the last half, extensively), cut, expanded, compressed, and recombined portions of the earlier version into a sequence of 255 unindented paragraphs, divided among thirty numbered sections. Except for Section 10, which is 1 paragraph long (the same fourteen-word sentence of the earlier version: "What works in the angle succeeds in the arc and holds in the chord" – which sounds like and possibly is a bit of Fourier's "calculus"), and in the final section, 30 (which is 2 paragraphs long – the second is one sentence), each section of the story consists of 9 four-line paragraphs. When the typescript was first sent to Johns Hopkins Press, all the lines in each paragraph were the same length, so that the words on the page looked like a series of bricks, each the same size and shape, each approximately the same (visual) texture. The shift from typescript to print changed that, of course (since the paragraphs were no longer the same length), but the overall effect – a series of building blocks, evenly spaced – persists in the published version. It is a device Davenport has used since, notably in the *Granta* version of "Fifty-Seven Views of Fujiyama" with a separate page for each paragraph,[12] and in "On Some Lines of Virgil" (*Ecl* 147–238). Among other things, it draws attention to the writing as a made thing, and to the manner of the making. Here is a paragraph from section 26 of "Au Tombeau de Charles Fourier" as it appears in *Da Vinci's Bicycle:*

> The center of the earth is the crabgrass seed. Balance of quinces, basket of oranges. Alice, tell me, tell me, Alice, how so settled a soul as I can be so giddy about *la gloire.* About what? says Alice. *La gloire.* You have it, says Alice, whatever it is.

In the *Georgia Review* the first of these sentences finished up a section devoted to Dogon cosmology, and "Balance of quinces" began the next, devoted to Gertrude Stein. The effect in the revised version is to dissolve the boundaries between the two making a sort of paratactic *apo koinou* working among sentences: the quinces and oranges can easily enough be read as part of the Dogon material, and to read it thus would not be a misreading. For the visual uniformity of the surface, making everything equivalent in the pattern of the composition, not only distances the reader from the materials themselves and their customary significance, but also dislocates the narrative. The juxtapositions of which this text is built are thereby rendered both obvious and yet fluid, uncertain, ambiguous, bordering on indeterminacy. One text merges with another in no identifiably causative way, for the uniformity of surface renders the perception of cause – which in more conventional work is heralded by the conventions of paragraph and chapter divisions – irrelevant even if possible. It is a visual flattening of surface, and it renders that surface opaque, and thus the writing draws attention to itself as writing, as medium, in a manner directly analogous to that of Cubism. Cubism, art historians are fond of remarking, drew attention to the opaque surface the painting actually is by placing pictorial elements (such as line, colour, plane, texture) on a two-dimensional surface. In the words of Robert Rosenblum, Cubism obliterated depth by asserting "the radically new principle that the pictorial illusion takes place upon the physical reality of an opaque surface rather than behind the illusion of a transparent plane."[13]

Such attention to surface emphasises that the objects or elements of this composition have been lifted out of their ordinary context and are, in Max Ernst's phrase, "on a plane apparently not suited to them."[14] There are sixteen pen-and-ink drawings in "Au Tombeau de Charles Fourier," each of them a sentence in the text, thirteen of them taking up a whole page, many of them apparently random groupings of images. Pen, and ink. Writing materials. Rosalind Krauss has remarked that Picasso's reliefs do not present "a moment of organisation that lies *beyond* the surface of the object. . . . He insists that there is a logic *in* that surface and that conception arises with experience rather than prior to or apart from it,"[15] a comment analogous to Davenport's that "the contemporary is without meaning whilst it is happening" (*Geog* 56). The flat opacity of surface in stories like "Au Tombeau" draws the reader into the immediacy of the composition, and at the same time reminds the reader that much of the material, removed from its customary or anticipated context (an essay, say, or a textbook) is quotation. David Antin has observed that in putting "real" objects in collages, moving them from "normal" contexts, Cubists created a visual space that "no longer yielded an iconic representation, even of a fractured sort, though bristling with significations."[16] Conception (and hence, *perhaps* meaning, i.e., the possibility of meaning) arises with experience; but it is an experience of dislocated objects, each carrying its contextual residue, in juxtaposition; an experience, if you will, of quotations; and it is this that makes Davenport's work seem at times bookish, even precious on occasion. Certainly the residual context carried by the "real" object, by the ready-made, by the quotation, has an effect in fiction similar to that of the Cubist "interplay between pictorial illusion and pictorial fact."[17] The writing demands both alertness (hence thought) and recognition (hence memory).

In a characteristically disingenuous response to a question about the form of his fiction, Davenport told Barry Alpert:

> If you're a teacher, you're constantly working with diverse materials. You may get up in the morning and you've got Keats's *Odes* to take some sophomores through, and you've got a chapter of

> *Ulysses* for your graduate students, and the mind gets in the habit of finding cross-references among subjects. This is the best way in the world to make my *assemblages,* as I call them. I don't think I've ever written a story. . . . [But] it looks pretentious to call them *assemblages,* which is a French word and taken from art history. (*Vort* 3)

If my description of "Au Tombeau de Charles Fourier" is at all accurate, then we must take Davenport at his word; it is indeed an assemblage. "Au Tombeau" started out as an attempt to get into English the information (about the Dogon) in Griaule's *Le Renard Pâle,* and from this he took a single idea, that "man is a kind of forager in an unknown universe." The other materials clustered around this central notion. "Nature's great forager is the wasp" (Davenport had been reading Spradbery's book on wasps);[18] Gertrude Stein riding in her T-model Ford is "something like a wasp out foraging"; Picasso is a kind of forager, "a kind of wasp as it were." Reading a book about the Wright brothers he "realized that what the Wright brothers had done was make a mechanical wasp, or bee. It's an insect, not a bird." All the elements in the story are examples of foraging: "Ogo the desert fox, which the Dogon feel is the very essence of the universe." And finally, as Davenport told Alpert, "there's the figure 8 to hold things together: everybody moves in a figure 8 the way a wasp flies. . . . I put them together without any hope that anybody would see this, or see how it fits together" (*Vort* 6). So what does it all mean? Like Ezra Pound in *Gaudier-Brzeska,* Davenport rejects "an ascribed or intended meaning";[19] as he wrote to me (3 July 1979), "What I'm writing *about* (you make your guess) is a pretty question. I trust to my instincts, but will find out one of these days." Conception arising with experience, then, and writing/composition as discovery.

*Assemblage* as a term in art history was devised by Jean Dubuffet in August 1953 to distinguish this kind of art, which fits together parts and pieces, from *collage* (literally pasting, sticking, gluing), a term he would reserve for the work of 1910–20. What is most striking about *assemblage* (besides, frequently, its three-dimensionality) is that its raw materials are often associationally powerful, almost always ready made, and *identifiable* (nails, dolls' eyes, photographs, dried flowers, old wood). That is to say, they retain much of their previous history (their contextual residue); it is also to say, in the words of one critic, that (compared to *collage*) "its ultimate configurations are so often less predetermined."[20] The interpolation of non-art material, indeed the exclusive use of such material, provides what art historians have come to call a "frame," by means of which no attempt is made to represent anything, but the actuality of "the world" is permitted to erupt within the environment of the work, and the boundaries between objects, categories, and activities dissolve. As Leo Steinberg has observed of the painting of Robert Rauschenberg, "the painted surface is no longer the analogue of a visual experience of nature but of operational process," and the work ends up as "a verification of its own experience."[21]

Davenport told *Contemporary Authors* in 1973 that his politics are "democrat and conservative." "It will be the business of literature and the arts to contain and transmit what culture survives the century. If any," he has said.[22] A tall order. *Collage* and *assemblage* are means of making art hold more different kinds of reality, and Davenport's contribution to the art of fiction may be that he has found, in *assemblage,* a means of informing the reader – in-forming the reader. Characteristically, he calls himself a "primitive." Yet the intelligence which drives through the writing, and which indeed makes the writing at all possible, insists – and here is the conservative – that one work within one's limitations, work with what one's got. Georges Braque once remarked that "Cubism . . . is a means . . . of putting painting within the range of my talents." It is not, I think, pressing too hard to suggest that *assemblage* is a means of putting fiction within the range of Davenport's.

# 13

# *And The Without*

## *An Interpretive Essay on Susan Howe*

*How do I exist in a language that doesn't want me to exist, or makes me exist as a fiction, as* la femme?

Nicole Brossard[1]

There's a deceptively literary or bookish flavour about Susan Howe's work, especially at the beginning of many of her sequences and books, prefaced as they often are with a quotation or quotations (e.g., *Hinge Picture, Articulation of Sound Forms in Time*); or opening with lines that have the feel of quotations, unmarked and unacknowledged, though the words may actually be Howe's (e.g., "Thorow"); or opening with a directly identified one.[2] Often, as in the case of *Cabbage Gardens* or *The Liberties,* the poem responds to the challenge explicit or implicit in the quotation, debunking or deconstructing the assumptions underlying and/or the circumstances giving rise to the words quoted. *Cabbage Gardens* is prefaced with Samuel Johnson deriding the notion of poems about cabbages whilst playing with the notion that the cultivation of the cabbage marks the history of civilization. *The Liberties* gives us Jonathan Swift writing the personal "little language" of the *Journal to Stella,* his writings to her preserved ("so adieu deelest MD MD MD FW FW Me Me / Fais I don't conceal a bitt. as hope sav'd"), hers to him destroyed, prefacing a poem that, in passionate rage, retrieves Hester Johnson (Stella) from her "liquidation."[3] Insofar as these works are bookish, they are revisionist. This is true, too, of those more explicitly radical works that seek to revise our notions of the world, and that are prefaced by quotation, such as *Articulation of Sound Forms in Time* and "The Captivity and Restoration of Mrs. Mary Rowlandson." I read the last-named work as a poem, for its direction is determined, much as the direction of Howe's astonishing *My Emily Dickinson* is determined, by her reading of language as an emblematic collection of signs, potential meanings, abbreviations, wonders, and terrors to which she is subject rather than of which she is "master." As George Butterick has observed, Howe "is another argument for the late start, like Olson," for "she does not make her earliest appearance with relatively predictable work, and then markedly develop from there."[4] I would add that her work is, too, all of one piece: It all makes one work, one life, one poem, but carrying with it a multiplicity of works, lives, poems.

It is in these terms that I take as thoroughly representative of Howe's writing the eight-poem sequence "Scattering as Behavior toward Risk," collected in *Singularities.* The first poem begins with an identified quotation from an American literary "classic" and the last ends with the words, significantly in upper case, "THE REVISER." The sequence itself is a further instalment in Howe's radical reassessment of canonical notions of history and of language, of patriarchal notions of women and of power and of truth. While her reassessment and indeed her poetics, rejecting the possibility of definitive statement, invite elliptical commentary (if they invite commentary at all), there are indeed identifiable and even definable concerns and themes recurring throughout Howe's work. I think that the great energy of Howe's writing arises from a series of tensions, between the more-or-less explicit themes and subject matter of the work, and the unstated verbal and schematic activity of the poem (between the algorhythmic and the heuristic might be one way to put it); between Howe's enchanted fascination with and desperate possession by history and with language, and her intense desire to be free of them; between her desire for the secure, the stable, and the defined, and her apprehension of them as essentially false; between her impassioned attraction to, and sheer terror of, the wilderness. What I offer is only *one* way of reading Howe. Here is the opening poem of "Scattering as Behavior toward Risk":

"on a [*p* < suddenly . . . on a > was shot thro with a dyed → < dyed → a soft]"*
(became the vision)(the rea) after Though [though]That
Fa

But what is envy [but what is envy]
Is envy the bonfire inkling?

Shackles [ (shackles) ] as we were told the . . . [precincts]

---

*_Billy Budd:_ The Genetic Text

In the course of the following pages, my remarks are largely confined to the opening three lines.

Bluntly uncompromising and problematic, the opening line emphatically and unabashedly draws attention to itself as text, as written rather than spoken language, indifferent to the reader. How, after all, can one voice this unfamiliar and cluttered-looking notation: Is it musical, with its *p*, its greater-than/less-than brackets? Is it conventional American–English literary orthography, with its quotation marks, lower-case beginning, square brackets, italics, elision marks, and asterisk? What are we to make of those arrows? Surely this is a code, though we cannot recognise which one: a computer text, perhaps? Voiced or not, it proceeds in bits and pieces, stops and starts, repeats. Problematic, and emphatically for the eye. So uncompromisingly is it removed from the forms and modes of "normal" discourse that there is a haze of uncertainty, what Howe elsewhere calls "a halo of wilderness" ("Illogic"), thrown about the line. We know – or at any rate trust – that it's verse, the look of the page tells us that, but how can we possibly voice it, how does one bit lead to the next? Are we to read "suddenly . . . on a" as grammatical subject to the verb "was shot"? What sorts of relationships are these, in this asyntactic writing? That "suddenly . . . on a" has something of the air of quick instruction on how to voice the first two words, and that closing "soft" looks like an echo, especially if we read the italicised *p* as *piano* (another voicing instruction). "Shot through with a dyed – [pause?] – dyed –": like shot silk, then? or to do with death? We do not know what we see, for we do not recognise it. (Yet we do know, of course. But there are no customary meanings here – or seem to be very few.)

The second line is similarly difficult, with its offbeat spacing, its variety of parentheses, its (apparently) fragmentary word/s, its use of upper case, and its equally problematic syntax. It's almost as though the notational system is continually being pushed (is falling?) off balance, subverting convention, undermining itself: The paired parentheses look like the mathematical notation for multiplication (and why are the *round* brackets such latecomers on the parenthetical scene?); the square brackets pushing that word "though" tight against "That" do not seem to be used the way they were in line 1; the large gap after "Though" comes as a welcome break for the eye after the headlong crowded impetus of the first line (the arrows forwarding, forwarding), but is difficult to interpret (a new breath? a second thought?). Parentheses and spacing mark words off into groups while signalling a tentative uncertain quality to them, and suggesting that the movement of thought in this writing need not necessarily be progress. Semantic grounds shift: "became" means turned into? Was fitting? Syntax continues to break down (*what* "became the vision"?) and indeed extends into the fragmenting and fracturing of words ("rea"; "[though]That"). The second line, like the first, gives us small islands of localised meaning, a haze of uncertain stumbling bursting into pockets of lucidity, clearings in the thicket, the movement toward coherence ("became the vision") shifting instantly to fragmentation and incompleteness ("the rea"), the lines diminishing down to the initial and terminal fragment "Fa" of line 3. Far? Father? Fate? The uncertain context makes all three (and a lot of others) possible, and the fragment suggests they might all be under erasure. It is worth recalling, though, that *Fa* is, according to both the *Oxford English Dictionary* and the *Century*, a musical term (the fourth note of the octave) – so the lines sing a diminishing music? The same sources tell us that *Fa* is an obsolete word for *few* and for *foe,* as well as Scottish for *fall*. If the word is complete, it is no less uncertain.

What is remarkable is not simply that the notation for the eye plays against and with that for the ear, but that moving toward fracture and fragment the syntax and the diction move also toward completion. The "rea" in line two invites us to read "Though" as similarly "incomplete," especially after the abbreviation "thro" in line one, yielding "thought" – an invitation reinforced by what comes next, the close-packed "[though]That" (a kind of *apo koinou* at the level of the letter). This itself gives rise to a rather complicated little movement in which, rhyming "thro" in line 1 with the "though" of line 2, the ear, reminded of Robert Duncan's habit of spelling "thought" *thot,* proposes a rhyme between the putative "Though[t] though" of line 2 with the "shot thro" of line 1. The ear hears what the eye does not see, and the movement of the poem depends upon and is a response to the shifts and uncertainties in the language.

So the lines are packed with transformations, and we see how, amid and because of the uncertainties, language generates text, the poem generates itself. The sheer closeness of the sets of parentheses incorporates the Rea(l) into the vision, making it vision*ary*. And what follows? another fairly dense play, this time predominantly semantic/lexical – "after Though." The upper case on "Though" makes it seem an afterthought, a substitution for "after," which immediately suggests (if we had not seen this already) that in these lines we are privy to the processes of writing, the processes of composition, the processes of *thought* – a word remarkable in these lines for its absence. As a conjunction or as an adverb expressing contrast (but here syntactically it seems to work as a noun?) *though* manifests thought – and after a gap, a pause (for thought?), the terminal group in the line emerges: "though[that]": *that,* deictic, pointing, a gesture toward the concrete object – or, as the *Century* dictionary says of *real,* "always importing the existent." So the last two words (one word?) of the line bring together the insubstantial/ nonmaterial (thought) and the actual/material (thing). The last two words bring together, then, enact, the vision and the real, the perceived and the thought.

"Fa" is a crux, encapsulating as it does the fracture and fragmentation of language in the very act of moving toward completion. Howe's work, from the very title of her first book (*Hinge Picture*) on, treads borders, boundaries, dividing lines, edges, invisible meeting points. Her language returns to such cusps again and again, for they mark extremities, turning points, limits, shifts, the nameless edge of mystery where transformations occur and where edge becomes centre. Hope Atherton, in *Articulation of Sound Forms in Time,* moves from the centre to the margin, to the wilderness, and (like Mary Rowlandson) thus marginalises the centre. "Extremities. Paths lost found forgotten. Border margin beginning. Birth/ Death. Inside/Outside. She/He. Moving/Staying. Finding/Losing" ("Armantrout" 209). Kings, Howe tells us in *My Emily Dickinson,* ruled by "divinely ordained decree, the allegorical point where God, the State, and human life met" (81), and King Lear "rashly gave his world away. Balance, confusion, naming, transformation –. Arrived at the point of initiation, stopped at the moment of conversion, instinct draws up short" (114). Mary Rowlandson, at sunrise "on a day of calamity, at the inverted point of antitypical history, looks out at the absence of Authority and sees we are all alone" (*CMR* 115). A cusp, where two curves meet and stop. Or do they. At the point where one realm meets another there is a crossover. And the great crossover place is language, always "at the blind point between what is said and meant" (*MyED* 82), always at the blind point between the static authority of name and the fluidity of nameless object. Language, moving toward definition, moving toward name, moving toward Authority, toward the arbitrary, toward Power, toward Noun, to assert control: "it was the primordial Adam to whom God gave the power of naming." But a world without names? "In the brave new world of Death there are no names" ("Armantrout" 211). Emily Dickinson and Emily Bronte entice Howe "away from comprehension to incommunicable mystery that may be essential harmony or most appalling anarchy" ("Women" 63). Mystery is nameless, incommunicable, pathless, wild, but irresistible. "Artists bow to no order" ("Olson" 6).

Hence the text is uncertain, indefinite; it resists description. How many words are there in line 2? How many groups? How many languages? Is "rea" a word? If "rea" is conventionally incomplete, is "Though"? If "though" is complete, is "rea"? You will not find *rea* in the *Oxford English Dictionary,* nor in the *Century.* But you will in Lewis and Short's *A Latin Dictionary.* It is a juridical word:

> I. Originally, a party to an action (*res*), either plaintiff or defendant; afterwards restricted to the party accused, defendant, prisoner, etc. II. In the stricter sense. A. A party obliged or under obligation to

do or pay any thing, or answerable or responsible for any thing, a bondsman, a debtor; one who is bound by any thing, who is answerable for any thing, a debtor. B. One who is accused or arraigned, a defendant, prisoner, a criminal, culprit.[5]

And it is *feminine,* a woman. *Rea* is also, as readers of Williams's *Paterson* find out, a Spanish word for whore. What vision what perception of women is this? Howe's poem is packed with transformations indeed, and the transformations are wrought by the apparent disorder of the language, the very irrationality of the text, out of which possible figurations and configurations of meaning emerge.

Unparaphraseable, these lines seem to register a process of perception and thought subject perpetually and continuously to re-casting, re-seeing, re-vision. They register a process of cogitating, meditating and exploring an old enigma, endemic perhaps to all human culture but especially acute in the history of New England, perpetually evoked and invoked by the complex of the known and the unknown, the seen and the unseen, the cultivated and the wild: The relations between the real and the visionary. Hesitant, seeking certitude and clarity, rejecting them as impossible, the vision immediately corrected (?), re-seen, re-assigned, to the necessarily and perpetually incomplete real. Caught in the field as it is, caught in the field of language, thought can progress no Farther. Fa. The doubleness of the movement is a doubleness of desire. Clarity and definition of deixis, of pointing, of *the,* lead only to fracture in language. "The" revised, surrounded by a halo of wilderness.

But there is more. The asterisk at the end of line 1 points to a text that proceeds through a series of more or less minor surprises, lurching, hiccupping, stopping and starting, stuttering and stammering along, casting jerkily around for words: "*Billy Budd.* The Genetic Text."[6] Line 1 is a quotation, a found text. Not – as the footnote carefully keeps clear – Melville's, but a coded text recording Melville picking his way in stops and starts through the writing of *Billy Budd,* a text recording Harrison Hayford and Merton M. Sealts picking *their* way through the tangled manuscripts of *Billy Budd.* Decoding it, not knowing at any given moment whether the words we read will two words later be crossed out, perhaps only to be restored a couple of pen strokes later, we discern a text "criss-crossed with erasures and corrections" (as Susan Howe wrote of P. Inman's *Platin* [9]), a text so urgently stumbling almost blindly along through a mind-boggling series of tentative and at times almost desperate castings-about for words and phrases that we are caught up in the sheer suspense the *processes* of the telling generate, a stuttering narrative of inarticulation unspoken within the narrative.

Howe's first line comes from the top of a left-hand page of the book

(412) – it stretches from margin to margin – and is just the sort of line that might catch the casual eye – or at least Susan Howe's – casting through flipped pages, or drawing the sorts. Decoded, it says:

> "on a [cross out in pencil all the words from 'suddenly' to 'on a'; insert, above the line and with a caret, the words 'was shot thro with a dyed'; cross out with (the same?) pencil the word 'dyed' and insert, above the line, with a caret, the words 'a soft']."

The first line of Howe's poem then, decoded, tells us that Melville's manuscript looks (more or less) like this:

~~suddenly dyed by the sun behind~~<br>
~~approaching near the horizon, took~~<br>
a soft<br>
was shot thro with a ^ ~~dyed~~ glory<br>
~~on a~~<br>
^

Such a translation of Howe's first line, thus made more or less coherent ("with a a soft glory"?) and intelligible, does not get us very far (but where were we going?). The meaning of the line, as it appears in the Genetic Text of *Billy Budd,* seems to be nothing like its meaning in Howe's poem (meaning is a function of context). The asterisk points us explicitly to this text, and what we have is a poem which in the act of inviting translation/decoding denies it, at the same time asserting the primacy of context and drawing the reader's attention to the processes of (Howe's) writing as well as of her/his reading. What is on the page is what we see. Yet the word "suddenly," one of the words the code tells us is crossed out, is not otherwise in Howe's line: it is, that is to say, present in its erasure. We see it in its absence. We see what we do not see.

The context from which this line comes might help if we're looking for clarity (whatever that might be) in Howe's poem, looking for a way of sorting out the syntax, the code. The sentence from which this line comes does afford a clue as to where that "(became the vision)" in the second line might have come from, but on the whole the context is not especially enlightening if we're looking for some sort of definitive meaning for Howe's text. Melville is describing the precise moment at which Billy Budd, that young man with something of the feminine in him, that young man Captain Vere has already called "an Angel," is being hanged:

> At the same moment it chanced that the vapory fleece hanging low in the East was shot through with a soft glory as the fleece of the

> Lamb of God seen in mystical vision, and simultaneously therewith, watched by the wedge of upturned faces, Billy ascended; and, ascending, took the full rose of the dawn. (124)

But how much clarity does this provide? Hayford and Sealts, in their commentary, say that "as to the implications of this . . . passage the critics are in wide disagreement" and "draw opposite conclusions from the [same] evidence" (192). Readers cannot agree on the meaning of Melville's text, though all seem to agree not only that the sentence from which Howe's line comes is of crucial significance in the narrative of *Billy Budd* but also that *Billy Budd* itself is a crucially significant document in the American literary canon (significance is a function of context). The text of *Billy Budd* is bristling with (unspecified) significations, but we hardly needed Howe's poem to tell us that. Why then does line one point outside the poem to the Genetic Text of *Billy Budd?*

This is not an easy question, even if part of the answer is to rejoin that the footnote dissolves the distinctions between a world inside the poem and a world outside the poem. It points to that set of attractions and repulsions I referred to in my second paragraph and establishes the quoted line as a boundary, a turning point of the visible and invisible. It may indeed look as though Howe is trying to eat her cake and have it, using the footnote reference as a source, using it to declare that this writing, so difficult to sort out and decipher, so uncompromising in its eschewal of conventional meaning, so determined in its rejection of conventionally intelligible syntax, is after all not eschewing or rejecting those things, but is instead actually decodeable, is indeed "about" something, does have a paraphraseable content. Perhaps those words and notations which lie so uncompromisingly opaque on the page, language, are after all transparent, and the poem is to be seen as forum, vehicle, and hence finally static. Perhaps the reference is a sort of apron string connecting the poem to the conventional world, making it intelligible in conventional terms. It may indeed look that way. The pull of the footnote is toward the conventional, toward the "intelligible," toward the "classic," toward "meaning," toward a paraphraseable "content," toward Noun. The pull of the syntax, of the weird notation on the page, is away from that, subverts and transforms the apparent stability of the transparent word, pulls toward Verb. The resulting tension is not only one source of energy for the poem, not only a source of the poem's passion – for this is indeed a poem of feeling as well as of thought; it also, in grounding the language of the poem in the perceived and physical world, reminds us that language is, itself, physical, the perceived and felt world.

In addition, it points to a complex of thought and feeling identifiable in that tension. The footnote points to the notations, the editorial apparatus and code, which clutter the line and which litter the Genetic Text. For significant as the Genetic Text (and Melville's manuscript) may be, it (and Melville's manuscript version) is also incoherent. Jerking and stuttering along and then bursting momentarily free into coherence and even lucidity

> Having settled upon h→<h→the cou→<the cou→his→this<Having . . . upon→Having determined upon the course to adopt, (371)

it is littered with misspellings and broken-off words

> [*p* <striker of the blow] Too well the thoughf →<thoughf→ thoughtful officer knew what his superior meant. [*p* <Too well . . . meant] (377)

and with omissions (the result, perhaps, of haste)

> what remains primeval in our formalized humanity may in
> end have caught Billy to his arms (400)

and with repetitions.

What this poem does, by making both Melville's and the Genetic Text visible, is point to the incoherence, the uncertainty, the groping of Melville's text – those features of his writing that are erased, made invisible, liquidated, in the Reading Text – and assert them as a compositional principle, insisting that we attend to the writer in the act of composition, responsive to the detailed notation of uncertainty's hesitation and accuracy's register. The first line of the poem insists that we read the Genetic Text the way Howe insists we read Emily Dickinson. "In the precinct of poetry," she says, "a word, the space around a word, each letter, every mark silence or sound, volatizes an inner law of form; moves on a rigorous line" ("Illogic" 7).

Yet one great interest of the Genetic Text of *Billy Budd* is that, unlike Melville's manuscript and unlike Howe's poem, it is indeed littered. It is littered by the editors who interrupt their coding with such editorial comment as "left incoherent," "revision leaves the sentence incoherent" (386, 367, and elsewhere). In the long run this means for the editors that even the Genetic Text, as they say of their own Reading Text transcribed from it, only "approximates Melville's final intention" because he might have engaged "in further expansion or revision" (*vi*). For the editors thus to conclude that the text of *Billy Budd* is indeterminate is to assume that a text is only determinate if it conforms to grammatical, syntactic, and even perhaps thematic and cultural conventions. It is also to assume that Melville had intentions for the text that either were clear to Melville himself and deducible or that conformed to an implicit but nevertheless clear set of grammatical, (etc.) conventions. Or both. Howe's poem assumes the contrary: that Melville's "litter" of emendations, faulty grammar and syntax, misspellings and incoherence is not litter at all – and neither, once it is before us, is the editorial apparatus. In transcribing Melville's manuscript the editors invented the Genetic Text, and in preparing a Reading Text they turned their backs on what they had wrought. For the Reading Text presents us with a composition whose order has been wrestled from an intractable text, from a Genetic Text that simply cannot be confined within the coherence imposed by the conventional obedience of the Reading Text. The Genetic Text bristles with tentativeness and is rich with possibility; it is thematically straitjacketed in a Reading Text which, like Captain Vere sacrificing Billy Budd to the principle of law, legislates away the sheer mystery of the Genetic Text and of Melville's actual writing encoded within it by seeking to control and to possess.

Thus Hayford and Sealts's edition of *Billy Budd Sailor (An Inside Narrative)* is, Howe's poem tells us, a trope. Within its covers we see enacted two conflicts: that between Melville and his "material" (the essentially inchoate story of Billy Budd); and that between the editors and Melville's text. It is a trope for a history in which "little by little grandmothers and mothers are sinking in sand while grandfathers and fathers are electing and seceding" ("Women" 69); a history of settlers exterminating the Indians and "redeeming" the souls of the Indians' captives by buying them; of the English repressing the Irish by force and by doctrine until, irreversibly divided, they begin to exterminate themselves in the name of certitude and righteousness; of the hegemony of an intellectual and economic power which would, by revising and acculturating the texts it recognises as central, marginalise and even abolish the actual texts as written because it seeks, by stabilising the world so that its processes are arrested or invisible, to manage it.[7] As Howe remarks of Emily Dickinson in "The Illogic of Sumptuary Values," "in a system of restricted exchange, the subject–creator and her art in its potential gesture, were domesticated and occluded by an assumptive privileged Imperative." It is a trope telling us, says the poem, that "malice dominates the history of Power and Progress. History is the record of winners. Documents were written by the Masters. But fright is formed by what we see not by what they say" ("Poetics" 13).

It thus enacts the essential human conflict, between the known and the unknown, the seen and the unseen, the cultivated and the wild. The two editors, wrestling the wildness of the manuscript into stable and definitive canonical shape, evoke the complex of the relations between the real and the visionary. Howe invites us to read *Billy Budd* as Melville wrote it, spasmodically erasing itself, constantly deconstructing and reconstructing itself. Throwing a halo of wilderness around the line from the Genetic Text with which it begins, the poem throws a halo of wilderness around *Billy Budd* itself and points to a textual, literary, intellectual and cultural arrogance which in homogenizing a work shackles it into invisibility. Here (again) are the last three lines of this opening poem:

> But what is envy [but what is envy]
> Is envy the bonfire inkling?
>
> Shackles [ (shackles) ] as we were told the . . . [precincts]

Howe sees that arrogance as patriarchal, and the conflict, between the world as is (wild) and the world as wanted (ordered), as devastating. A cincture is a girdle, a belt, a barrier, an enclosure, and a fence. While the text longs for resolution, it insistently demands that its disorder not be dissipated in mere definition. The blankness of the page surrounding each poem in the sequence – and indeed Howe's deeply ingrained necessity to compose in units of one page – is essential to the poem's decontextualizing of utterance, forcing us to read Genetic Texts (surely each poem itself is one) without translating the code, so the eye sees and attends everything on the page without hierarchising or invisibilising according to the demands of the canon. Eyes pre-cinct the poem. As the last line of the poem suggests, our history, what we were told, precincts the text and our reading.

Such a thematic view of the opening of "Scattering" as a radical rereading of *Billy Budd* sees the poem as a further stage in Susan Howe's archaeological retrieval of lost or straitjacketed American texts, in her retrieval of historical persons (women especially, but also writers) straitjacketed or obliterated by being textualized and then erased: Hester Johnson, Mary Rowlandson, Thoreau, the emblematically named Hope Atherton, Emily Dickinson. "I write to break out into perfect primeval Consent," she told the New Poetics Colloquium in 1985. "I wish I could tenderly lift from the dark side of history, voices that are anonymous, slighted – inarticulate" ("Poetics" 15). They have been hidden by a utilitarian, canonizing, and classicizing impulse; they have willy-nilly succumbed – like Cordelia in *The Liberties* – to an authoritative "rationalization" which, patriarchal, seeks to possess the text by removing or rationalizing all "accidentals," confining it to a single body of meaning, to a single role, to a single order of understanding. It does so by reshaping and "correcting" the text in the interests of tidiness, in order that it conform to notions of formal ("literary") decorum. It rejects outright the notion of world as text, world as language, world as trope, viewing the world instead as a series of fixed categories of meaning whose validity is determined by the rationality of the forms of discourse in which that meaning is couched. It confines Mary Rowlandson in a "familiar American hierarchical discourse of purpose and possession" (*CMR* 116) and, rhetorically, appropriates her march "away from from Western rationalism deeper and deeper into limitlessness" (*CMR* 116) until she "excavates and subverts her own rhetoric" (*CMR* 117) lest she be false to her sense of the world and to herself. Such a convention-ridden view of writing not only confines value to conformity but also finds incomprehensible and reprehensible the notion that Emily Dickinson's work is as great as it is *because* it is like Melville's *Billy Budd* and like angelic Billy Budd. It stammers and stutters and jerks along, more silent than it is loquacious, breaking and breathing in awkward places, violating customary syntax and vocabulary and diction, occasionally incomprehensible, often incoherent, perennially uncertain because it articulates a world where, as Howe says of Rowlandson, "all illusion of volition, all individual identity, may be transformed" (*CMR* 116). And perennially incomplete, unfinished. So Dickinson appends to her poems alternative versions as "a sort of mini-poem" ("Illogic"); she obeys not the traditional rigidities of the quatrain, but the topography of the poem's composition, the page. Line breaks and stanza breaks, shifts of attention and energy resulting from reaching the edge or the end of the page, from turning the paper over and starting a new page, affect the course of the poem's breathing, and thus of the poem's making, and the course of our reading. "Specialists want to nail things down," Howe says in an essay on Charles Olson (himself notably inarticulate and incoherent). "Poets know to leave Reason alone" because "all power, including the power of Love, all nature, including the nature of Time, is utterly unstable."[8]

"What does not change / is the will to change" (Olson, "The Kingfishers"). For Howe this is not a matter of will (save in that Nature might be willful), but of necessity to which one must submit. And the impulse to disorder in the world leaves its mark in the sheer isolation of Howe's poems on the page, surrounded by white: a visible trope of Howe's tough and difficult feminism. There are figurations in these figures who are figured against no *ground,* who move away from ground, who move *without.* Such a movement, to be free of the burden of ground, freed of definition by others, freed of singularity, freed of language, freed of the necessity to be sane or to be mad, freed of history, is terrible and is exhilaration. But it is impossible and doomed. Howe knows that the primeval (that "lost prelapsarian state") "may have existed only in the mind" ("Armantrout" 209) if it existed at all; that we all suffer violent "primal exile from the mother" (*MyED* 107); and that we can never escape "that language outside language we are all entangled in" ("Women" 61). Always one balances on the edge, on the turning point, on the move to without. Always one carries language, desire, history. One balances, as she said of Emily Dickinson, between and in "reverence and revolt" on the cusp of the present, carrying "intelligence of the past into future of our thought" (*MyEd* 85). Caught between loss and desire, Howe's vision is difficult, uncompromising:

> No hierarchy, no notion of polarity. Perception of an object means loosing and losing it. Quests end in failure, no victory and sham questor. One answer undoes another and fiction is real. Trust absence, allegory, mystery – the setting not the rising sun is Beauty (*MyED* 23).

Howe is, more than any American writer I can think of except perhaps Melville or Henry Adams, burdened by history: The burden, of retrieving from erasure and marginality those (women) who have been written out, without (as Howe puts it in her prose introduction to "Thorow") appropriating primal indeterminacy, is compounded by the drift of the primal toward the immediate, toward the abolition of history (and hence of language) altogether. History, like language, is not and cannot be linear. Her writing is essentially religious, devoted to a lively apprehension of the sacramental nature of our experience of the world, and of the sacramental nature of the world. Like Emily Dickinson she is an utterly astringent formalist.

# Notes

## PREFACE

1 Maurice Merleau-Ponty, "Indirect Language and the Voices of Silence." *Signs,* trans. Richard C. McCleary (Evanston, Ill.: Northwestern UP, 1964) 43.

## INTRODUCTION

1 Letter to Edmund Wilson, 8 October 1923. *The Letters of Gertrude Stein and Carl Van Vechten 1913–1946,* ed. Edward Burns (New York: Columbia UP, 1986) 88.
2 William Carlos Williams, "Objectivism," *Encyclopedia of Poetry and Poetics,* ed. Alex Preminger (Princeton: Princeton UP, 1965) 582; L. S. Dembo, "The Objectivist Poet: Four Interviews" *Contemporary Literature* 10.2 (Spring 1969): 160.
3 Louis Zukofsky, "Preface – 'Recencies' in Poetry," *An "Objectivists" Anthology* (Dijon: To Publishers, 1932) 24–5. This important essay is collected in an abridged and revised version, conflated with the essay "Program: 'Objectivists' 1931" (*Poetry* 37.5 [February 1931]: 268–72) in *Prepositions: The Collected Critical Essays,* expanded ed. (Berkeley: U of California P, 1981) 12–18 as "An Objective." In downplaying the coherence of the Objectivists as a group, Zukofsky was somewhat disingenuous: There is at the Harry Ransom Humanities Research Centre, University of Texas at Austin, a set of typescript notes for a talk he gave at the Poetry Centre of the YMHA in New York on "The Objectivist Program," 23 January 1941.
4 Michael Heller, *Conviction's Net of Branches: Essays on Objectivist Poets and Poetry* (Carbondale: Southern Illinois UP, 1985); Michael Palmer, "On Objectivism," *Sulfur* 26 (Spring 1990): 117.
5 In their material and phenomenal enactment, of course, nouns are no more static within reading and writing than any other part of speech: As Steve McCaffery points out, "verb and noun partake equally in syntactic movement and the syllabic, metric (hyper and hypo) dynamics entailed in their alphabetic constitution" – sound, rhythmic movement, graphics – the range

of qualities Julia Kristeva assigns to the *genotext* (letter to Peter Quartermain, 18 July 1990).

6 Gertrude Stein, "Poetry and Grammar," *Lectures in America* (New York: Random House, 1935) 209–46; the quotation is from 210.

7 Williams, "Introduction to *The Wedge,*" *Selected Essays* (New York: New Directions, 1969) 256.

8 *Century Dictionary and Cyclopedia,* 10 vols. (New York: Century, 1902) entry for *machine,* Definition 7. The *Century* is, for the purposes of this book, preferable to the *Oxford* simply on the grounds that it is an American dictionary of English. It is also the dictionary Louis Zukofsky habitually used from about 1950 on.

9 Charles Olson, "Projective Verse," *Human Universe and Other Essays,* ed. Donald Allen (New York: Grove, 1967) 52.

10 Jonathan Monroe, *A Poverty of Objects: The Prose Poem and the Politics of Genre* (Ithaca: Cornell UP, 1987) 10, 25.

11 For its first two issues the subtitle of *Sagetrieb* was "A Journal Devoted to Poets in the Pound–Williams Tradition"; it then became devoted to poets in the "Pound–H. D.–Williams Tradition" until Volume 6, Number 1 (Spring 1987), when its subtitle was changed to "A Journal Devoted to Poets in the Imagist/Objectivist Tradition."

12 Sir William Rowan Hamilton, "Quaternions," ms. notebook entry for 16 October 1843, *The Mathematical Papers of Sir William Rowan Hamilton,* Vol. 3: *Algebra,* ed. H. Halberstam and R. E. Ingram (Cambridge: Cambridge UP, 1967) 103–5; Karl Marx: *Capital,* 4th German ed., trans. Eden and Cedar Paul, introduction G. D. H. Cole, addendum Murray Wolfson (London and New York: J. M. Dent [Everyman's Library], 1974) Part 1, Chapter 1, *passim.*

13 Charles Olson, "The Songs of Maximus," *The Maximus Poems,* ed. George F. Butterick (Berkeley: U of California P, 1983) 19.

14 Paul Valéry, "Literary Reminiscences," *Leonardo, Poe, Mallarmé,* trans. Malcolm Cowley and James R. Lawler, *The Collected Works of Paul Valéry,* ed. Jackson Mathews, Vol. 8 (Princeton: Princeton UP, 1972) 324.

15 William Carlos Williams, "Measure – a loosely assembled essay on poetic measure," *Spectrum* 3.3 (Fall 1959): 149 (Williams's italics).

16 Niels Bohr, *Atomic Theory and the Description of Nature* (Cambridge: Cambridge UP, 1961) 54.

17 J. Robert Oppenheimer, *Science and the Common Understanding* (New York: Simon and Schuster, 1954) 40.

18 Henry Adams, *The Education of Henry Adams* (New York: Modern Library, 1931) 382; quoted partially in Louis Zukofsky *Bottom: On Shakespeare* (Austin: U of Texas P, 1963) 345.

19 Marshall Berman, *All That Is Solid Melts into Air: The Experience of Modernity* (New York: Simon and Schuster, 1982) 345.

20 Bertrand Russell, *Our Knowledge of the External World as a Field for Scientific Method in Philosophy* (Chicago and London: Open Court Publishing, 1915) 28. (Italics added.)

21 Henry Adams, *Education* 457; Gertrude Stein, "A Seltzer Bottle," *Tender Buttons,* in *Selected Writings of Gertrude Stein,* ed. Carl Van Vechten (New York: Modern Library, 1962) 466; William Carlos Williams, *Selected Letters,* ed. John C. Thirlwall (New York: McDowell Obolensky, 1957) 23–4.

22 John Seed, "Living the Storm: George Oppen's 'Songs of Experience,'" *Not Comforts / But Vision: Essays on the Poetry of George Oppen,* ed. John Freeman (Budleigh Salterton: Interim, 1985) 14.

23 Louis Zukofsky, "American Poetry 1920–1930," *Prepositions* 148.

24 William Carlos Williams, "Prologue to *Kora in Hell,*" *Imaginations,* ed. Webster Schott (New York: New Directions, 1970) 14.

25 Bob Perelman, "The First Person," *Hills* No. 6–7 (*Talks,* ed. Bob Perelman) (1980):156.

26 Ulla Dydo has in a series of remarkable essays traced the genesis of many Stein works, putting the lie to any reading that seeks to "translate" Stein's "meaning" by decoding it in the manner of Rebecca Mark in her "Introduction," *Lifting Belly* (Tallahassee: Naiad, 1989) *xi–xxxiii.* Ulla E. Dydo, "*Stanzas in Meditation:* The Other Autobiography," *Chicago Review* 35 (Winter 1985): 4–20, with its companion piece "How to Read Gertrude Stein: The Manuscript of *Stanzas in Meditation,*" *Text: Transactions of the Society for Textual Scholarship* 1 (1981): 271–303, establishes the highly coded and intentionally private nature of Stein's text and at the same time demonstrates the peripheral relationship of the code to the act of reading. For a similarly useful reading of late Zukofsky work, see Michele J. Leggott, *Reading Zukofsky's Eighty Flowers* (Baltimore: Johns Hopkins UP, 1989).

27 William Carlos Williams, "The Work of Gertrude Stein," *Selected Essays* 117–18. (My italics; for my discussion of the authorship of this essay, see Chapter 5, Note 13.)

28 Basil Bunting, "The Lion and the Lizard," ts., Zukofsky papers, Harry Ransom Humanities Research Centre, University of Texas at Austin, 2; "Some Limitations of English," *The Lion and Crown* 1.1 (October 1932): 28.

29 William Carlos Williams, letter to Zukofsky, 2 April 1928, *Selected Letters* 94.

30 Dembo 161.

31 William Carlos Williams, *In the American Grain* (New York: New Directions, 1956) 219, 220.

32 Robert Duncan, *As Testimony* (San Francisco: White Rabbit, 1964) 7, 12.

33 Susan Howe, "The Illogic of Sumptuary Values" (unpublished typescript). On Stein, see for example Wendy Steiner, *Exact Resemblance to Exact Resemblance: The Literary Portraiture of Gertrude Stein* (New Haven: Yale UP, 1978) 111–16.

34 Dembo 213; Basil Bunting, in Sally Beauman, "Man of Plain Words [interview]," *Daily Telegraph Magazine* 244 (13 June 1969): 33.

35 I take these words from Carl Van Vechten's letter to Gertrude Stein, 22 February 1923: "you are a classic & have imitators & DISCIPLES!" *Letters of Gertrude Stein and Carl Van Vechten* 66.

36 Bruce Andrews, "Poetry as Explanation, Poetry as Praxis," *The Politics of Poetic Form: Poetry and Public Policy*, ed. Charles Bernstein (New York: Roof, 1990) 29.

37 Oscar Cargill, cited by Richard Bridgman, *Gertrude Stein in Pieces* (New York: Oxford UP, 1970) 125n.

38 Louis Zukofsky *Bottom* 22; for the exact wording of Zukofsky's comments to Niedecker, 9 November 1935, see Barry Ahearn, *Zukofsky's "A": An Introduction* [Berkeley: U of California P, 1983) 75, and Ron Silliman, "Why the MLA Can't Read," *The New Sentence* (New York: Roof, 1987) 143. Permission to quote refused by Paul Zukofsky.

39 Beauman, "Man of Plain Words," 32. According to Barry Ahearn, when Zukofsky was writing "A" – 8 (circa 1936) Bunting sent him materials about "Welsh metrics of Selwyn Jones" (*Zukofsky's "A"* 231). Among Zukofsky's papers at the Harry Ransom Humanities Research Center, University of Texas at Austin, is a four-page set of notes in Zukofsky's hand titled "Bunting on Jones," in which Zukofsky records Bunting's characterisation of Persian music. Zukofsky is possibly transcribing notes made during conversation, in which case they could date as early as 1930–1 or as late as 1938–9.

40 Ezra Pound, "Studies in Contemporary Mentality . . . XIX. –? Versus Camouflage," *New Age* 22.11 (10 January 1918): 209. Andrew Parker, "Ezra Pound and the 'Economy' of Anti-Semitism," *Postmodernism and Politics,* ed. Jonathan Arac (Minneapolis: U of Minnesota P, 1986) 70–91, offers an extremely valuable analysis of the linguistic basis of Pound's fascism.

41 Bruce Andrews, "Misrepresentation," *L=A=N=G=U=A=G=E* 12 (June 1980): [5]. As Andrews uses the term, "behavioural" includes bodily behaviour (eye movement, breath, arm gesture, and so on); my own emphasis is more on cognitive behaviour than his seems to be, though not excluding the physical: how the words seem to behave in relation to one another as we process the reading, how syntactic, aural, and other linguistic aspects and effects determine (and often problematise) the cognitive process.

42 Henry James, *The Question of Our Speech: The Lesson of Balzac. Two Lectures* (Boston: Houghton Mifflin, 1905) 39. Further references are noted parenthetically in my text.

43 The 1907 figures are taken from *Reports of the Immigration Commission (1907–1910),* 41 vols. (Washington, D. C.: Government Printing Office, 1911) 3, *Statistical Review of Immigration 1820–1910: Distribution of Immigrants 1850–1900:* 8–43, but especially 43, 46; the average for 1905 is derived from 1, *Abstracts of the Reports of the Immigration Commission:* 5, where a total of 8,795,386 immigrants is reported for the ten years 1901–10. Vols. 1,2, and 3 are especially useful, as is Department of Commerce and Labor, Bureau of the Census (S. N. D. North, director), *A Century of Population Growth from the First Census of the United States to the Twelfth, 1790–1900* (Washington, D. C.: Government Printing Office, 1909).

44 *Thirteenth Census of the United States Taken in the Year 1910: Population,* 4 vols. (Washington, D. C.: Government Printing Office, 1913), but especially

Volume 1; 30 percent (nearly nineteen million) of a native-born white population of just over sixty-eight million were born of "foreign or mixed parentage" (i.e., one or both parents born outside the United States), and an additional thirteen million were foreign born (1: 129–35, but see also especially 961–4). Of the thirty-two million born of "foreign white stock" only 31 percent had "English or Celtic" as their "mother-tongue," while of the foreign born, only 23 percent spoke English or Celtic as their mother-tongue (961–4). The same Census reported that 22 percent of the foreign-born white population ten years of age and over were "unable to speak English so as to be understood in an ordinary conversation" (1265–72). By 1930, after nearly fifteen years of stricter controls on immigration, this proportion had dropped to just over 8 percent (*Fifteenth Census of the United States Taken in the Year 1930* [Washington, D. C.: Government Printing Office, 1933] 2: 1349).

45 Louis Zukofsky, *Autobiography* (New York: Grossman, 1970) 33.

46 For a fuller discussion of Stein, Williams, and Zukofsky, see Chapter 5, Note 26. Reznikoff rather sparsely records his bilingual childhood in his poem "Early History of a Writer" (*Poems 1937–1935,* Vol. 2 of *The Complete Poems,* ed. Seamus Cooney [Los Angeles: Black Sparrow Press, 1978], especially 143–7), and in his interview with Reinhold Schiffer, "The Poet in his Milieu," *Charles Reznikoff: Man and Poet,* ed. Milton Hindus (Orono: National Poetry Foundation, 1984), 117 and 124, from which the quoted passages come. Reznikoff's childhood differs from Stein's, Williams's, and Zukofsky's in that his "mother's discipline was we should learn English." Another Objectivist poet, Carl Rakosi, was born in Berlin and at the age of one moved with his family to Hungary, where they lived until 1910, when he was six (Dembo 178). Even Basil Bunting felt dissociated from his language. Sent at the age of sixteen to Leighton Park School in the south of England, he found his Northumbrian identity put him at odds with the South and with the standard British koiné: "there must be some great underlying difference between North & South," he wrote to the Headmaster in October 1916; "people with Southern manners are, for me, utterly 'impossible' & hateful." (Xerox ms., Mountjoy Collection, Durham University. The original ms. is at Leighton Park School.)

47 William Carlos Williams "The Poem as a Field of Action," *Selected Essays* 286. For accounts of Pfaff's bar and restaurant see Albert Parry, *Garrets and Pretenders: A History of Bohemianism in America* [1933] (New York: Dover, 1960); and Gay Wilson Allen, *The Solitary Singer: A Critical Biography of Walt Whitman* (New York: Macmillan, 1955) 229–31, 269–70.

48 Charles Bernstein, "Three or Four Things," *Content's Dream: Essays 1975–1984* (Los Angeles: Sun & Moon, 1986) 25.

49 Jacques Attali. *Noise: The Political Economy of Music,* tr. Brian Massumi (Minneapolis: U of Minnesota P, 1985) 34.

50 Defining the tone-standard as "a clear criterion of the best usage and example" (16), James defended the "principle of taste" on the grounds that "there are, you see, sounds of a mysterious intrinsic meanness, and there are sounds of a mysterious intrinsic frankness and sweetness" (29).

51 Louis Zukofsky, *Collected Fiction* (Elmwood Park, Ill.: Dalkey Archive, 1990) 12. Permission to quote refused by Paul Zukofsky.
52 L. S. Dembo, "Oppen on His Poems: A Discussion," *George Oppen: Man and Poet,* ed. Burton Hatlen (Orono: National Poetry Foundation, 1981) 213.
53 *A Century of Population Growth,* 128–30.
54 Lorine Niedecker, *From This Condensery: The Complete Writings,* Robert J. Bertholf, ed. (Highlands, NC: Jargon, 1985) 48. The same question is asked in Louis Zukofsky, "Chloride of Lime and Charcoal" (written 1949), *Complete Short Poetry* (Baltimore: Johns Hopkins UP, 1991) 125. Such cultural amnesia is not, of course, peculiarly American. Basil Bunting, teaching a course on Mediterranean history to coal miners in 1939, recorded being asked "few questions, only one jewel of half-knowledge: 'Please, what was the connection between this Caliph Omar and 'Omer that wrote the Iliad?' " (Letter to Zukofsky, 18 December 1939, Harry Ransom Humanities Research Center, University of Texas at Austin.) D. H. Lawrence suggested that it is "industrial, really" (*Lady Chatterley's Lover* [New York: Grove Press, 1959] 189).
55 Basil Bunting, "1910–1920," ts. lecture given at Newcastle University, 1968, p. 10. Ts. in the possession of Peter Quartermain.
56 William Carlos Williams, *Kora in Hell, Imaginations* 46. At the end of the second World War Gertrude Stein noted how the GI of 1944 had, when compared to the Doughboy of 1918, come into an *American* language. "I think of the Americans of the last war, they had their language but they were not yet in possession of it, and the children of the depression as that generation called itself was beginning to possess its language but it was still struggling but now the job is done, the G. I. Joes have this language that is theirs, they do not have to worry about it." (*Wars I Have Seen* [New York: Random House, 1945] 259.)
57 "Thanks to the Dictionary," *It Was* (Kyoto: Origin P, 1961) 99–132. Zukofsky reworked the text intermittently throughout his career. The manuscript in the Harry Ransom Humanities Research Center, University of Texas at Austin, which identifies the dictionaries as *Funk and Wagnall's Practical Standard Dictionary* and *Webster's Collegiate Dictionary,* is dated 1932, but the manuscript at the University of Illinois shows evidence of reworking in 1934 or even later; in 1951 Zukofsky reworked it for (abortive) publication in a magazine called *Possibilities,* and rearranged the text yet again in 1959–60. Basil Bunting's carbon copy of a ts. draft, in the Mountjoy Collection, Durham University Library, is titled "Parts of a Novel."
58 Gertrude Stein, *Narration: Four Lectures,* introduction Thornton Wilder (Chicago: Chicago UP, 1935) 10; *Lectures in America* 53.
59 Laura Riding, "The New Barbarism and Gertrude Stein" (originally published in *Transition* 3 [June 1927]), *Contemporaries and Snobs* (Garden City: Doubleday Doran, 1928) 189, 194.
60 William Carlos Williams, *Kora in Hell, Imaginations* 59.
61 W. B. Yeats, "What Is Popular Poetry?" *Essays and Introductions* (New York: Macmillan, 1961) 6.
62 Title of Chapter 3, *The Philosophy of Rhetoric* (New York: Oxford UP. 1936).

63 Malcolm Cowley, *Exile's Return* (New York: Viking, 1956) 18.
64 Malcolm Cowley and Slater Brown, "Comment: To the Editors of The Dial," *Broom* 6.1 (January 1924): 30.
65 Andrews, [7].
66 L. S. Dembo, "Oppen on His Poems" 213.
67 John Berger, *Ways of Seeing* (London: Penguin, 1972) 32.
68 Louis Zukofsky, "Preface," *An "Objectivists" Anthology* 21, 14, 24, 18. Permission to quote refused by Paul Zukofsky. Though Zukofsky dropped the analogy of the desk from *Prepositions,* he frequently associated instrumental readings of poetry with the predatory.
69 *Mystery Train,* dir. Jim Jarmusch, 1989; *Teen-Age Mutant Ninja Turtles,* dir. Steve Barron, New Line Cinema, 1990. The television programme of which Barron's film was an offshoot was produced specifically for children; the film, written by Todd W. Langen and Bobby Herbeck, seems to have been made for a less clearly defined audience. See the review in the *New York Times* 30 March 1990: C, 8.
70 Williams, *Spring and All* (1923), *Imaginations* 100.
71 Steve McCaffery, "Intraview," *L=A=N=G=U=A=G=E* 2 (April 1978): [22]; reprinted in *The L=A=N=G=U=A=G=E Book,* ed. Bruce Andrews and Charles Bernstein (Carbondale: Southern Illinois UP, 1984) 189.)
72 Steve McCaffery, "An Intention To Be Wrong," *V Beyond the Ideo,* videotape (Toronto: Underwhich Editions, 1983).
73 Bruce Andrews, *Give Em Enough Rope* (Los Angeles: Sun & Moon, 1987); Steve McCaffery, *The Black Debt* (London, Ontario: Nightwood Editions, 1989).
74 McCaffery, "Intraview" 189.
75 Basil Bunting, letter to Alan Neame, 16 April 1951, quoted in part in bookseller's catalogue *Modern First Editions* (Warwick: R. A. Gekowski, 1984). There is a carbon copy of the complete typescript among Dorothy Pound's papers at the Lilly Library, Indiana University.
76 Jack Spicer, "from The Vancouver Lectures," *Caterpillar* 12 (July 1970): 183. Further references are noted parenthetically in my text.
77 Williams, "The Invisible University," *Trend* 1.1 (January 1942): 4.
78 So, too, Duncan, in "Passages 26," incorporates his own hesitations, doubts, observation of and commentary on the writing process into the writing, as in

"life writes
Mao's mountain of murderd men
the alliteration of ms like Viet Nam's burnd villages
irreplaceable . . . "

("Some Versions of Passages 26," *Audit* 4.3 [1967]: 62–3. The final published text, in *Bending the Bow* [New York: New Directions, 1968] 113, is slightly different).
79 Williams, "Introduction to *The Wedge,*" *Selected Essays* 257; letter to Louis

Zukofsky, 22 October 1935, quoted in Zukofsky, "William Carlos Williams," *Prepositions* 48.

80 Charles Olson, "Projective Verse," 52.

81 William James, "A Suggestion about Mysticism," *Collected Essays and Reviews* (London: Longmans, Green, 1920) 500–1.

82 Bruce Andrews and Marjorie Perloff, "An Interview," *American Poetry* 7.3 (Spring 1990): 94.

83 I borrow the pun from Bruce Andrews, in conversation.

## *CHAPTER ONE*

1 Gertrude Stein, "Sentences," *How To Write* (New York: Dover, 1975) page numbers as given. The quotation in the title is from "Regularly Regularly in Narrative," *How To Write* 243. I owe a great deal in the preparation of this essay to Ulla E. Dydo of CUNY Bronx, and to Mava Jo Powell of the University of British Columbia. I thank them both.

2 Jayne L. Walker, *The Making of a Modernist: Gertrude Stein from Three Lives to Tender Buttons* (Amherst: U of Massachusetts P, 1984) *xix*.

3 *Deixis* (Greek, *pointing*) refers to "the location and identification of persons, objects, events, processes and activities being talked about, or referred to, in relation to the spatio-temporal context created and sustained by the act of utterance and the participation in it, typically, of a single speaker and at least one addressee." John Lyons, *Semantics* (Cambridge: Cambridge UP, 1978) 2: 636.

4 Stein's work abounds in examples of this sort of thing. So in *Patriarchal Poetry* there is the apparently nonsensical sequence "What is the difference between a fig and an apple. The one precedes the other" (*Yale Gertrude Stein*, ed. R. Kostelanetz [New Haven: Yale UP, 1980] 128). Stein asks a question which conventionally demands a qualitative answer (appleness, figness) but provides another sort: fig precedes apple positionally in the question. Stein thus renders absurd a possible hierarchy implicit in the question through a means closely similar to the brilliant "A wish is an article not followed by a noun," where the latent pun in *article* enjoins the reader to redefine *noun*.

5 Gertrude Stein, *Tender Buttons*, in *Selected Writings of Gertrude Stein*, ed. Carl Van Vechten (New York: Modern Library, 1962) 490. I take the dates of composition of Stein's work from Ulla E. Dydo, "Must Horses Drink. or, 'Any Language Is Funny If You Don't Understand It'," *Tulsa Studies in Women's Literature* 4 (Fall 1985): 276–77 and 279, Note 13.

6 Hal Levy, notes on Stein's lectures, 1935; quoted Dydo 274.

7 Gertrude Stein, *Tender Buttons* 476. I need hardly point out that not all the poems in *Tender Buttons* are structured the same way. And, of course, since by the time "Book" appears the reader has already read fifty-four "Objects" some of the procedures I outline here will already be familiar. My analysis of "Book" is indebted in some of its details to conversations with Bruce Comens and with Michele J. Leggott.

8 "The definite article, when it is used deictically, . . . is to be understood as instructing, or inviting, the addressee to find the referent in the environment,

without however directing his attention to any particular region of it." Lyons 2: 655–6.

9 Sara Mills, "No Poetry for Ladies: Gertrude Stein, Julia Kristeva and Modernism," *Literary Theory and Poetry: Extending the Canon*, ed. David Murray (London: Batsford, 1989): 101.

10 See M. A. K. Halliday and R. Hasan, *Cohesion in English* (London: Longman, 1976) for a detailed treatment of linking as a formal agent in language. In some languages such patterns as Stein uses (like vowel infixes occurring inside consonantal lexemes) signal grammatical meanings of various kinds.

11 For the dating and place of composition of *Lifting Belly* see Virgil Thomson's introductory note to the poem in Gertrude Stein, *Bee Time Vine and other pieces (1913–1927)* (New Haven: Yale UP, 1953) 63. Page references to *Lifting Belly* and to *Patriarchal Poetry* in my text, however, are to these poems as printed in *The Yale Gertrude Stein*.

12 If we read the words "Part II" on Page 5 as a paragraph of text rather than as a division number (as Virgil Thomson suggests we should) then *Lifting Belly* consists of 1,812 paragraphs. If we define a sentence as everything that appears between periods (or before one, in the case of the first sentence) and/or before a paragraph break, *Lifting Belly* consists of 2,074 sentences. This count treats the two lines ending with a comma on Pages 46 and 47 as sentences. The second paragraph on page 10 ("Do you please m.") is not the only evidence that there may be misprints in this (and other) Yale texts; there is obviously need for a properly edited version of Stein's work.

13 My own rough count yields 7 one-line paragraphs that do not terminate in a period or a comma (most of those are in the final pages) and only twelve commas in the whole of *Lifting Belly*. There are some 126 paragraphs with more than one sentence; in many of these there is no particular reason to assign each sentence to the same voice.

14 The great bulk of them (55) is in Section 1.

15 Ulla E. Dydo, "Gertrude Stein: Composition as Meditation." *Gertrude Stein and the Making of Literature*, ed. Shirley Neuman and Ira B. Nadel (London: Macmillan, 1988) 56.

16 Other word counts in this paragraph are as follows: *method*, 22; *hears*, 17; *is*, 12, but it does not appear until the 52nd word; *and*, 8, but all of them between the 37th and 57th words inclusive (i.e., 8 times in 21 words); and *to*, 5, all in first 15 words.

It is perhaps worth noting in addition the two sentences following this, completing Stein's paragraph:

> Unified in their expanse. Unified in letting there there there one two one two three there in a chain a chain how do you laterally in relation to auditors and obliged obliged currently.

The paragraph glosses its own activity.

17 "Anaphora . . . depends ultimately upon deixis" (Lyons 2: 657). For a discussion of pronouns as shifters and of the relationship between anaphora and deixis see Lyons, Chapter 15, where he draws on R. Jakobsen, *Shifters, Verbal Categories, and the Russian Verb* (Cambridge, Mass.: Harvard UP, 1957). Shifter is Jakobsen's term.

18 *Portraits and Prayers* (New York: Random House, 1936) 57–8.
19 I am indebted to Mava Jo Powell for this formulation, which comes from Stephen C. Levinson, *Pragmatics* (Cambridge: Cambridge UP, 1983) 55.
20 For a discussion of "quasi-English," see Lyons 2: 461 and the pages following.
21 *Yale Gertrude Stein* 3.
22 For a reappraisal of Stein's "realism" as a form of composition by multidimensional field grounded in language and the perception of language, see Lyn Hejinian, "Two Stein Talks," *Temblor* 3 (1986): 128–39.
23 *Lectures in America* (Boston: Beacon Press, 1957) 215.
24 *Finnegans Wake* (New York: Viking, 1939) 519.5
25 For a full-length treatment of Joyce's work as text-intrinsic system, see Lorraine Weir's radical reassessment *Writing Joyce: A Semiotic of the Joyce System* (Bloomington: Indiana UP, 1989).
26 Laura Riding, "The New Barbarism and Gertrude Stein" (originally published in *Transition* 3 [June 1927]), *Contemporaries and Snobs* (Garden City: Doubleday Doran, 1928) 189, 194.
27 T. S. Eliot, "Charleston, Hey! Hey!" [review of *Composition as Explanation* by Gertrude Stein] *Nation and Athenaeum* 40 (29 January 1927): 595. Eliot's italics.
28 Gertrude Stein, *Wars I Have Seen* (London: Batsford) 170.
29 Arthur Power, *Conversations with James Joyce* (London: Millington, 1974) 93.
30 W. B. Yeats, "America and the Arts," *Uncollected Prose Volume 2: Reviews, Articles and Other Miscellaneous Prose: 1897–1939,* Ed. John P. Fraye and Colton Johnson (New York: Columbia UP, 1976) 341.
31 Yeats, "Mr. Rhys' Welsh Ballads," *Uncollected Prose* 2:92.
32 Stan Brakhage, letter to Jane Brakhage, 17 May 1963, *Metaphors on Vision,* ed. P. Adams Sitney, *Film Culture* 30 (Fall 1963), unpaged (Brakhage's ellipsis). The entire issue is devoted to *Metaphors on Vision.*
33 Gertrude Stein, "Farragut," *Useful Knowledge* (Barrytown, NY: Station Hill, 1988) 13.

## *CHAPTER TWO*

1 Pierre Boulez, *Notes of an Apprenticeship,* texts collected by Paul Thevenin, trans. Herbert Weinstock (New York: Knopf, 1968) 381.
2 Louis Zukofsky, *Complete Short Poetry* (Baltimore: Johns Hopkins UP, 1991) 82–3. Further references abbreviated *CSP.* Other works by Zukofsky are abbreviated as follows:

*Prepositions: The Collected Critical Essays,* expanded ed. (Berkeley: U of California Press, 1981), as *Prep.;*
*Bottom: On Shakespeare* (Austin: U of Texas P, 1963), as *Bottom;*
*A Test of Poetry* (New York: Jargon/Corinth, 1964), as *A Test;*
*"A"* (Berkeley: U of California P, 1978) as *"A".*

Other frequently cited works are abbreviated as follows:

Marcella Booth, *A Catalogue of the Louis Zukofsky Manuscript Collection* (Austin: U of Texas, 1975), as Booth;

Celia Zukofsky, *A Bibliography of Louis Zukofsky* (Los Angeles: Black Sparrow, 1969), as CZ.

3 See CZ 37, and *Prep* 152. Paul Zukofsky is the source of information for the submarines, in a letter to C. Scarles, 7 June 1991; Hugh Kenner told me about the bombsights.

4 William Carlos Williams, "A Novelette," *Imaginations,* ed. Webster Schott (New York: New Directions, 1970) 273.

5 H. A. Lorentz, *The Theory of Electrons and Its Applications to the Phenomena of Light and Radiant Heat. A course of lectures delivered in Columbia University, New York, in March and April 1906,* 2nd ed. (Leipzig: Teubner; New York: Stechert, 1916) 1–2.

6 Neither *capacitor* nor *capacitance* appears in the *Oxford English Dictionary*. The 1933 *Supplement to the O. E. D.* records that *capacitance* was "recommended" in 1916 by the Institute of Electrical Engineers as the term for "electrostatic capacity," but there is still no entry for *capacitor. Webster's New International Unabridged Dictionary,* 2nd edition, 1935 defines *capacitor* as "Electrical term. A condenser." *Webster's Third* and *A Supplement to the O. E. D.* (1976) have entries for both terms.

7 *Encyclopaedia Britannica,* 14th edition (1939). Article on "Condenser (Electrical)."

8 Philip R. Coursey, *Electrical Condensers: Their Construction, Design and Industrial Uses* (London: Pitman, 1927) 51, 61.

9 Coursey 13–14.

10 *Webster's 2nd,* entry for *electricity*. Charles Olson, "Projective Verse," *Human Universe and Other Essays,* ed. Donald Allen (New York: Grove Press, 1967) 52.

11 *"A"* 24. Permission to quote refused by Paul Zukofsky.

12 Bertrand Russell, *Our Knowledge of the External World as a Field for Scientific Method in Philosophy* (Chicago and London: Open Court Publishing, 1915) 28.

13 Boulez 204.

14 William Carlos Williams, *I Wanted to Write a Poem,* reported and ed. Edith Heal (Boston: Beacon Press, 1958) 29. For a valuable discussion of Davis's drawing in relation to *Kora in Hell* see Roy A. Miki, *The Prepoetics of William Carlos Williams's* Kora in Hell (Ann Arbor: UMI Research P, 1983) 95–107.

15 John Cage, *Silence: Lectures and Writings* (Cambridge: MIT Press, 1966) 194. (Emphasis added.)

16 Henry Adams, *The Education of Henry Adams* (New York: Modern Library, 1931) 457. Further references abbreviated *Education.*

17 Lorine Niedecker, "The Poetry of Louis Zukofsky," *From This Condensery: The Complete Writing,* ed. Robert J. Bertholf (Highlands: Jargon Society, 1985) 293.

18 Barry Ahearn, "Origins of 'A': Zukofsky's Materials for Collage," *ELH* 45 (Spring 1978): 155.

19 "Sincerity and Objectification," *Poetry* 37 (February 1931): 280.
20 Ezra Pound, *ABC of Reading* (New York: New Directions, 1960) 52.
21 Niedecker 296.
22 Boulez 24. (Emphasis added.)
23 Russell 29.
24 Boulez 201.
25 Lorentz 133. Quoted in *CSP* 104.
26 Letter to Cid Corman, 25 August 1960, *Origin* second series, 1 (April 1961): 63; quoted in Cid Corman, "In the Event of Words," *Louis Zukofsky: Man and Poet,* ed. Carroll F. Terrell (Orono, Maine: National Poetry Foundation, 1979) 326.
27 I adopt "practice" from Donald Wesling, *The Chances of Rhyme: Device and Modernity* (Berkeley: U of California P, 1980), Chap. 1, but especially 6–12.
28 Ezra Pound, "Berlin," *The Exile,* 4 (Autumn 1928): 114.
29 William Carlos Williams, *The Selected Letters of William Carlos Williams,* ed. John C. Thirlwall (New York: McDowell, Obolensky, 1957) 126.
30 William Carlos Williams, "A New Line Is a New Measure," *New Quarterly of Poetry* 2 (Winter 1946–7): 8. (Emphasis added.)
31 H. R. Mackintosh, "Grace," *Encyclopedia of Religion and Ethics,* ed. J. Hastings (New York: Scribner's. 1921) 6: 364.

## *CHAPTER THREE*

1 Louis Zukofsky, *"A"* (Berkeley: U of California P, 1978) 214. All further references are to this edition.
2 Basil Bunting, conversation with Peter Quartermain, 24 October 1971.
3 *"A" 1–12* was originally published by Cid Corman in Japan (Kyoto: Origin Press, 1959); the English edition (London: Cape) appeared in 1966 and the American (New York: Doubleday/Paris Review) in 1967; *"A" – 14* was separately published as a book in 1967 (London: Turret) two years before *"A" 13–21* appeared (London: Cape; New York: Doubleday/Paris Review, 1969). Unless otherwise stated, all references to *"A"* in this essay are to the one-volume edition (Berkeley: U of California P, 1978).
4 The manuscript of "A" – 7 is dated 4–7 August 1930 (date of completion; Zukofsky began work on the poem 10 October 1928); the first section of "A" – 8 to be completed (ending at line 5, *"A"* 49), is dated 5 August 1935 – an interval of almost exactly five years. See items C7 and C8 in Marcella Booth, *A Catalogue of the Louis Zukofsky Manuscript Collection* (Austin: U of Texas, 1975) 51–2.
5 See the "Year by Year" section of Celia Zukofsky, *A Bibliography of Louis Zukofsky* (Los Angeles: Black Sparrow Press, 1969) 48.
6 Louis Zukofsky, letter to the editor, *Poetry* 43 (May 1933): 117.
7 Louis Zukofsky, *Prepositions: The Collected Critical Essays,* expanded ed. (Berkeley: U of California P, 1981), 16 (Zukofsky's italics). Further references cited *Prep*. For further elaboration of this point about "A" – 7 see

Peter Quartermain, "Louis Zukofsky – Re: Location," *Open Letter,* 2nd ser., 6 (Fall 1973): 54–64.

8 Hugh Kenner, "Of Notes and Horses," *Poetry* 111 (November 1967): 112.

9 Louis Zukofsky to Ezra Pound, 12 December 1930, in Barry Ahearn, ed., *Pound/Zukofsky: Selected Letters of Ezra Pound and Louis Zukofsky* (New York: New Directions, 1987) 79. (Further references abbreviated *Pound/Zuk.*) Ezra Pound, "Cavalcanti," *Literary Essays of Ezra Pound,* T. S. Eliot, ed. (London: Faber, 1954) 168. In the same essay Pound called the double canzone "the grand bogey of technical mastery" (170). A carbon copy of the 1935 typescript *Workers' Anthology* is among Basil Bunting's papers, Mountjoy Collection, Durham University Library.

10 Louis Zukofsky letter to Cid Corman, 11 July 1960, *Origin* 2nd. ser., 1 (April 1961): 46

11 According to Bunting (conversation with Peter Quartermain, 20 December 1971), Pound edited *Active Anthology* to set before the public work by Bunting, Marianne Moore, William Carlos Williams, and Zukofsky, with a few others to round out the book. Bunting selected the work by Moore and Williams, and eight pages of "Fragments from *Eimi*" by E. E. Cummings. Pound selected the rest. Pound's correspondence with Zukofsky indicates Zukofsky's role in the editorial process, too (see *Pound/Zuk xiii,* and 141–9).

12 The letter is at the Harry Ransom Humanities Research Center, the University of Texas at Austin. For the exact wording of what is here paraphrased see Peter Quartermain, "I am Different, Let Not a Gloss Embroil You," *Paideuma* 9.1 (Spring 1980): 204. Permission to reprint refused by Paul Zukofsky.

13 "Imagism." *The New Review* 1.2 (May–June 1931): 160–2; partially reprinted in *Prepositions* 135.

14 The letter is at the Harry Ransom Humanities Research Center, the University of Texas at Austin. For the exact wording of what is here paraphrased see Quartermain, "I Am Different" 204–5. Permission to reprint refused by Paul Zukofsky.

15 The letter is at the Harry Ransom Humanities Research Center, the University of Texas at Austin. For the exact wording of what is here paraphrased see Quartermain, "I Am Different" 206. Permission to reprint refused by Paul Zukofsky.

16 There are, however, the important exceptions of the notebooks for "A" – 22, "A" – 23, and *80 Flowers.* In her *Reading Zukofsky's "80 Flowers"* (Baltimore: Johns Hopkins UP, 1989) Michele Leggott suggests that Zukofsky specifically preserved these notebooks as instruction manuals for readers of those poems.

17 Louis Zukofsky, "'Recencies' in Poetry," *An "Objectivists" Anthlogy* (Le Beausset, Var: To, Publishers, 1932) 21–2; *Prep.* 17.

18 The Dedication to Celia Zukofsky was originally designed as a transition from "A" – 23 and so placed to smooth over the joint between separate volumes of the book. Its move to the end of the poem preserves the discontinuity, the abrupt shift, between the volumes, and points the reader to an index which, originally prepared by Zukofsky (and at first consisting

only of entries for "a," "an," and "the"), was expanded by Celia Zukofsky, and then revised by him.

19 Giorgio di Santillana and Hertha von Dechend, *Hamlet's Mill: An Essay on Myth and the Frame of Time* (Boston: Gambit, 1969) *xiii*.

20 I am indebted to Hugh Kenner for the identification of this as a found poem. In a letter, 20 September 1979, he told me of remembering it "in an anthology called *Humor among the Clergy*, Anglican whimsy from some English publisher." I am unable to identify the source more precisely.

21 The relevant papers – drafts, notes, correspondence with prospective publishers – are scattered, the bulk of them in the Harry Ransom Humanities Research Center, University of Texas at Austin and in the American Literature Collection, Beinecke Rare Book and Manuscript Library, Yale University, with the remainder in the Poetry Collection, SUNY Buffalo. For more detailed documentation, see Chapter 5, Note 13.

22 William Carlos Williams, "The Work of Gertrude Stein," *Selected Essays* (New York: New Directions, 1969) 115. Further references abbreviated *SE*.

23 Louis Zukofsky to Cid Corman, 12 July 1963. The letter is at the Harry Ransom Humanities Research Center, the University of Texas at Austin. For the exact wording of what is here paraphrased see Peter Quartermain, "'Only Is Order Othered. Nought Is Nulled': *Finnegans Wake* and Middle and Late Zukofsky," *ELH* 54.4 (Winter 1987): 961. Permission to reprint refused by Paul Zukofsky.

24 *Bottom: On Shakespeare* (Austin: U of Texas P, 1963) 22 (emphasis added).

25 The publication, of course, did nothing of the sort. Zukofsky's English text (Chapters 1 and 3) were serialised in *The Westmінister Magazine* 22.4 (Winter 1933): 9–50; and 23.1 (Spring 1934): 7–46. Taupin's French translation of Zukofsky's text (including Chapter 2, "Le Poete Resuscite," Zukofsky's selection of Apollinaire's work) was published as *Le Style Apollinaire* (Paris: Les Presses Modernes, 1934), but the bulk of the edition was destroyed in a warehouse fire. For the exact wording of Zukofsky's remark to Rakosi here paraphrased (the letter is at the Harry Ransom Humanities Research Center, the University of Texas at Austin) see Peter Quartermain, "I am Different, Let Not a Gloss Embroil You," *Paideuma* 9.1 (Spring 1980): 206. Permission to reprint refused by Paul Zukofsky.

26 "The Poet," *The Collected Works of Ralph Waldo Emerson*, Vol. 3, *Essays: Second Series*, ed. Joseph Slater, Alfred R. Ferguson and Jean Ferguson Carr (Cambridge: Belknap P of Harvard UP, 1983): 11.

## *CHAPTER FOUR*

1 John Dryden, "Notes and Observations on *The Empress of Morocco*," *Prose 1668–1691, An Essay of Dramatick Poesie and Shorter Works*, Vol. 17 of *The Works of John Dryden*, ed. Samuel Holt Monk (Berkeley: U of California P, 1971) 182.

2 *First Half of "A" – 9*, New York 1940. Further references abbreviated *First Half* only when the material cited is peculiar to this edition. The poem itself, without the apparatus included in *First Half*, is in *"A"* (Berkeley: U of

California P, 1978) 106–8. Other work by or referring to Zukofsky is abbreviated as follows:

*Bottom: On Shakespeare* (Austin: U of Texas P, 1963), as *Bottom;*
*Prepositions: The Collected Critical Essays,* expanded ed. (Berkeley: U of California P, 1981), as *Prep.;*
Marcella Booth, *A Catalogue of the Louis Zukofsky Manuscript Collection* (Austin, Texas: Humanities Research Center U of Texas, 1975), as Booth.

When *"A" – 9* was published as a broadside ("Futura 9," Stuttgart: Mayer, 1966) Zukofsky reiterated his earlier (and lamentable) decision that *First Half* is "not to be reprinted."

3 Zukofsky's correspondence with Dahlberg and Corman relating to these copies is at the Harry Ransom Humanities Research Center, The University of Texas at Austin. According to Barry Ahearn copies "were still to be had for the asking in the 1960's." *Zukofsky's "A": An Introduction* (Baltimore: Johns Hopkins UP, 1983) 100.
4 *First Half* 40. For the exact wording of Zukofsky's text, see Peter Quartermain, "'Not at all Surprised by Science': Louis Zukofsky's *First Half of A – 9.*" Carroll F. Terrell, ed. *Louis Zukofsky: Man and Poet* (Orono, Maine: National Poetry Foundation, 1979), 204.
5 *Henry Adams: Detached Mind and Poetic Undertow* was substantially complete by May 7, 1924, and was Zukofsky's M. A. thesis at Columbia University. Not only was it, as Zukofsky himself noted, the first full-length study of Adams, it was written within six years of the publication (in 1918) of Adams's *Education,* and still awaits publication in book form. Initially serialised in three instalments in *The Hound & Horn* in 1930, it was substantially abridged for its inclusion in *Prepositions.*
6 Henry Adams, *Mont-Saint-Michel and Chartres,* introduction by Ralph Adams Cram (Princeton: Princeton UP, 1981) 383. Further references abbreviated *MSM.*
7 Michel Foucault, *The Order of Things: An Archaeology of the Human Sciences* (London: Tavistock, 1970) 328.
8 Robert Duncan, "Notes on Poetics Regarding Olson's Maximus," *Fictive Certainties: Essays* (New York: New Directions, 1985) 71.
9 William Richard Lethaby, *Architecture: An Introduction to the History and Theory of the Art of Building,* with new preface by Basil Ward, 3rd ed. (London: Oxford UP, 1955) 153. Further references abbreviated *Architecture.* Zukofsky quotes part of this passage in *Bottom,* 183–4.
10 Hugh Kenner, "Of Poetry and Horses," *Poetry* 111 (November 1967): 112.
11 Of the twenty-four movements of *"A"*, the last completed were "A" – 22 & 23; the manuscript at the Harry Ransom Humanities Research Center, the University of Texas at Austin, is dated 17 April 1974.
12 Ezra Pound, "Cavalcanti," *Literary Essays,* ed. with an introduction by T. S. Eliot (London: Faber and Faber, 1954) 170. Further references abbreviated *LE.* Ezra Pound's *Gaudier-Brzeska A Memoir* (New York: New Directions, 1970) will be abbreviated *G-B.*

13 Letter to Peter Quartermain, 18 October 1968. For the exact wording of what is here paraphrased see Quartermain, "'Not at all Surprised'," 208. Permission to reprint refused by Paul Zukofsky.

14 *"A"* 48–9; originally published in *New Masses* 27.6 (3 May 1938):14 as "March Comrades. Words for a workers' chorus."

15 The only surviving portion of Zukofsky's aborted *Workers' Anthology* is a 1935 carbon-copy typescript which Zukofsky sent to Basil Bunting, now in the Mountjoy Collection, Durham University Library. Zukofsky included a little less than half of its contents in *A Test of Poetry*.

16 Described in Booth 52, item C8a. There is also a balancing of patternings amongst the nine stanzas; 1, 5, and 9, for instance, are almost identical.

17 See Hugh Kenner, "Too Full For Talk: 'A' – 11," *Louis Zukofsky: Man and Poet,* ed. Carroll F. Terrell (Orono, Maine: National Poetry Foundation, 1979) 195–202 for a careful discussion of this poem.

18 *Capital,* 4th German ed., trans. Eden and Cedar Paul; introduction G. D. H. Cole, addendum Murray Wolfson (London and New York: J. M. Dent [Everyman's Library], 1974) 47. Further referred to as *Capital*.

19 Of course, a "sought effect" might indeed be *per se* a proposition, or received as one, and "effects" might well generate "propositions" anyway. The matter is discussed *passim* in *Bottom*.

20 Lawrence of Aquilegia, *Speculum Dictaminis;* quoted in James M. Murphy, introduction, *Three Medieval Rhetorical Arts* (Berkeley: U of California P, 1971) *vii*. I am grateful to Meredith Yearsley for showing this to me.

21 Robert Creeley, *A Quick Graph: Collected Notes and Essays* (San Francisco: Four Seasons Foundation, 1970) 130. Further references abbreviated *AQG*.

22 Guy Davenport, "Zukofsky." *The Geography of the Imagination: Forty Essays* (San Franscisco: North Point, 1981) 103.

23 William Blake, "On Virgil," *Complete Poetry and Prose,* ed. D. Erdman, commentary by Harold Bloom; rev. ed. (Berkeley: U of California P, 1982) 270.

24 Ludwig Wittgenstein, *Tractatus Logico-Philosophicus* (London: Kegan Paul, Trench, Trubner, 1922) 27.

25 "Notes on Contributors," *New Directions, 1938* (Norfolk, Conn.: New Directions, 1938), unpaginated. James Laughlin told me in conversation, 16 March 1982, that he wrote the "Notes."

26 For the text of "A Foin Lass Bodders," Zukofsky's slang version, see *Paideuma* 7.3 (Winter 1978): 409–11.

27 "*U. S. A.: Poetry:* Louis Zukofsky." National Educational Television programme filmed 16 March 1966.

28 Robert Duncan, "The Sweetness and Greatness of Dante's *Divine Comedy,*" *Fictive Certainties: Essays* (New York: New Directions, 1983) 142–61, but especially 143–6.

29 For the text of Reisman's second (and final) stanza see Hugh Kenner, "Loove in Brooklyn," *Paideuma* 7.3 (Winter 1978): 417.

30 Ezra Pound, "Brancusi," *LE* 444.

31 Thomas Sprat, *The History of the Royal-Society of London, For the Improving*

*of Natural Knowledge* (1667), ed. Jackson I. Cope and Harold W. Jones (St. Louis: Washington U, 1958) 113. Further references abbreviated *History*.

32 H. Stanley Allen, *Electrons and Waves: An Introduction to Atomic Physics* (London: Macmillan, 1932) 43. Further references abbreviated *E&W*.

33 Hugh Kenner, *The Counterfeiters, An Historical Comedy* (Bloomington: Indiana UP, 1968) 129. Much of the argument in this paragraph is indebted to this book, hereafter cited as *Counterfeiters*.

34 William Carlos Williams, *Paterson* (New York: New Directions, 1963) 95.

35 "Value is the word I use for the intrinsic reality of an event," Alfred North Whitehead wrote in *Science and the Modern World* (1925). "Value is an element which permeates through and through the poetic view of nature." In January 1950 (when he was writing the second half of "A" – 9), Zukofsky appended these words (with quotations from nine other writers) to the manuscript of his essay "A Statement for Poetry" under the heading "Other Comments."

36 Jacques Roubaud, "Poétique comme exploration des changements de forme," *Changement de Forme: Révolution Langage*, ed. Jean Pierre Faye and Jacques Roubaud, Vol. 1, *Change de Formes: Biologies et Prosodies* (Paris: Union générale d'éditions, 1975) 75.

37 Eric Mottram, "1924–1951: Politics and Form in Zukofsky," *Maps* 5 (1973): 98–9.

38 Robert Duncan, "Reading Zukofsky These Forty Years," *Paideuma* 7.3 (Winter 1978): 427.

## *CHAPTER FIVE*

1 William Carlos Williams, letter to Louis Zukofsky, 2 April 1928, in William Carlos Williams, *Selected Letters*, ed. John C. Thirlwall (New York: McDowell, Obolensky, 1957) 94. Further references abbreviated *SL*. Other works by Williams are documented parenthetically in the text as follows:

*CP1 Collected Poems of William Carlos Williams*, Vol. 1: *1909–1939*, ed. A. Walton Litz and Christopher MacGowan (New York: New Directions, 1986);
*CP2 Collected Poems of William Carlos Williams*, Vol. 2: *1939–1962*, ed. Christopher MacGowan (New York: New Directions, 1988);
*KIH Kora in Hell: Improvisations*, in *Imaginations*, ed. Webster Schott (New York: New Directions, 1970);
*ML Many Loves and Other Plays* (New York: New Directions, 1961);
*Pat Paterson* (New York: New Directions, 1963);
*SE Selected Essays* (New York: New Directions, 1969).

2 Louis Zukofsky, *Complete Short Poems* (Baltimore: Johns Hopkins UP, 1991) 216. Further references abbreviated *CSP*. Other works by Zukofsky are documented parenthetically in the text as follows:

*"A" "A"* (Berkeley: U of California P, 1979).
*Bottom Bottom: On Shakespeare*, 2 vols. (Austin: Ark P, 1963).

*Prep. Prepositions: The Collected Critical Essays,* expanded ed. (Berkeley: U of California P, 1981).

References to Marcella Booth, *A Catalogue of the Louis Zukofsky Manuscript Collection* (Austin: Humanities Research Center, 1975) are abbreviated as "Booth."

3 The letter is at the Harry Ransom Humanities Research Center, the University of Texas at Austin. For the exact wording of Zukofsky's remarks here paraphrased see Peter Quartermain, "'Actual Word Stuff, Not Thoughts for Thought': Louis Zukofsky and William Carlos Williams," *Credences* 2.1 (Summer 1983): 104. Permission to reprint refused by Paul Zukofsky. Quotations from the letters of Lorine Niedecker are copyright the estate of Lorine Niedecker, Cid Corman executor; from William Carlos Williams are copyright William Eric Williams and Paul Williams. Quotations and citations from these letters and manuscripts appear by courtesy of their owners as follows:

The Harry Ransom Humanities Research Center, the University of Texas at Austin (documented parenthetically in the text as TxU);
American Literature Collection, Yale University (documented as CtY);
Poetry/Rare Books Collection, State University of New York at Buffalo (documented as NBuU).

From about 1930 on, Louis Zukofsky scrupulously dated the manuscripts of his work, always with the date of completion, occasionally with the date of beginning as well. Dates of completion, when given, are from the manuscript source.

4 See, for example, *"A"* 214–15; 226. For the exact wording of Zukofsky's words to Niedecker here paraphrased see Quartermain, "'Actual Word Stuff": 104. Permission to reprint refused by Paul Zukofsky.

5 As, for example (to pick some poems from *CSP* virtually at random), "Michtam 4" quotes Basil Bunting; "Light 5" quotes Lenin; "Light 8" quotes Celia Zukofsky; "Xenophanes" quotes Xenophanes; "Her Face the Book of" quotes Robert Duncan, Henry Birnbaum, and Lorine Niedecker; "*Anew* 18" quotes the Emperor Hirohito; and "29 Songs, 1" quotes Thomas Jefferson.

6 Such as Williams's review of 55 *Poems,* "An Extraordinary Sensitivity," *Poetry* 60 (September 1942): 338–40; his untitled review of *An "Objectivists" Anthology* in *The Symposium* 4 (January 1933): 114–16; and his review of *Anew,* "A New Line is a New Measure," *The New Quarterly of Poetry,* 2.2 (Winter 1947–8): 8–16. On his side, Zukofsky wrote on Williams in "American Poetry 1920–1930," *The Symposium,* 2 (January 1930): 60–84; "Beginning again with William Carlos Williams," *The Hound and Horn* 4 (Winter 1931): 261–4; "Poetry in a Modern Age," *Poetry* 76 (June 1950): 177–80; "The Best Human Value," *The Nation* 186 (31 May 1958): 500–2; "An Old Note on William Carlos Williams," *The Massachusetts Review* 3 (Winter 1962): 301–2; many of these were considerably revised or cut when published in *Prep.*

7 In addition to "A" – 17, so numbered to coincide with Williams's birthday, 17 September, there are "Songs of Degrees" (*CSP* 148–51), and "*Anew* 42" (*CSP* 99–102).

8 Williams sent Zukofsky the typescript drafts of what was to become *The Wedge* on 21 March 1943 (TxU), with further exchanges through 11 April 1943 (TxU); on 10 September 1943 (TxU) Williams sent *The Wedge* back to Zukofsky for further revisions; on 24 September Cummington Press accepted *The Wedge* for publication, and on 5 October 1943 (TxU) Williams asked Zukofsky for yet further revisions. Emily Mitchell Wallace records, in *A Bibliography of William Carlos Williams* (Middletown, CT: Wesleyan UP, 1968) 53, that *The Wedge* was published on 27 September 1944. For a clear recounting of Zukofsky's hand in the make-up of *The Wedge* see Neil Baldwin, "Zukofsky, Williams, and *The Wedge:* Toward a Dynamic Convergence," in Carroll F. Terrell, ed., *Louis Zukofsky: Man and Poet* (Orono, ME: National Poetry Foundation, 1979) 129–42.

9 William Carlos Williams, "Zukofsky," in Louis Zukofsky, *"A" 1–12* (Kyoto: Origin Press, 1959) 291–6; reprinted in *Agenda,* 3.6 (December 1964): 1–4.

10 Much of this exchange is still buried, and the extent of Williams's indebtedness to Zukofsky may never be amply documented. The Harry Ransom Humanities Research Center, the University of Texas at Austin, holds some 490 letters and cards from Williams to Zukofsky, some 40 from Florence Herman Williams to Zukofsky, and copies of a handful of letters from Zukofsky to Williams. Most of Zukofsky's letters to Williams (there are not many) are at SUNY Buffalo and at Yale University.

11 The evidence is largely inferential, and I doubt whether Zukofsky got paid. But see for example Zukofsky to Williams, 28 August 1931, where Zukofsky reports that he may have sold some of Williams's poems to *Hound and Horn* (NBuU). (For Zukofsky's exact words, here paraphrased, see Quartermain, "'Actual Word Stuff": 120, note 11. Permission to reprint refused by Paul Zukofsky.) Williams persisted in job hunting for Zukofsky, however; on 7 November 1942, for example, he sent Zukofsky to Clayton Hoagland, whom he thought might have a job for him at the New York *Sun*.

12 Zukofsky completed "Mantis: An Interpretation" on 4 November 1934 (MS at TxU). For the exact wording of Zukofsky's letter to Williams on 27 October 1934 (TxU) and 22 October 1941 (TxU), here paraphrased, see Quartermain, "'Actual Word Stuff": 105. Permission to reprint refused by Paul Zukofsky. Similarly, Williams had on 27 December 1928 (CtY) commented in some detail on "A" – 1 and (like Pound) objected to the original opening ("A / thousand fiddles playing Bach"). There is, in the Centre for Pound Studies at Yale, a typescript of the first two pages of "A" – 1 extensively marked up by Pound.

13 Williams to Zukofsky, 3 November 1929: "Your notes have been of great assistance to me in revising the Stein thing" (CtY), and Zukofsky to Carl Rakosi, 16 January 1931, stating flatly that he and Williams cooperated on the essay (TxU). (For Zukofsky's exact words, here paraphrased, see Quartermain, "'Actual Word Stuff": 120, Note 13. Permission to reprint refused

by Paul Zukofsky). Other references to Zukofsky's revisions of the essay on Stein are in Williams's letters to Zukofsky 15 September 1929, 10 October 1929, 22 October 1929, 22 November 1929, and 4 December 1929 (all at TxU). Williams sent his essay on Pound for comment and possible revision on 23 February 1931 (CtY).

14 For example, Mrs. Arnold's four-line "aria" (as Zukofsky called it) "Sorrow! sorrow little child!" in Act 1, Scene 2 (*ML* 328) is by Zukofsky (MS at TxU); the poem "Alba" (*CSP* 134; see also Booth 63) was written for *The First President* – Zukofsky discarded it in 1934 and rewrote it in 1952 (TxU). The synopsis of Act 3 is at NBuU, as is the MS of Williams's "Under the Stars," a dialogue between Washington and Lafayette which was later discarded from *The First President* and published separately in *UKCR* 11 (Autumn 1944): 26–8 after extensive reworking by Zukofsky. Writing *The First President* proved a nightmare for Williams, as the correspondence (scattered among CtY, NBuU, and TxU) shows; at one stage Williams enlisted the help of Zukofsky's friend Jerry Reisman as well as that of Zukofsky.

15 Anton Reiser, *Albert Einstein: A Biographical Portrait* (New York: Albert and Charles Boni, 1930); moderately successful, the book was published in November 1930, with a second printing in January 1931, and an English edition the same year (London: Thornton Butterworth, 1931). In a note on the inside cover of the TxU copy of Reiser's book, Zukofsky records that he did not wish to have his name as translator appear in the book, which (but for Einstein's preface) was, so far as he was concerned, simply a job to be done in the winter and spring of 1929–30. Zukofsky told Rakosi he was writing a ghost book on Apollinaire for $50.00 a month (2 March 1932; TxU). Williams read the manuscript of *The Writing of Guillaume Apollinaire* in May 1933 (Williams to Zukofsky 31 May 1933; TxU) and commented enthusiastically on it in a letter of 28 March 1934 (TxU). (For Zukofsky's exact words here paraphrased, see Quartermain, "'Actual Word Stuff": 120, Note 15. Permission to reprint refused by Paul Zukofsky). See also Barry Ahearn, ed. *Pound/Zukofsky: Selected Letters of Ezra Pound and Louis Zukofsky* (New York: New Directions, 1987).

16 "Swivel-hipped Amazon" is at TxU; the remainder (so far as I can determine) are at NBuU. Whilst teaching at Madison, Wis. in 1930–1 as a "two-thirds" Assistant Professor, Zukofsky reworked Williams's "A Democratic Party Poem" – see, for example, in addition to the MSS at NBuU, Zukofsky to Williams 10 July 1931 (CtY).

17 For example, Zukofsky's notebook for "A" – 22 and 23 at TxU closes with an addendum (obviously predating the composition of "A" – 22 and 23) consisting of some ten drafts of the "dedication" to "A" – 24, which date from 17 September 1968 to 27 September 1969 when he finally decided not only on the published version but that it should serve as what he called "transition from A 23." The California edition of *"A"* prints this *after* "A" – 24, on 806. The insistent care with which Zukofsky dated his manuscripts from 1930-or-so on suggests the urgency of his concern to preserve the history of his writing, of the compositional process, of his text. Williams, on the other hand, seems to have been indifferent to the history of his.

18 Text of *Go Go* (1923), *Spring and All* (1923), *Collected Poems 1921–1931* (1934), *Complete Collected Poems* (1938), and *Selected Poems* (1949).

19 Zukofsky's copy, at TxU, is inscribed by Williams with the date 11 April 1928. See also "The Best Human Value," *The Nation* 186 (31 May 1958): 501 and *Prep* 47.

20 Gertrude Stein, *Lectures in America* (Boston: Beacon Press, 1957) 221.

21 'απο κοινοῦ, literally, *in common* or *shared*. See Liddell and Scott, entry for κοινός, definition VI, 4: "in Grammar and Rhetoric." Like "quantity," it seems to be a device largely neglected for some 400 years in English verse; it occurs frequently in such writers as Thucydides and in such poems as *Beowulf*.

22 The first two of Williams's "Calypsos," when they first appeared in *The New Yorker* (14 September 1957): 85 as "Puerto Rican Songs," were heavily punctuated.

23 This technique, refined and exaggerated, seems to be the basic principle of composition in "A" – 22 and "A" – 23, where its effect is virtually to remove the author's own voice entirely from the poem, so that in effect the poem is *authorless*, simply (!) a play of language in which, or out of which, meanings are constructed.

24 Paul Zukofsky was born on 22 October 1943; the poem was completed on 19 July 1960 (ms. at TxU).

25 Zukofsky uses a lot of quotations; there are, too, very often *unquoted* quotes which resonate among the words, songs we already know or – more often – cultural icons like plays by Shakespeare or by the Greeks and Romans.

26 As Gertrude Stein records on the opening pages of *Wars I Have Seen* (London: Batsford, 1945) she heard "Austrians German and French French" between 1875 and 1879; that is, from when she was eight months old (when the family moved to Vienna) to when she was four-and-a-half (when the family moved to Paris) to when she was five (when the family moved to New York and then Baltimore, "where emotions began to feel themselves in English"). In his *Autobiography* (New York: Grossman, 1970) 33 Zukofsky records that he first learned English when he went to school, at Chrystie and Hester Streets. In Chapter 1 of *William Carlos Williams: A New World Naked* (New York: McGraw-Hill, 1981), Paul Mariani gives the evidence for the predominance of Spanish in William George Williams's household when William Carlos was a small child. William George, who spoke Spanish fluently, was rarely at home; Elena, whose native language was Spanish, learned French and preferred it because it was a sign of culture, and disliked English, learning it only slowly and imperfectly; Emily Wellcome also spoke Spanish, having lived in Santo Domingo and Puerta Plata for over twenty years. That Spanish was alive in the house is testified in part by the large box of postcards written nearly all in Spanish, some in French, the odd one in English, which Paul Mariani found at 9 Ridge Road when working on his book; William George conversed in Spanish when he was at home, though as William Carlos grew older he spoke more and more English in the home. In the letter to me (9 March 1982) in which he gives this information, Mariani says that "Williams learned much of his English from his

grandmother and of course from the neighborhood, but always there was the plash of Spanish in the house, so that Pound's insight that Williams was a 'Dago,' i.e., the outsider looking in on a new world of language is correct. Since Williams was a slow and also a meticulous learner, the words – the English words – struck his consciousness as words – signs – with a texture. Which helps explain his particular love of Gertrude Stein. Words as words as words. Pop Williams was away nearly all of Williams's life, certainly up till a year or two before his death by cancer of the colon on Christmas Day 1918."

Laura Riding acutely remarked in *Contemporaries and Snobs* (New York: Doubleday Doran, 1928), 189 that "None of the words Miss Stein uses have ever had any experience. They are no older than her use of them. . . . None of these words . . . has ever had any history." I think this applies equally well to both Williams and Zukofsky.

27 Letter to Cid Corman, 27 December 1959 (TxU); (for Zukofsky's exact words here paraphrased, see Quartermain, "'Actual Word Stuff": 114. Permission to reprint refused by Paul Zukofsky).

28 Letter to Allan Stroock, *Hound and Horn* papers, CtY; (for Zukofsky's exact words here paraphrased, see Quartermain, "'Actual Word Stuff": 115. Permission to reprint refused by Paul Zukofsky).

29 Letter to Cid Corman, 17 August 1959 (TxU); to Lorine Niedecker, 1941 fragment (TxU); and to Niedecker, c. 1950 fragment (TxU). (For Zukofsky's exact words here paraphrased, see Quartermain, "'Actual Word Stuff": 120, note 15. Permission to reprint refused by Paul Zukofsky).

30 George Bowering, *Allophanes* (Toronto: Coach House Press, 1976), [9].

31 "The Objectivist Program: Lecture at the Poetry Center of the YMHA, NY. 23 Jan 1941," typescript at TxU. (For Zukofsky's exact words, here paraphrased, see Quartermain, "'Actual Word Stuff": 116. Permission to reprint refused by Paul Zukofsky).

32 Paul Valéry, "The Future of Literature: Will It Be a Sport?" *New York Herald Tribune* (Book section), 22 April 1928: 1, 6. A somewhat different version, "The Future of Literature," is in *The Collected Works of Paul Valéry,* ed. Jackson Mathews, Vol. 11, *Occasions,* trans. Roger Shattuck and Frederick Brown, with an introduction by Roger Shattuck (Princeton: Princeton UP, Bollingen Series 45.11, 1970) 151–7. Zukofsky completed this passage on 7 January 1937 (TxU).

33 Valéry's four essays on Descartes are collected in the aptly titled volume *Masters and Friends,* trans. Martin Turnell, introduction by Joseph Frank, of *The Collected Works of Paul Valéry,* Vol. 9 (Princeton: Princeton UP, Bollingen Series 45.9, 1968).

34 It might be argued that *Paterson* reflects Rimbaud and Baudelaire as much as it does Apollinaire; certainly it echoes neither Laforgue nor Valéry. Other than the generic resemblance of *Pat* 137 to work in *Calligrammes,* at best suggestive of Apollinaire (but also reminiscent of work in the later issues of *Transition*), there are parallels, echoes, and possible quotations which suggest a fairly close acquaintance with and use of Apollinaire. Not only do dogs and unicorns run all through *Alcools* (as do, I might add, the sea,

and rivers), but in that book Apollinaire specifically links the act of creation to wine and fire, drunkenness and life; the bottle mauled by fire in Book 3 (and especially *Pat* 117) is reminiscent of the opening and closing lines of "Nuit Rhénane," a poem in which occur the yellow and green of the library's flames in *Paterson* Book 3. Similarly, *Pat* 107's "And the river / passes but I remain" echoes the refrain of "Le Pont Mirabeau," while the "thought" of those lines and the ones immediately following generally reechoes that of Apollinaire's poem. So too "stale as a whale's breath" (*Pat* 20) occurs in a context very similar to that of the "mammoth's dull taste" in "Palais." Apollinaire and Williams both share a concern for everyday language (see, e.g., "Cortege"); much of the flavour of *Paterson*'s disconnectedness and collagelike quality is also the flavour of *Alcools,* and both poets evoke smells, breath, and stench throughout their work. It is tempting, of course, to overstate the parallels, but they are worth following up.

35 Zukofsky felt, as he told Rakosi on 4 April 1932 (TxU), that his discovery of those writers major to him, Adams, Apollinaire, and Pound, was sheer luck, a matter of stumbing across them. He completed *The Writing of Guillaume Apollinaire* on 19 April 1932 (for Zukofsky's exact words here paraphrased, see Quartermain, "'Actual Word Stuff'": 122, Note 32. Permission to reprint refused by Paul Zukofsky).

36 The opening paragraph of "A-bomb and H-" is discussed in Chapter 6. For a careful and detailed analysis of Williams's discovery of how to "write carelessly" in *Kora in Hell,* and of its central role in his poetic, see Roy Miki, *The Prepoetics of William Carlos Williams Kora in Hell* (Ann Arbor: UMI Research P, 1983).

37 In his Introduction to *The Yale Gertrude Stein* (New Haven, 1980), Richard Kostelanetz acutely observes that, just as "no event is more important than any other" in *The Making of Americans,* so (through repetition) Gertrude Stein's clauses "have equal weight within the whole" (*xvii–xviii*).

38 "Things are not seen, therefore they are not things known." *Picasso* (Boston: Beacon Press, 1959) 35.

39 *Lectures in America,* 209–10. Such a distrust of nouns as inert and lifeless has a long history in American writing, especially but not only in the moralist/revivalist protestant tradition, from at least Jonathan Edwards if not Thomas Hooker on. Emerson's 1844 remark (in "The Poet") that "every word was once a poem" has its later parallel in Gertrude Stein's desire, in *Tender Buttons,* for a form in which the poem, taking on all the activities and shifts of verbs, engaging perception, will itself redeem nouns by becoming one.

## *CHAPTER SIX*

1 George Borrow, *The Romany Rye: A Sequel to "Lavengro",* 6th (definitive) ed., (London: John Murray, 1900) 90. The quotation in my title is from James Joyce, *Finnegans Wake* (New York: Viking, 1958) 613.13–14. Further quotations from this work will be cited parenthetically by page and line number. In the preparation of this chapter I owe much to numerous conversations with Dr. Michele Leggott of the University of Auckland and Dr.

Lorraine Weir of the University of British Columbia. Zukofsky's letters and (carefully dated) manuscripts referred to in this essay are, along with Celia Zukofsky's "pony" of Catullus, in the Louis Zukofsky Manuscript Collection at the Harry Ransom Humanities Research Center, University of Texas at Austin.

2 See Marcella Booth, *A Catalogue of the Louis Zukofsky Manuscript Collection* (Austin: Humanities Research Center, University of Texas, 1975) 223, 239–40. For a full description and discussion of this project, see Joseph Evans Slate, "The Reisman–Zukofsky Screenplay of 'Ulysses': Its Background and Significance," in *Joyce at Texas: Essays on the James Joyce Materials at the Humanities Research Center,* ed. Dave Oliphant and Thomas Zigal (Austin: Humanities Research Center, 1983) 107–39

3 Louis Zukofsky, *"A"* (Berkeley: University of California Press. 1978); *Complete Short Poems* (Baltimore: John Hopkins UP, 1991); *Bottom: On Shakespeare* (Austin: The Ark Press, 1963). Quotations from these works will be cited parenthetically.

4 Louis Zukofsky, *Initial* (New York: Phoenix Book Shop, 1970).

5 James S. Atherton, *The Books at the Wake: A Study of Literary Allusions in James Joyce's Finnegans Wake* (London: Faber and Faber, 1959) 34.

6 *The Century Dictionary & Cyclopedia,* 10 vols. (New York: Century, 1902). Further quotations are from this edition.

7 Bruce Comens, "Soundings: The 'An' Song Beginning 'A' – 22," *Sagetrieb* 5 (Spring 1986): 95–106 points out that the "I'm" in "Time" is bracketed by the "ear" in "Era" and "Year," and that "Year" itself rhymes with "yere," an archaic form of "ear." He also gets at the difficult syntax of the opening lines of *Initial,* especially that exasperating "others letters."

8 Charlton B. Lewis and Charles Short, *A Latin Dictionary* (Oxford: Clarendon Press, 1879). Further quotations are from this edition.

9 Michele J. Leggott, *Reading Zukofsky's 80 Flowers* (Baltimore: Johns Hopkins UP, 1989) 34–52.

10 Diogenes Laertius, *Lives of Eminent Philosophers,* trans. R. D. Hicks, 2 vols. (Loeb Classical Library; London: Heinemann; Cambridge: Harvard Univ. Press, 1929) 2: 329.

11 Louis Zukofsky to Cid Corman, 12 July 1963. The letter is at the Harry Ransom Humanities Research Center, The University of Texas at Austin. For the exact wording of what is here paraphrased see Peter Quartermain, "'Only is Order Othered. Nought is Nulled': *Finnegans Wake* and Middle and Late Zukofsky," *ELH* 54.4 (Winter 1987): 961. Permission to reprint refused by Paul Zukofsky.

12 For a representative Zukofsky manuscript, see Cathy Henderson, "Supplement to Marcella Booth's 'A Catalogue of the Louis Zukofsky Manuscript Collection," *Lawrence, Jarry, Zukofsky: A Tryptich – Manuscript Collections at the Harry Ransom Humanities Research Center,* ed. D. Oliphant and G. Dagel (Austin: University of Texas, 1987), 88; also published in enlarged full-colour facsimile as "An Alphabet of Subjects (contents this notebook)" (Vancouver, B.C.: Slug Press, 1979).

13 Adeline Glasheen, *A Third Census of Finnegans Wake: An Index of the Characters and Their Roles* (Berkeley: University of California Press, 1977) 7.
14 James Joyce, *Letters*, ed. Stuart Gilbert (New York: Viking, 1957) 258.
15 Louis Zukofsky, *Prepositions: The Collected Critical Essays,* enlarged ed. (Berkeley: Univ. of California Press, 1981) 167. Further citations will be abbreviated *Prep*.
16 On the rivalry of ear and eye in the *Wake*, see Lorraine Weir, "Permutations of Ireland's Eye in *Finnegans Wake*," *Canadian Journal of Irish Studies* 4.2 (December 1978): 23–32.
17 Quoted in Donald Phillip Verene, *Vico's Science of Imagination* (Ithaca and London: Cornell Univ. Press, 1981) 26.
18 Quoted in Richard Ellman, *James Joyce*, rev. ed. (New York: Oxford Univ. Press, 1982) 554.
19 Roland McHugh, *Annotations to Finnegans Wake* (Baltimore: Johns Hopkins Univ. Press, 1980) 281. Further quotations will be cited parenthetically.
20 Ezra Pound, *Personae: The Collected Poems* (New York: New Directions, 1926) 187.
21 Verene 212.
22 H. Stanley Allen, *Electrons and Waves: An Introduction to Atomic Physics* (London: Macmillan, 1932).
23 Zukofsky wrote "A" – 13 in 1960, and again shelved work on further movements of *"A"* until 1963, when he wrote "A" – 16, 17, and 20. But it is all one work, as Robert Creeley observes: "a poet writes one work all his life, a continuing *song*, so that no division of its own existence can be thought of as being more or less than its sum" ("'Paradise / our / speech . . . ,'" in *A Quick Graph: Collected Notes and Essays*, ed. Donald M. Allen [San Francisco: Four Seasons Foundation, 1970] 124).
24 This device, of incongruous juxtaposition of vocabularies, is an extension of the techniques Zukofsky employed to somewhat different ends in *The First Half of "A" – 9* in 1938–40. Permission to quote the first four sentences of "A-Bomb and H-" refused by Paul Zukofsky as "gratuitous."
25 Martin Heidegger, *What Is Called Thinking?*, trans. J. G. Gray (New York: Harper and Row, 1968) 71.
26 Thus I adapt "fecund incoherence," a term Marianne DeKoven uses of Gertrude Stein in her essay "Gertrude Stein and Modern Painting: Beyond Literary Cubism," *Contemporary Literature* 22 (1981): 83.
27 McHugh *v*.
28 Fritz Senn, *Joyce's Dislocutions: Essays on Reading as Translation*, ed. J. P. Riquelme (Baltimore: Johns Hopkins Univ. Press, 1984).
29 Celia and Louis Zukofsky, trans., *Catullus (Gai Valeri Catulli Veronensis Liber)* (London: Cape Goliard, 1969); reprinted in *CSP* 241–319 without the Latin *en face*. Further references are cited parenthetically. As she told Burton Hatlen, Celia Zukofsky did the groundwork, transcribing the complete Catullus on alternate lines of a notebook, noting above each line of Latin the quantity of every vowel and every syllable, and writing

out below each line "the literal meaning of meanings of every word indicating gender, number, case and the order or sentence structure" (Burton Hatlen, "Zukofsky as Translator," in *Louis Zukofsky, Man and Poet,* ed. C. F. Terrell [Orono: National Poetry Foundation, 1979] 347. Further quotations are cited parenthetically). Zukofsky then worked out his version of each line on the opposite page, on alternate lines, and Celia then made a fair copy on the line above. She worked one notebook ahead of him; he started on 8 February 1958 and worked steadily through the whole of Catullus's work in order, skipping Number 64 ("Peliaco quondam"), with which he completed the sequence on 1 February 1966. During the last three of these six years he also wrote "A" – 14 through 20, and as soon as he'd finished he began "A" – 21, a line-by-line translation of Plautus's *Rudens.* The first poems in *Catullus* are quite straightforward clear translations; as the book progresses, however, the cross-linguistic punning increases and the syntax gets more and more unconventional. Parts of Poem 63 ("Attis") lose sentence structure altogether, moving into Attis's mad incoherence.

30 F. W. Cornish, et al., trans., *Catullus, Tibullus, and Pervigilium Veneris* (Loeb Classical Library; London: Heinemann; Cambridge: Harvard Univ. Press, 1962) 179.

31 *CSP* 317, where there is a small typo here silently corrected.

32 C. L. Neudling, *A Proposopography to Catullus* (Oxford: Iowa Studies in Classical Philology, 1955) 131.

33 Robinson Ellis, *A Commentary on Catullus* (Oxford: Clarendon Press, 1876) 131; further quotations will be cited parenthetically. Kenneth Quinn, ed., *Catullus, The Poems,* 2nd ed. (London: St. Martin's Press, 1977), 451.

34 Marjorie Perloff, "Poetry as Word-System: The Art of Gertrude Stein," *American Poetry Review* 8.5 (September/October 1979): 37. Further quotations are cited parenthetically.

35 Reading *Catullus,* Ian Hamilton Finlay commented (in a letter to Zukofsky, July 1963) that "the point is somehow to do with nouns, and structure – to eliminate the forward pull of syntax." Zukofsky agreed. (Both letters are in the Harry Ransom Humanities Research Center, the University of Texas at Austin.)

36 Meredith Yearsley, "Gertrude Stein," in *Dictionary of Literary Biography: American Poets 1880–1945,* Volume 54: *Third Series, Part Two,* ed. Peter Quartermain (Detroit: Gale Research, 1986) 443.

37 Charles Bernstein, "Time Out of Motion: Looking Ahead to See Backward," *American Poetry* 4 (Fall 1986): 86. Further quotations are cited parenthetically.

38 James Joyce, *A Portrait of the Artist as a Young Man* (New York: Viking, 1956) 189.

39 Louis Zukofsky, "Thanks to the Dictionary," *Collected Fiction* (Elmwood Park, Ill.: Dalkey Archive 1990) 270–300.

40 Gertrude Stein, *Picasso* (Boston: Beacon Press, 1959) 24.

41 Quoted in Ellman 546, 397.

## CHAPTER SEVEN

1 George Kubler, *The Shape of Time: Remarks on the History of Things* (New Haven: Yale UP, 1962) 1. Ezra Pound calls poetry "an art originally intended to make glad the heart of man" in *ABC of Reading* (New York: New Directions, 1960) 13. In the course of this essay I refer to conversations with Bunting and to stories he told. From September to December 1970 he taught at the University of British Columbia, Vancouver, B. C., and from September 1971 to April 1972 at the University of Victoria, Victoria, B. C. During these two periods we saw a great deal of each other, and talked a lot.

2 William Carlos Williams, *Sappho* (San Francisco: *Poems in Folio,* 1957). A somewhat different version of the text is in *Paterson* Book 5, Part 2.

3 Charles Dickens, *Hard Times,* ed. David Craig (Harmondsworth, Middlesex: Penguin Books, 1969) 50.

4 Basil Bunting, "Mr. Ezra Pound," *New English Weekly* 1 (26 May 1932): 138.

5 Lawrence Richardson, "Ezra Pound's Homage to Propertius," *Yale Poetry Review* 6 (1947): 23.

6 J. P. Sullivan, *Ezra Pound and Sextus Propertius* (Austin, Texas: U of Texas P, 1964) 57, 23 (emphasis added). Further references parenthetically documented in my text.

7 T. S. Eliot, "Introduction: 1928," *Selected Poems* by Ezra Pound (London: Faber and Faber, 1949) 20.

8 Basil Bunting, "Prince of Poets," *Sunday Times* [London], 12 November 1972.

9 Jonathan Williams and Tom Meyer, "A Conversation with Basil Bunting (1976)," *Poetry Information* 19 (Autumn 1978): 38.

10 Eric Mottram, "Conversation with Basil Bunting on the Occasion of his Seventy-Fifth Birthday," *Poetry Information* 19 (Autumn 1978): 6. It would be interesting indeed to read that essay.

11 I wish to thank Meredith Yearsley, whose analysis of these passages helped me very much.

12 This is a very difficult area indeed, where one must in the long run rely on intuition. There is a *vast* literature, but a good introduction is Roman Jakobson, "Why 'Mama' and 'Papa'?" *Selected Writings 1: Phonological Studies* (The Hague: Mouton, 1962) 538–45.

## CHAPTER EIGHT

1 Quotations without documentation are from conversations with Basil Bunting or from his letters to me. All other quotations, unless otherwise indicated, are from the following collections, permission to print as coded:

CtY: Collection of American Literature, Beinecke Rare Book and Manuscript Library, Yale University;

ICU: Department of Special Collections, the University of Chicago Library;
InU: Lilly Library, Indiana University, Bloomington, Indiana;
NBuU: Poetry Collection, State University of New York at Buffalo;
TxU: Harry Ransom Humanities Research Center, University of Texas at Austin.

 The words quoted as epigraph are from a letter to me, 19 July 1971.

2 Letter to Louis Zukofsky, 20 August 1947 (TxU).
3 Letter to Ezra Pound, 28 November 1954 (CtY).
4 "83 Answers . . . and Some Questions" BBC television programme first broadcast on BBC North East, 1983; repeated on BBC 2, 11 May 1985.
5 Letter to Dorothy Pound, 9 June 1949 (InU).
6 Letter to Marian Bunting, 9 November 1938 (TxU).
7 Sally Beauman, "Man of Plain Words," *Daily Telegraph Magazine* 244 (13 June 1969): 32.
8 "Folk-Song in London," *The Sackbut* 8.9 (April 1928): 272.
9 Letter to Marian Bunting, 30 December 1937 (TxU).
10 "Folk-Song in London" 274.
11 Letter to Jonathan Williams, 22 August 1977 (NBuU).
12 Letter to Louis Zukofsky, 25 July 1944 (TxU).
13 Letter to Louis Zukofsky, 27 October 1953 (TxU).
14 Letter to Ezra Pound, [April 1954] (CtY).
15 Letter to Dorothy Pound, 28 August 1948 (InU).
16 Letter to *Contempo,* 5 February 1932 (TxU).
17 Letter to Ezra Pound, 21 March 1934 (CtY).
18 Undated letter to Ezra Pound, [1934] (CtY).
19 Letter to Ezra Pound, 6 April 1935 (CtY).
20 Letter to Ezra Pound, 31 December 1935 (CtY); after three years of increasingly exasperated correspondence on both sides, Bunting broke with Pound with an angry and uncompromising letter written on 16 December 1938 (CtY).
21 Letter to Ezra Pound, 21 March 1934 (CtY).
22 Beauman, "Man of Plain Words" 30.
23 Letter to Jonathan Williams, 27 January 1976 (NBuU).
24 Letter to Louis Zukofsky, 3 February 1951 (TxU).
25 Editorial, *Times* 14 April 1952: 7.
26 Letter to Dorothy Pound, 17 May 1948 (InU).
27 Undated letter to Ezra Pound, [1934] (CtY).
28 Bunting showed me this letter the day he received it, when I immediately copied it from memory in my notebook. So far as I know Bunting destroyed the original.
29 Letter to Dorothy Pound, 8 January 1947 (InU).
30 Letter to Louis Zukofsky, 13 March 1951 (TxU).
31 Letter to Louis Zukofsky, 19 April 1951 (TxU).

32 Brian Butters, "Don't Keep Poetry to Yourself – Read It Aloud," *Victoria Daily Times* (13 October 1971): 3.
33 Letter to Dorothy Pound, 14 April 1949 (InU)
34 Letter to Dorothy Pound, 17 December 1947 (InU).
35 Letter to Dorothy Pound, 17 December 1947 (InU).
36 Letter to Louis Zukofsky, 29 March 1953 (TxU).
37 Letter to Ezra Pound, 17 March 1953 (InU).
38 Letter to Ezra Pound, 9 July 1953 (CtY).
39 Letter to Louis Zukofsky, 18 June 1953 (TxU).
40 Letter to Louis Zukofsky, 28 September 1953 (TxU).
41 Letter to Louis Zukofsky, 6 August 1953 (TxU).
42 Printed as "Perche no spero" in *Collected Poems* (Mt. Kisco, N. Y.: Moyer Bell, 1980) 12.
43 Letter to Louis Zukofsky, 3 February 1951 (TxU).
44 "I think I'm best pleased with the fowler et seq. Or least discontent anyway. Or the musicians?" Letter to Dorothy Pound, 20 July 1951 (InU).
45 Letter to Louis Zukofsky, 6 August 1949 (TxU).
46 Letter to Louis Zukofsky, 16 September 1964 (TxU).
47 Working draft of the opening lines of "A New Moon," sent to Peter Quartermain, 9 April 1973.
48 Letter to Louis Zukofsky, 27 April 1934 (CtY).
49 Letter to Louis Zukofsky, 12 November 1950 (TxU).
50 Letter to Harriet Monroe, 20 November 1932, *Poetry* Magazine Papers, 1912–36, Box 30, Folder 23 (ICU).
51 "The Lion and Lizard," ts. 2 (TxU).
52 Letter to Louis Zukofsky, June "the newmoonth" 1953 (TxU).

## *CHAPTER NINE*

1 Kurt Schwitters, "Banalitäten," *Merz* 4 (1923), translated in Werner Schmalenbach, *Kurt Schwitters* (New York: Abrams, 1977) 202.
2 Charles Reznikoff, *The Complete Poems,* ed. S. Cooney, 2 vols. (Los Angeles: Black Sparrow, 1978) 2: 209. All further references cited parenthetically as *CP*.
3 William Carlos Williams, *Paterson* (New York: New Directions, 1963) 225.
4 Ezra Pound, *Selected Letters, 1907–1941,* ed. D. D. Paige (New York: Harcourt Brace, 1950) 124.
5 William Carlos Williams, *The Collected Poems of William Carlos Williams. Vol. 1: 1909–1939,* A. Walton Litz and C. MacGowan, ed. (New York: New Directions, 1986) 451, 453, 224.
6 Cleanth Brooks, "Poetry since *The Waste Land*" (1964), *A Shaping Joy: Studies in the Writer's Craft* (New York: Harcourt Brace Jovanovich, 1972) 64.
7 Ezra Pound, "Dr. Williams's Position," *Literary Essays,* ed. T. S. Eliot (London: Faber and Faber, 1945) 394.

8 Hayden Carruth, "A Failure of Contempt," *Poetry* 107 (March 1966): 397; William Dickey, "The Thing Itself," *Hudson Review* 19 (Spring 1966): 152.
9 William Carlos Williams, "Prologue to *Kora in Hell,*" *Selected Essays* (New York: Random House, 1954) 11.
10 August Kleinzahler, "The Walker," *Sagetrieb* 1.1 (Spring 1982): 103.

## *CHAPTER TEN*

1 John Taylor (of Caroline), *An Inquiry into the Principles and Policy of the Government of the United States* (1814), introduction by Roy Franklin Nichols (New Haven: Yale UP, 1950) 482.
2 Robert Creeley, *For Love: Poems 1950–1960* (New York: Scribner's, 1962) 41. Further references are abbreviated *FL*.
3 William Carlos Williams, *In The American Grain,* introduction by Horace Gregory (New York: New Directions, 1956) 114. Further references are abbreviated *IAG*. Other works by Williams to which I refer are abbreviated in the text as follows: *Selected Essays* (New York: Random House, 1954) as *SE; Spring and All,* in *Imaginations,* ed. Webster Schott (New York: New Directions, 1970) as *S&A*.
4 Cited in Ludwig Wittgenstein, *Philosophical Investigations,* trans. G. E. N. Anscombe (Oxford: Blackwell, 1953) 18. Further references are abbreviated *PI*.
5 Robert Creeley, *A Quick Graph: Collected Notes and Essays,* ed. Donald Allen (San Francisco: Four Seasons Foundation, 1970) 71. Further references are abbreviated *QG*.
6 Gertrude Stein, *Lectures in America* (Boston: Beacon, 1957) 235; *Narration: Four Lectures* (Chicago: U of Chicago P, 1935) 25. Further references to *Lectures in America* are abbreviated *LIA*.
7 Jacques Roubaud, *Autobiographie, chapitre dix* (Paris: Gallimard 1977).
8 "The Lover" is dated 1953 in Mary Novik, *Robert Creeley: An Inventory, 1945–1970* (Kent, Ohio: Kent State UP, 1973) 86.
9 Quoted by Creeley in a letter to Cid Corman, 15 November 1950, *Origin* 2 (Spring 1951): 74.
10 Michael McClure, *Meat Science Essays,* 2nd ed. enlarged (San Francisco: City Lights, 1966) 10.
11 Louis Zukofsky, *Bottom: On Shakespeare* (Austin: U of Texas P, 1963) 64. Further references are abbreviated *Bottom*. See *PI* 29, for Wittgenstein.
12 Robert Creeley, *Contexts of Poetry: Interviews 1961–1971,* ed Donald Allen (Bolinas: Four Seasons Foundation, 1973) 87.
13 Plato, *Theaetatus,* 201e–202b, trans. with notes by John McDowell, *Clarendon Plato Series* (Oxford, Clarendon, 1973) 94–5. Wittgenstein, *PI* 21, quotes a somewhat different version of this passage.
14 Charles Olson, *Causal Mythology* (San Francisco: Four Seasons Foundation, 1969) 2.
15 Robert Creeley, *Presences: A Text for Marisol* (New York: Scribner's, 1976) [unpaginated].

16 Robert Creeley, *The Gold Diggers and Other Stories* (New York: Scribner's, 1965) 47.
17 Bertrand Russell, "Logical Atomism," *Logic and Knowledge,* ed. Robert C. Marsh (London: Allen & Unwin, 1956) 337.

## *CHAPTER ELEVEN*

1 Ludwig Wittgenstein, preface, *Tractatus Logico-Philosophicus* (London: Routledge, 1922) 27. The quotation in the title is from Charles Olson, "The Songs of Maximus," *The Maximus Poems,* ed. George F. Butterick (Berkeley: U of California P, 1983) 19.
2 "A Preface prepared for MAPS #6. The Issue," *MAPS* 6 (1974): 8.
3 Thus I conflate "A Preface," 9–10, with "Ideas of the Meaning of Form," *Fictive Certainties: Essays* (New York: New Directions, 1985), especially 92–5.
4 "A Preface" 12.
5 "Rites of Participation [*The H. D. Book* Part 1, Chapter 6]," *Caterpillar* 1 (October 1967): 7.
6 "Ideas of the Meaning of Form" 95.
7 Conversation, 30 January 1966.
8 Wayne Nyberg and Dennis Wheeler, interviewers, "Robert Duncan: On His Mind," *Ubyssey* [student newspaper, U of British Columbia] (21 January 1966): 6.
9 Louis Zukofsky, *Bottom: On Shakespeare* (Austin: U of Texas P, 1963) 164.
10 Letter to Peter Quartermain, 21 August 1970. All parentheses are Duncan's.
11 "The Truth and Life of Myth," *Fictive Certainties* 50.
12 "A Preface" 1.
13 "Robert Duncan: On His Mind" 6.
14 [Untitled Essay] *Magazine of Further Studies* 6 [(1969): 40].
15 "*U. S. A.: Poetry* Robert Duncan and John Wieners" ts. version of television programme produced by KQED, San Francisco, 1966, 5.
16 "From *The H. D. Book* [Part 2, Chapter 8]." *Credences* 1.2 (July 1975): 88.
17 *Bottom* 183.
18 "The Truth and Life of Myth" 50.
19 "Notes on Poetics Regarding Olson's *Maximus,*" *Fictive Certainties* 71.
20 "Interview/Workshop with Robert Duncan," *Soup* [1] (1980): 32.
21 "Introduction," *Bending the Bow* (New York: New Directions, 1968) *v*.
22 "Robert Duncan: On His Mind" 6.
23 Robert Duncan, preface, *Letters* (Highlands: Jargon, 1958) *iii*.
24 *U. S. A. Poetry* 7.
25 Letter to Peter Quartermain, 16 June 1970.
26 "Rites of Participation (Part 2) [*The H. D. Book* Part 1, Chapter 6]," *Caterpillar* 2 (January 1968): 140.
27 "There Could Be a Book without Nations in Its Chapters," *Derivations: Selected Poems 1950–1956* (London: Fulcrum) 78.

### *CHAPTER TWELVE*

1 Gabriel Arbouin, "Devant l'Idéogramme d'Apollinaire," *Les Soirées de Paris* 26 (July 1914): 383–4. "Most commentators," says S. I. Lockerbie, "have assumed erroneously that Arbouin was a pseudonym of Apollinaire's" (Introduction, Guillaume Apollinaire, *Calligrammes: Poems of Peace and War [1913–1916],* trans. Anne Hyde Greet [Berkeley: U of California P, 1980] 10).

2 Letter to Peter Quartermain, 11 March 1978. Subsequent quotations from letters are identified parenthetically by date, and are copyright Guy Davenport.

3 Guy Davenport, *The Geography of the Imagination: Forty Essays* (San Francisco: North Point, 1981) 366. Further references abbreviated *Geog.* Other books by Davenport are abbreviated as follows:

*Tatlin! Six Stories* (Baltimore: Johns Hopkins UP, 1982); reprint of 1974 edition, as *Tat!;*

*Da Vinci's Bicycle: Ten Stories* (Baltimore: Johns Hopkins UP, 1982); corrected reprint of 1979 edition, as *DaV'sB;*

*Eclogues: Eight Stories* (San Francisco: North Point, 1981), as *Ecl;*

*Herakleitos and Diogenes,* trans. Guy Davenport (Bolinas: Grey Fox, 1979), as *Her.*

Barry Alpert, "Guy Davenport – An Interview," *Vort* 9 (1976): 3–17 is abbreviated *Vort.*

4 Fernand Braudel, *The Mediterranean and the Mediterranean World in the Age of Philip II,* 2 vols., trans. S. Reynolds (New York: Harper and Row, 1972); Ezra Pound, *ABC of Reading* (New York: New Directions, 1960) 17.

5 Guy Davenport, *The Intelligence of Louis Agassiz: A Specimen Book of Scientific Writings,* Foreword by Alfred S. Romer (Boston: Beacon, 1963). Pound would no doubt appreciate that irony.

6 Ezra Pound, *Selected Prose 1909–1965,* ed. William Cookson (New York: New Directions, 1973) 323.

7 George Steiner, "Rare Bird," *New Yorker* (30 November 1981): 201.

8 Siegfried Giedon, *The Eternal Present: A Contribution on Constancy and Change,* 2 vols. (New York: Bollingen Foundation, 1962) 1:6.

9 Louis Zukofsky, *Bottom: On Shakespeare* (Austin: U of Texas P, 1963) 10.

10 Zukofsky, *Bottom* 164. Emphasis added.

11 Catherine O'Neill, "An Alchemist of History and Invention," *Chronicle of Higher Education* (2 April 1979): R4.

12 "Fifty-Seven Views of Fujiyama," *Granta,* 4 (1981): 5–62; the version in *Apples and Pears and Other Stories* (San Francisco: North Point, 1984) 21–51, has been slightly revised.

13 Robert Rosenblum, *Cubism and Twentieth-Century Art* (New York: Abrams, 1961) 80.

14 Max Ernst, *Beyond Painting, and Other Writings by the Artist and His Friends* (New York: Wittenborn, Schultz, 1948) 22.

15 Rosalind E. Krauss, *Passages in Modern Sculpture* (New York: Viking, 1977) 48.
16 David Antin, "Some Questions about Modernism," *Occident* 7 (Spring 1974): 21.
17 Rosenblum 101.
18 J. P. Spradbery, *Wasps: An Account of the Biology and Natural History of Solitary and Social Wasps,* Foreword by O. W. Richards (Seattle: U of Washington P, 1973). From a conversation with Guy Davenport in November 1978.
19 Ezra Pound, *Gaudier-Brzeska, A Memoir* (New York: New Directions, 1970) 86.
20 William C. Seitz, *The Art of Assemblage* (New York: Museum of Modern Art, 1961) 25.
21 Leo Steinberg, *Other Criteria: Confrontations with Twentieth-Century Art* (New York: Oxford UP, 1972) 84.
22 Quoted by John Shannon, "Dianoia," *Margins* 13 (August–September 1974): 21.

## *CHAPTER THIRTEEN*

1 Nicole Brossard at The New Poetics Colloquium, Vancouver, 23 August 1985.
2 In what follows I refer to the following titles by Howe, abbreviated as indicated.

"Armantrout" "Rae Armantrout: Extremities," *The L=A=N=G=U=A=G=E Book,* ed. Bruce Andrews and Charles Bernstein (Carbondale: Southern Illinois UP, 1984) 208–10.
*ASFT* *Articulation of Sound Forms in Time* (Windsor, Vt.: Awede, 1987).
*CG* *Cabbage Gardens* (n.p. Fathom Press, 1979).
*CMR* *"The Captivity and Restoration of Mrs. Mary Rowlandson," Temblor* 2 (1985): 113–21.
*HP* *Hinge Picture* (New York: Telephone Books, 1974).
"Illogic" "The Illogic of Sumptuary Values" (unpublished typescript).
*Liberties* *The Liberties,* reprinted in *The Defenestration of Prague* (New York: Kulchur Foundation, 1980) 64–127.
*MyED* *My Emily Dickinson* (Berkeley: North Atlantic Books, 1985).
"Olson" "Where Should the Commander Be," *Writing* 19 (November 1987): 3–20.
"Scattering" "Scattering as Behavior toward Risk," *Singularities* (Hanover, NH and London: Wesleyan UP/ UP of New England, 1990) 61–70.
"Owen" "Howe on Owen," *L=A=N=G=U=A=G=E* 13 (December 1980): [28–30].

| | |
|---|---|
| *Platin* | "P. Inman: *Platin*," *L=A=N=G=U=A=G=E* 12 (June 1980): [8–10]. |
| "Poetics" | "[Statement]," *Poetic Statements for the New Poetics Colloquium, August 21–25, 1985* (Vancouver: Kootenay School of Writing, 1985) 12–15. |
| "Women" | "Women and Their Effect in the Distance," *Ironwood* 28 (Fall 1986): 58–91. |

3 The words "little language" are Swift's, as are those in parentheses. They are quoted by Howe (*Liberties*, 66); Part 1 of *The Liberties* is titled "Fragments of a Liquidation."

4 George F. Butterick, "The Mysterious Vision of Susan Howe," *North Dakota Quarterly* 55 (Fall 1987): 313. Rachel Blau DuPlessis, "Whowe: An Essay on Work by Susan Howe," *Sulfur* 20 (Fall 1987): 157–65, is, like Butterick's essay, essential for anyone interested in Howe's work. She manages that difficult task of elucidating Howe's poetic without in the least diminishing the deep rage and pain so intrinsic to it.

5 Charlton T. Lewis and Charles Short, *A Latin Dictionary* (Oxford: Clarendon, 1879) entry for *reus*.

6 Herman Melville, *Billy Budd Sailor: An Inside Narrative. Reading Text and Genetic Text,* ed. Harrison Hayford and Merton M. Sealts, Jr. (Chicago: U of Chicago P, 1962) 412.

7 Howe's insistence on reading Melville's works as Melville left them is an act of reading markedly close to Zukofsky's retrieval of the Shakespearean canon: Lacking canonical certainty, the forty-four items of the canon must be treated as one work, no matter when written, no matter how moot Shakespeare's authorship. Viewed thus the work is longeval as a unity which is (in Shakespeare's words) from "itself never turning" (*Bottom: On Shakespeare* [Austin: U of Texas P, 1963] 13; permission to quote refused by Paul Zukofsky). Zukofsky amplifies this view throughout *Bottom,* but especially in "Definition" (266–341).

8 "Olson" 17; *MyED* 116. Guy Davenport says of Olson that "his poetry was inarticulate. His lectures achieved depths of incoherence" in *The Geography of the Imagination: Forty Essays* (San Francisco: North Point, 1981) 81.

# Index

Boldface is used to distinguish major references.